ECHOES

ECHOES

MEMOIRS OF
ANDRE KOSTELANETZ

by

Andre Kostelanetz

in collaboration
with
Gloria Hammond

Harcourt Brace Jovanovich, Publishers
New York and London

Requests for permission to make copies of any
part of the work should be mailed to: Permissions,
Harcourt Brace Jovanovich, Publishers, 757 Third Avenue,
New York, N.Y. 10017.

Library of Congress Cataloging in Publication Data
Kostelanetz, Andre, 1901–
Echoes: memoirs of Andre Kostelanetz.
Includes index.
1. Kostelanetz, Andre, 1901–
2. Conductors (Music)—Biography.
I. Hammond, Gloria. II. Title.
ML422.K693A3   785'.092'4 [B]   81–6825
ISBN 0–15–127392–8   AACR2

Printed in the United States of America

First edition

B C D E

Contents

ILLUSTRATIONS ARE BETWEEN PAGES 58 AND 59
AND BETWEEN 154 AND 155.
PICTURE CREDITS ARE ON PAGE 249.

PART ONE

Lessons

I have come to think of my past as two separate lives. The first, though the furthest back in time and the shortest in years—it began with my birth in St. Petersburg, Russia, in 1901 and "ended" twenty-one years later—has the clearest echo in my memory. Whenever I think of it, I fall easily into its present, watching in my mind's eye the events of those years as one might see remembered scenes from a particular play or film.

The distance between then and what came after is not only a matter of miles and time but the distance that naturally falls between the stopping of a whole way of life and the starting of a new. I learned about self-reliance in that first life, about true friendship and love, about the unspeakable cruelties of civil war. And most of all I learned to concentrate on finding the beauty in the world around me, in nature and in people, to appreciate every revelation of that beauty.

It is not sentiment, then, that makes the echo of my first life so strong and clear, but rather the fact that those early experiences taught me the value of choosing life—over existence, over resignation, negativeness, fatalism, death. That one lesson has shaped all the intervening days and years since, and has made me count myself among the most fortunate of men.

FINLAND

Lake Ladoga

Gulf of Finland

● ST. PETERSBURG
(LENINGRAD)

ESTONIA

Volga

LATVIA

LITHUANIA

● MOSCOW

R U S S I A   (U. S. S. R.)

EAST
PRUSSIA

● VILNA
(VILNIUS)

● MINSK

● WARSAW

POLAND

Don

ROSTOV-NA-DONU ●

ASTRAKHAN

Caspian Sea

RUMANIA

Crimea

● ARMAVIR

● NOVOROSSIYSK

● KISLOVODSK

● YALTA

Black   Sea

Caucasus

Georgia

BULGARIA

CONSTANTINOPLE
(ISTANBUL)

Armenia

TURKEY

SYRIA

Sea of Marmara

GREECE

| 0 | | 200 | | 400 | miles |

| 0 | 200 | | 400 | | kilometers |

WESTERN RUSSIA – 1922

IT IS COLD IN THE railroad car and dark, except for one candle. There is tea in a samovar at one end of the car if I want it. The server is there, in his small enclosure just behind the samovar. This *provodnik* and I haven't spoken yet, in three days and nights.

What brought me here was not courage or resourcefulness or political sensibility, but luck and adaptability. It is the beginning of the fifth year of the Bolshevik Revolution. Yet until these days and nights alone I had not experienced it in my soul. I simply moved within the upheaval, changing my direction when I had to but not taking a stand. Against the daily obstacles—shortages of food and fuel, lack of communication, travel difficulties—my main idea was to go on, get through as best I could. I was not alone. I had aunts and uncles in Petrograd—the name given St. Petersburg in 1914—and my friends at the Opera, where I worked coaching. The worst thing was the knowledge that any night it could be our turn to be taken away, without explanation. Each day the list would be posted, like the cast of some new opera, and we would read the names of those who would not be seen again.

We tried to offset the horror of that specific danger by living as close to the old familiar pattern as possible. It was a means of controlling our fear, and it worked as long as we could make a living. But the want of fuel finally forced the Opera to close. And finally, too, I was forced to confront the Revolution because it had ruptured my life. I decided to take a stand, to leave Russia and thus begin my personal fight.

These three days in the railroad yards of Minsk are the first step.

Someone will come for me and take me to the Polish border. Maybe tomorrow or even tonight. There will be a tap on the window and I will go. I have a fur coat, and I have gone to the home of friends twice for a meal and a bath. But from now on, I've decided, I will wait here. Now it does not matter whether it is day or night. Time has collapsed. The immediate problem is to stay awake enough to hear the tap when it comes.

My parents lived an apolitical life in St. Petersburg, privileged Jews in an essentially anti-Semitic city. They did not participate in the Revolution. They may have been conscious of the forces that finally clashed, but they were not directly affected by the preliminary events, the warning signs, and so they overlooked them. They were no different from other *kulturny* of the day.

Our family had money, and we were able to enjoy the cultural vitality of the capital, the Russian "window to the West." The signals of changes to come were perceived as cause for some caution, no more. After the Kerensky Revolution, in the spring of 1917, my father decided that the safe thing to do would be to send my mother to the Caucasus with my sisters, Mina and Maria, and brother, Boris, for a while. When the Bolshevik Revolution came, in October of 1917, he felt the turmoil would very shortly run itself out but that in the meantime he would go to Helsinki, where he had business connections. Just for two weeks or so. Father took only enough funds for that length of time and, typical for a successful businessman of his social rank, one change of formal attire. No gentleman of his day traveled without his dinner jacket.

As the elder son I was to remain in the city in our apartment on Karavanaya Oolitza, number 2. The schools had been closed, but I would be able to continue studying music privately. And there were aunts and uncles nearby.

I was almost sixteen when I said good-by to my father. I was twenty-one when I saw him again.

I realize now that the Revolution probably averted a crisis between my father and me. He had never been pleased at my musical ambitions. To his way of thinking there was only one course for me, to follow in his footsteps. I was just as determined in my own ideas and firm about what I wanted to do. Although we didn't argue over it constantly, I was aware of his disapproval all through my childhood and adolescence.

I think the day he discovered I had marked five keys on the piano to correspond to the lines of the staff—"1" on the E key, and so on—he was pretty certain I was serious. And that was quite early on, when I was about six and had begun piano study with my first teacher. I waited until she had left one day before penning the numbers onto the keys. Later, I tried to wash them off—I must have had some doubt that the cleverness of my idea would be appreciated—but the ink had soaked right into the ivory. The family was horrified, the teacher was horrified. But I think it made more than one impression.

My father was a real estate broker, a member of the Bourse—the St. Petersburg Stock Exchange—and had dealings with the royal house as well as with titled gentry. It was understandable that he felt I should have the advantages of his achievements when the time came. A career in music would mean that I would be just a second- or third-class citizen. Only a few musicians ever achieved the highest artistic rank. Father was a practical man. He could not see any point in his son throwing away an opportunity for virtually guaranteed success. I think I must have inherited his stubbornness and singleness of purpose, for I was just as determined to make music my life. For as long as I can remember, it was the most important thing in the world to me.

In any case I had him to thank for my early appreciation of music in the first place. If I had been born into a less fortunately situated family, I probably would not have known its joys until much later. My parents had subscription seats at the Mariinsky Opera for both operas and ballets. Although Father did not play an instrument, he followed opera closely and knew many by heart.

Perhaps because Mother played the piano herself she was sympathetic to my interest in it. She would never oppose my father openly, but some time after the inking-of-the-keys incident, she decided to take me to see Madame Koskova, a teacher at St. Petersburg Conservatory and a pupil of its founder, Anton Rubinstein.

And one afternoon there we were in Madame's apartment. She served tea, and then I played for her, something by Mendelssohn. Afterward she asked me to show her my hands. "They are Rubinstein's hands," she said. A decisive remark. It did not make an enthusiast of my father, but neither did he forbid my having lessons. After that I began studying with one of Koskova's assistants.

We children would sometimes be taken to a ballet or an opera. I liked the ballets. The music was so beautiful. And in the Mariinsky orchestra all the principal parts were played by His Majesty's soloists. You would suddenly see a person come in, sit down, play, and then leave! Only the best performers played the solos.

I was not particularly taken with opera, but one that absolutely fascinated me was *Carmen*. The day I finally got hold of the score I was very excited. I immediately found my sister Maria and played it for her. I was about ten, and she was two and a half years younger. She listened very attentively, but in the end she did not share my enthusiasm: "This is very remarkable, but don't you think it is rather vulgar music?" I was surprised—but then I remembered how young she was.

When I was five I contracted scarlatina. Immediately everyone was moved from the house, and I was left there in the care of a nurse. She was a very pretty girl, very sweet to me. One evening as I lay in bed the most beautiful sounds began to drift into my consciousness. The nurse was playing the piano in the living room, Schubert's Impromptu in A-flat, and very well, as I know now. I remember feeling enveloped in the sweetness and comfort of those sounds. If there was a single moment when I first became aware of music and of wanting to make music myself, that was it. After that the nurse played often, and I listened and watched with rapt attention.

Sometimes I wonder at those circumstances and whether, if any one of them had not been what it was, the effect would have been the same: if the nurse hadn't been so pretty—I think she was my first crush—and hadn't played so well; if I had not been so young; if I had not gotten sick in the first place. It was the first of many times in my life when certain elements seemed to combine and

ignite one another and force a particular result. My only participation was to risk crossing the bridge once I had been swept to it.

The dark silence of this railroad car is no stranger to me. It is
the natural companion of the Russian winter days, when there are
very few hours of light and, always, a muting blanket of snow.

Rozanchiki, soft rolls in the shape of "tiny roses." They were as
much a part of our childhood winter mornings as the darkness and
the silence. Each warm "petal" could be pulled away and spread
with butter and jam, or caviar. We ate them and drank tea. That
was our breakfast. It was just the governess, Mina, Maria, and I at
this early-morning meal. On school days we never saw Mother and
Father until dinner time, and both meals were eaten pretty much
in silence. Whatever conversation there was had to be spoken in
the language we were learning at the moment. That was the role
of the governess. First, we had a French girl, Mademoiselle d'Orsy,
who lived with us for two years. She was lovely, and her sister,
who would sometimes come to visit, was even more beautiful—we
heard she was mistress of the prime minister. Next came a German
girl, just as pretty and just as adept at teaching us her language.

We walked to school. Mina and Maria went in one direction, to
the Lohvinsky Scalon, a fashionable school for the education of
young girls, and I went to St. Peter's School. We would leave
about seven-thirty.

The streets were still as dark as night. The only life was the
activity around the government vodka stores. They opened very
early, and there would always be a few *muzhiks* skillfully striking
the bottoms of the small bottles in just the right spot and with just
the right pressure so that the cork flew out but the vodka stayed in.
Heads would tilt back, and the vodka would be quickly dispatched
straight down the throat. The empty bottles were then tossed into
the snow, and the peasants would be on their way to work.

St. Peter's was an all-boys school. We wore military uniforms
and, accordingly, we were to conduct ourselves with an orderly

rhythm of model behavior. We marched into the classroom; in perfect unison we stood and greeted the teacher; two by two we marched to the lunchroom.

I seemed to absorb this pattern readily. My friend Efrem was fond of reminding me that I even marched home! (He, meanwhile, would be galloping ahead of me through the snow.) I suppose the discipline of the school was only a slightly sharper reflection of my life at home. And then there were the casual loud good times I discovered at Efrem's house. It had never occurred to me that other people lived differently. Our studies were all-important. Everyone in my family was always either reading or working on some project of enlightenment. But at the Kurtzes' all was gaiety. The whole family was musical, so, of course, there was a piano. I found myself drawn to their vitality and to their love for music. I could play to my heart's content, without having to think of my father's feeling that I spent too much time at the piano. Efrem "conducted," and his brother Arved played the violin.

Efrem was very tall, taller than most of the other boys and much taller than I. He sat right next to me all through our school years. I could not resist teasing him that the reason he was so successful in his studies was obviously that he had only to glance down from his advantageous height and copy my work!

It was a joke, of course, but the fact is I was the better pupil, first in the class every year. My father felt I should excel, and I did, but it did not come easily. I spent many extra hours at study. And after a while I came to agree with him. I began to enjoy the feeling of being bright and well educated. I wanted to be first, not waste time being adequate. So I did not have as much free time as Efrem did, but I spent all I did have with him and his family.

Later, when my own family had left Petrograd, Efrem's mother would often insist that I eat dinner with them—a very important invitation because in most cases there would be no dinner for me otherwise. They did not seem to worry about the source of their next meal, or about much of anything. If one of the family happened somehow to come by a precious extra pound of sugar, there was no question of rationing it. Mrs. Kurtz would use it right up making batches of wonderful candies. Their flair for living was not diminished by the deprivations of those times.

Our musical evenings would very often go beyond the eight o'clock curfew. It was quite a long walk home for me, and the utter quiet of the streets made it seem even longer. I took comfort in the rhythmic echoing of my own footsteps.

It was the early fall of 1917 that my father left for Helsinki. Mother, Mina, Maria, and my little brother, Boris, were already in the Caucasus. I stayed alone in the huge apartment. The family money had been "appropriated" almost simultaneously with their departure, but I managed, with the help of my aunts and uncles.

It seems much more dramatic to look back on that time than it was to live through it: World War I had been raging since 1914. Czar Nicholas left the capital for field headquarters to take charge of the troops. Rasputin, the notorious and ill-fated monk, was then unencumbered in wreaking his sinister influence on Czarina Alexandra, and by the time of his murder in July, 1916, support for Nicholas had been destroyed. The czar was forced to abdicate in March, 1917, and before that year was over the provisional government would be dissolved and the Bolsheviks would be in power. Tremendous events, but they did not have immediately devastating effects on our family life. The upheaval was total in the end, but it came slowly.

In that early fall of 1917, as I began my life alone in Petrograd, there were not great differences in the round of days. The shortage of food was something we had all been living with since the beginning of the war. Now there was a night curfew and "requisitioning," but they did not affect my daily existence. I was forced to grant these realities a place in my life, but I did not dwell on them. I was not at an age where it really seemed to matter.

The schools were closed, but I continued practicing my music. Skipping lunch did not bother me—there was always tea, made now with some sort of grass, to get through on.

One day I read in the paper that all private cars were to be requisitioned. I thought of the Benz my father had: why not use it for a final fling, have a picnic in the country? It would be a novelty for me because in all the time my father had the car I remember that we all took only one ride in it. I began to make plans. Somewhere there was a black market. I could get bars of chocolate to hide in the car for my guests to find.

It was a beautiful day. I had arranged with Julius, who had been our chauffeur, to drive my party out into the country. There were no cars on the roads. We could have been stopped any minute, but we were not. It was the last carefree time I can remember in that city.

On the way home the car began to *puck, puck, puck*. Julius pulled to the curb and said we were out of gas. That was the end of our afternoon.

The family had not been gone for long then. I still believed, as they had, that the political changes would not be irrevocable, that our lives would return to normal. The days went on, historic days, but we did not see that then. And gradually, despite what we wished to believe, our lives were being changed. Every day there were fewer reasons for clinging to our unrealistic belief that nothing was different, and yet we did cling. It seemed the old way was the only way we could live. Fear had blinded us to reality and at the same time protected us from it. Our instinct to survive told us to lie low, not accept anything as real danger unless it entered our front door, so to speak, as when, on a hot July day in 1918, the news came of the murder of the former czar, Nicholas II, his wife, Alexandra Feodorovna, and all their children. It shocked us. By then the czar was totally unpopular, but the whole family just being shot in a cellar. . . . Still, everybody was afraid to say a word. Just as there had been no outcry when the Bolsheviks, the so-called Reds, staged their coup the previous October, or when they disbanded the short-lived constituent assembly three months later and became the Russian Communist Party, or when the dreaded Cheka began its liquidating activities.

Word came from Kislovodsk that my mother and the children had no money left. They had been gone nine months. Something had to be done, and I decided, as the man of the family now, that I would somehow get to her with help.

I sent word to my father in Helsinki, and he directed me to a banker friend in Petrograd who gave me a few thousand rubles. The next step was to figure a way of traveling to the Caucasus without encountering the fighting in the south between the Reds and the moderate Whites. Kislovodsk was famous for its sparkling water, *narzan*, and was in a popular resort area easily accessible from the north, a three-day train trip straight south. But I didn't think the trains would be allowed through the front, and even if they were, I didn't want to risk it. My plan was to go southeast by train to the Volga and then by ship south to Astrakhan, the mouth of the Volga on the Caspian Sea. I wasn't sure yet how I would get from there southwest to Kislovodsk.

The first part of the trip went smoothly enough. I stayed in Astrakhan for two days, and by that time I had fallen in with a group of about fifteen who had the same intention as myself, to get to the Caucasus. None of us was sure what our next means of travel should be, but part of the active front lay between us and Kislovodsk, so we would have to stay close to the Caspian while traveling farther south and then turn west for our final destination. We could go overland, but it would require not only a more exact knowledge of the area than any of us had but also the risk of meeting up with armed groups who were certain to be unsympathetic to our intentions. Then someone suggested taking a boat down the western side of the Caspian, staying as close to shore as possible.

Of course, at that point there were no regularly scheduled ferries just waiting to take us wherever we wanted to go. We would have to buy a boat. The idea grew more appealing by the minute. No one seemed bothered by the fact that there was not one sailor among us. We put some money together and went to the dock.

The first boat we saw that we thought we could afford was a sailboat. There were three sailors on it, and we approached the one who looked the most in command. He turned out to be the captain, and he agreed with our plan to buy the boat and their services with it, and to charge us a price in line with the fact that we would return the boat at our destination. We would begin our voyage the next morning.

The boat was small, with no railing. We slept on deck. All went well for several days. The worst danger was that you could roll right overboard in your sleep some night.

One afternoon the sky began to blacken. It looked like a tremendous storm would be over us any minute. I went to the captain to ask what his plan was, but I soon saw that he was quite drunk. The two sailors were in the same condition. I don't think they knew what danger we were in. The rest of us held a short meeting and decided beaching the boat was the only thing to do. Immediately. We managed to ground it in the shallows, and then we waded to shore. The timing was unbelievably propitious, because the top of the storm was suddenly right there. I am not sure exactly where we landed, but it looked like a desert. The sand was blowing in huge whorls. We lay down and covered our faces.

The storm didn't last long. The wind died down, and we took stock of our situation. The first thing we realized was that we were fifteen again: the captain and the two sailors were gone. We never saw them or the boat again.

We began to make our way toward some huts in the near distance. They belonged to a group of nomads, and we asked if they could take us to the nearest railroad station. I was hoping it would be Mineralny Vody ("Mineral Waters"), where one railway goes to Georgia and the other to the spa resorts of the Caucasus. They said it was a long way but that they had camels. Well, none of us knew how to ride a camel, but then none of us had known how to sail, either.

Four camels were brought out and some very simple wagons, which the camels could drag. Some of us could ride the beasts and some the wagons. Two men would accompany us. We agreed to pay, again striking a bargain based on the condition that the means of transportation would be returned in the end.

It took us the rest of the day to organize the trek. We agreed to use as little water as possible, since there would be only one canister available. I was glad there were no children in the group.

The days were very hot, the nights very cold. On several nights there was a phenomenon I had never seen: huge bolts of lightning that looked as if they were coming right at you out of a clear sky, literally. And there was no sound at all.

The trek went on and on. I lost track of time. Finally we met another group of nomads. They were Kalmyks, I think, judging from their Mongolian faces and from the difficulty we had in trying to speak with them. We did manage to communicate, though, and they asked us if it was true that there was a revolution going on, and then they invited us to join them in one of their *yurtas* for some tea. Another man and I accepted, but everybody else decided to keep walking. We had our tea, which was as much melting grease as anything else, and then stepped out of the lattice-frame tent into the desert twilight. We thought we would catch up easily, but total darkness came with breath-taking suddenness and we were alone without any sense of which direction to take. The ferocious dogs the Kalmyks kept picked that moment to inspect us. We could not see them, but their snarling growls and snortings seemed to be all around us. Eventually we did find a nomad—or, more likely, he found us—who brought us to our group.

The next morning we found railroad tracks, and that was as good as a station. All we had to do was follow them. It had been eight days since we'd left the Caspian shore, so there was no pondering which direction to follow. We just went. That same day we arrived at a small station. And there was a train standing there. What a fantastic sight! It was made up of fourth-class cars, one of which was, unbelievably, marked for Kislovodsk. We climbed aboard and some hours later reached the resort town.

There was an immediate official hullabaloo: For what purpose had we come? Did we have anything to declare? Naturally, I didn't tell them about the money, but I realized that I had better distract them with something so I handed over a precious eighth pound of tea—instantly pronounced "contraband"—that I had brought as a present for my mother.

The family was staying in a hotel then, and I walked there. Of course, they were enormously surprised to see me, for there had been no way I could tell them I was coming. The next thing I did was go to the spa and bathe in the *narzan*. Afterward I slept for eighteen hours.

I had no idea that it would be eighteen months before I would return to Petrograd. By then the civil war would be pretty much burned out.

———————

The wagon-lit seems quieter than ever. Perhaps because the candle has gone out. In the faint dawn glow I can see the wick afloat in the still warm melted wax. It is so cold, and in this early-morning semidarkness I think again of my school days.

I was a serious student at school. I had to work hard to stay at the top of my class, something Father expected. It was not that I was unaware of the opportunities for mischief, but I was more aware of the risk I would be taking. Then, one day, I made up for all the temptations I had passed by. The thrill of making mischief lasted only a few seconds, but there was an unexpected thrill that I never forgot: the experience of loyalty.

The inspiration for my prank was our German teacher, Herr Schwanbach, which means "swan brook." The rule was that when he entered our classroom for the lesson we rose and greeted him with, *"Guten Morgen,* Herr Schwanbach." My idea was to tell about twelve boys that they were not pronouncing his name correctly, that it should be Schweinbach, which is "swine brook."

Well, the professor walked in and was greeted by the "corrected" pronunciation. He stopped still and then turned and walked out. Very soon it was clear that the head of the school knew all about the matter, except for the identity of the villain. Disclosure would have meant my expulsion. I did not confess. I am not sure expulsion wouldn't have been preferable to the awful fear that one of the boys would tell, but not one of them ever did.

"Bread is the most useful article of food" is the one English sentence I remember from my childhood lessons in that language. We never had an English-speaking governess live with us. English was not regarded as something we would ever have need of, and even in school it was taught only in advanced classes. Somehow it was not taken seriously, but I do remember our teacher. His name was Walter Scott, and it was his book we used, a reader-grammar that contained that oddly memorable sentence.

Hebrew was another language that was not given any attention in our home, not in our earlier years anyway. We were Jews, but we were not in any way attentive to it. That is why Mina and I were so unprepared for Father's sudden conviction that we should learn Hebrew. Mina was about thirteen, and I was a year and a half younger.

One day Father summoned us to his study and showed us a map of Palestine and presented us with a copy of the Old Testament written in Hebrew. He felt we would need these because we would be learning to speak and write the language of the Prophets. We were amazed. He might as well have said: Tomorrow you will begin to learn Sanskrit! It wasn't that he knew Hebrew himself or that he wanted us to go to synagogue. He was not then especially religious. The whole thing sounded far-fetched to us.

It was quite a challenge. Not only because the language was so different from what we were used to learning, but in all of St. Petersburg virtually nobody spoke it. Finding a teacher was thus difficult, but Father did. His name was Solodouho, and he would come for about two hours every day. As we struggled through the Old Testament stories he pointed out the places on the map where they occurred. In that way we could project ourselves into the past, even "hear" the people speak. Mina and I made good progress.

But one day Solodouho didn't come. We read in the paper that he had been arrested. He was a pharmacist and, in filling a prescription intended for a child, he made a mistake, and it turned out to be poisonous. Luckily, the child survived, but Solodouho was made out to be a virtual murderer. The fact that Solodouho was a Jew did nothing to offset this construction of his character. Eventually he was released, but he was no longer allowed to practice his profession. Solodouho resumed teaching us, and perhaps he had other pupils, too, who would afford him a living. We never found out.

Mina and I became fluent in Hebrew. And we found a use for it after all: whenever we wanted to hide something from other ears we simply lapsed into our new language. Nobody in our whole family spoke it, nor did any of our friends.

Finally it was decided that I would be confirmed. After the ceremony my grandfather invited some of the most distinguished Jews of the city, about fifteen people. I had prepared a speech, all in Hebrew and lasting about half an hour! The time came, and I began to speak. In just a few minutes I realized that not one person there understood a word I was saying!

Our apartment house in St. Petersburg was on the corner of Karavanaya Oolitza and Circus Square. From our windows on the top floor we could see the palace of the mother of the czar to the left, and, right across from us, the circus. The circus was very popular and open ten months a year. Yet, in all the years we lived there, none of us ever went. I do not remember that any of us longed to go, either. We simply didn't feel the lack of anything we had not experienced. Friends, for instance. I made a few friends in school, but they never came to the house. In our home free time was spent in studying, reading, serious pursuits.

On birthdays there were parties, virtually all-family affairs. Cousins would spring out of nowhere for these occasions. Otherwise we were insulated against nonproductive distractions.

In the winters my parents would go away for a vacation, to either the French or Italian Riviera. Father would talk of retiring there, although I never could imagine such a thing as my father retiring anywhere. It was a long way away, a four-day train trip, and they were gone for a month and a half. I always felt very lonely during those winter weeks. I missed my mother's tremendous warmth and tenderness.

In the summer we would all go to the country or to my grandparents' estate, about a hundred miles from the city, where my mother's father had built a house for each of his children. I think Grandfather and Grandmother looked forward to these few weeks in summer when all the family would be together as much as we did. These were my favorite grandparents. I loved their dignity and kindness. My grandmother was a woman of great heart. If anything disappeared in her house—a gold spoon or a small piece of jewelry—she would not permit any investigation or prosecution. If something is missing, she would say, it means only one thing: that person needed it more than you. And Mother told us how she learned that lesson in charity of spirit. When she was a girl she was trying on a new dress and the maid admired it. My grandmother told her daughter to take it off and give it to the maid. My mother began to cry, but nothing could be done. That was the law!

Those summer days were a wonderful time. There seemed to be an endless group of cousins to play with, and we all became quite close. Much later, when everything had changed and I was living in Petrograd after the family had left, one of these cousins and I took the train out to the estate. Our grandparents had left, but we hoped to bargain with the peasants who had stayed to take care of the place. We had brought two gold watches to offer in return for some flour and other staples. The caretakers saw us as we came up the hill on our way from the railroad station, and they rushed to meet us. Perhaps they thought the Revolution was over, because, one by one, they took us aside to give an accounting of our various possessions. "Vasily took your piano," one said, and, "Ivan has your bed"—just telling on each other! (My grandmother might have said, "Well, Vasily and Ivan needed them more than you. . . .") We explained that the Revolution was still going on and that we needed food. They gave us so much that it was difficult to conceal it, which we had to do as we approached the station in Petrograd. It was against regulations to bring in so much food, but we managed by hiding it under our coats.

Just now this railroad car, my waiting place, seems darker than before. It must be the silence. Complete, almost tangible. I feel wrapped in it, like a mummy. Death is here, in the darkness, and for the moment I'm not aware of anything else.

Despite the turmoil of revolution all around me, I had never seen death up close or felt it as a threat before I got to Kislovodsk.

But a few days after my arrival the front moved south, and suddenly we were trapped in the fighting, running from the crossfire in town, hiding in cellars. And I saw dead people for the first time. They were lying in the streets. We had to be careful when running not to trip over these corpses. And when we would get to some dark hiding place and crouch down, the memory of what I had just seen would push out all other thoughts and make my head throb. I knew it was war and that death is part of war, but that didn't seem enough of an explanation for the awful finality and the waste. And this was a civil war, Russians killing Russians. Some of those people had died without even understanding the argument. . . .

The siege didn't last for more than a few days. In between the times we were caught in the violence we never spoke about what each of us must have felt. It was as if it was so overpowering a fact that it was beyond being a mere topic of discussion. I felt the shock of seeing how cruel and mindless the human being can be as a searing of my whole being, a brand I would wear all my life.

After that period of steady violence the days began to run together in a pattern of survival. The fact that most of our family was together helped to relieve the uncertainty of our existence. The fineness of the weather and the romantic beauty of the surrounding hills sometimes faded the war from our minds for days at a time. Our staple food was yogurt. It was plentiful, delicious, and never failed the test for the proper consistency: a spoon must stand by itself in it.

When the money supply began to get critically low, I wrote to the manager of a factory in Rostov-na-Donu that my father had once owned, asking if he could help us. He replied that if I could get there he could give me some money. By this time my mother decided it was time for us to leave Russia. The first step would be to get to Novorossiysk, then to Yalta on the Black Sea, Constantinople, Athens, and finally the United States. We had word that my father had already managed to get to New York, where my uncle Ilya was a minor official at the Russian consulate. I would go to Rostov-na-Donu and get some money. The family would meanwhile go to Novorossiysk and, instead of going back to Kislovodsk, I would join them there.

I got to Rostov without any trouble. The manager was kind and very generous. He came to the station with me and wished me good luck. My first destination was a transfer point for Novorossiysk. The journey began smoothly. There were several stops along the way, and at one of the longer ones, Armavir, quite a few of us had the idea of getting off the train for a little exercise.

I have tried in vain to remember if there was any clue, any unusual movement, any suspicious-looking person, that would have prepared us for what happened next. Without warning there was a human blockade all around us, and it tightened quickly. We were so many fish in a net. There were no questioners or challengers among us—we were too stunned. I still do not know if our captors were Reds or Whites. They did not identify themselves or show any sort of credentials. They said nothing at all.

We were taken to a large building several miles away. It looked as if it might have been a warehouse of some sort. There was a maze of corridors and stairs inside, but it was too dark to see more than that. We were left in an enormous hall. Huge columns supported the ceiling, and they cast long shadows in the dimness so that, at first, I didn't notice the fifty or sixty people already there. The windows were as big as doors, and there was no glass in them, only iron gates. An armed guard stood near each. It was cold and still, except for the crackling of small fires that some of the people had managed to get going. Nobody seemed curious. There was no conversation at all. A dungeon of silent strangers.

The hours went by. I felt as if I were in a terrible dream. The silence was awful. The fear was too deep and too dreadful even to draw us together. I began to think that if I made any attempt to find out what was going on the result might be worse than my imaginings. Perhaps that was what the others felt, too.

There were no beds or chairs. We had to use whatever extra clothes we had to make a place to rest on the stone floor. From time to time a strange gruel was distributed as food.

Every night there was a roll call. The people whose names were read were taken out. Even then there was no discussion. No one appeared concerned. Of course, there was always reason to hope they were released, but then we always heard a few shots afterward. . . .

Oddly, I had not been searched—none of us had—so I still had the money. I began to stroll around the room, hoping it would appear that I was just trying to give myself something to do. But what I really wanted was to examine the face of each guard. One had a very young, appealing-looking face. He seemed about my age. Perhaps I could take a chance on him. I settled down and, on a page from a notebook I carried, wrote a message to the manager in Rostov, telling him where I was as nearly as I could. I had been keeping the money in an envelope, which I now used for the note. I let a few hours go by. Finally I went up to the boy and asked if I were to pay him would he mail a letter for me, and he said he would. I gave the envelope to him with some money. I made sure it was a good deal more than he would need for stamps.

Three days went by, formless hours of pacing, trying to keep a fire going, bracing myself for the evening roll call. And on the third evening I heard, "Kostelanetz!" This was it, then. The shocking current of fear I'd expected did not come, only a strong sense of relief. The waiting was over, and in those moments before I knew why my name had been called, I could relish the feeling of hope that had been blocked by unending numbing hours of confinement.

I was led out with several others. We were taken downstairs, along corridors, and finally into a brightly lit room. And there he was, my father's associate from Rostov, rushing toward me! What was I doing here? I told him I had no idea. To this day I have no idea.

The commander of the prison apologized profusely for my situation and said I was free to go.

My father's friend took me to the public baths, and I told him the skimpy details. He told me what he knew. We ate a huge meal, and the next morning he came with me to the railroad station, this kind man who had twice rescued me. There was one train there, and it was going to Kislovodsk. More than anything I wanted to move on, away from this place, so I boarded the train. I didn't know for certain if my mother had left for Novorossiysk. I would take a chance that she hadn't.

———

There is a white sea of snow visible through the window, and above it the purple-black night. I see nothing that tells me I am in a railroad yard in Minsk, waiting. There is a face moving through the blackness, a young woman's face, and she is smiling. Satik Mikirtichef.

Satik had found me unconscious in the tiny house in Kislovodsk. The door was open when I arrived, and I saw that the house was empty. Mother had kept to the agreement and gone to Novorossiysk. That had been all that registered before I fainted.

I woke in a hospital bed. Satik, I learned later, had brought me there. I had typhus, very contagious, so I did not see her for forty-eight days. Once in a while she would send a note. I passed the fourteen-day crisis all right, but due to a shortage of disinfectant I had developed an infection, probably from an unsterilized needle.

Every few hours bodies were being taken away, corpses, victims of typhus dying around me. I experienced the most melancholy time of my life in that hospital. I kept remembering the open door and the empty house inside. No message, no trace at all of my mother or sisters and brother. Were we really ever there? I was beginning to think that our time together was nothing more than a trick the typhus fever had played on my mind. I couldn't be certain what the reality was beyond the hospital walls. The profound isolation I felt was worse than the aloneness I'd experienced as a prisoner at Armavir. But the days passed and with them the worst of my depression.

It wasn't until I was released from the hospital that I saw Satik for the first time. She had the kind of beauty that makes one forget everything for a moment. Pushkin and Lermontov have written about the women of that part of the world—the special tone of the skin, like coffee lightened with cream, and the glossy deep black hair. Satik was my first capitulation. She was Armenian, very young, small boned. We met every day, and before long we could lose ourselves in each other and forget that there was a civil war right at the edge of our world.

I had met a man named Roichel in the hospital, a doctor. He seemed to sense how isolated and uncertain I was, for he befriended me, which for him meant making me his responsibility. He gave me some money—what I'd had left was stolen in the hospital—and introduced me to his friends. The most wonderful discovery of all was that he played the violin. Among the friends we visited was a kind, beautiful woman with two lovely daughters; we would play sonatas for them. At one of those evenings Alexander Aslanof was part of the gathering. He had been conductor of the Mariinsky Opera in St. Petersburg—Petrograd—and was one of several prominent opera people who were now living as escapees in Kislovodsk. Aslanof had already organized an opera company, and his wife, who was a famous singer, had a studio for voice students. It was in that studio as an accompanist that I first worked in my chosen field. My pay was not much, but that was all right with me. I felt I should be the one to pay because of all the operatic scores I was learning.

One day Aslanof told me he needed a pianist for the opera—in Russia the title is concertmaster, but it means coach and assistant conductor—and he asked if I would take the job. What an opportunity it was—so many wonderful singers from Moscow and Petrograd. The very first day I had to coach a tenor in *Faust*, and I also had to play the organ backstage for the performance. I was able to keep my job at the studio as well. It seemed to me that I couldn't have had a better beginning in my career, even if there had been no war, no upheaval.

But I have a thought now—and it seems almost a blasphemy to me—that it was in fact just because of the war that I found myself in so fortunate a situation. I don't mean to suggest there is anything good about war. I am only too aware it is still in effect out there beyond the white-planed rail yard. The fighting is over now; still, the devastation, the disruption of people's lives, will be felt for a long time. But war does speed up time, increases the number of events, and that rush of events left me little time to decide what the next step should be. Sometimes I made a deliberate decision— taking the train back to Kislovodsk instead of waiting for one to Novorossiysk—but more often I was swept along in a tumult of experiences caused by forces outside my life.

It occurs to me that I am still very young, and yet I have already a great deal of life to look back on. These thoughts are my only companions in this solitude of waiting, and I am glad of them. My best memories are of summer. The silence of winter was broken. The days were so long, golden, and there were discoveries to be made.

Mother would always take us children away to the seaside for a few of those precious summer weeks. Several years in a row we went to a beach town close to the city, on the Bay of Finland. The water was very calm, so Mother confidently sent us to the beach for the day by ourselves. But once I discovered the local band musicians rehearsed in the afternoons, I spent less time at the shore.

It seemed astounding to me that so many separate sounds could retain their separateness even while they were blending into one single sound, with a life of its own. Sometimes I would concentrate on each musician in turn and try to distinguish his particular instrument's sound within the whole. Other times I just closed my eyes and let the music take its shape in the air around me. Often my younger sister, Maria, would come with me, for moral support. She would always have a large seashell, a conch, with her, and at intermission she would put it to her ear and listen to the music of the ocean. After the rehearsal we put in a token appearance at the beach and then went home.

I don't know if Mother knew about these detours, and I did not tell her. She would not have minded, probably, but I was fascinated enough not to risk the possibility of having to disobey her outright. But perhaps Mother did know of these secret afternoons after all—it is certainly true that children do not fool their parents as often as they would like to think—and only nodded to herself, remembering my first exposure to a group of musicians. It was a summer when the family went to the German beach town of Krantz. I don't remember many details because it happened when I was about five, but I feel as if I do, since my mother enjoyed telling the story of how her son "conducted" an all-brass band.

Each afternoon there would be an outdoor concert. It was a casual affair, with the band playing under a cupola and people strolling about or just sitting in some shady spot. Every day my mother would settle herself for a chat with some friends, and I would begin to move toward the band, always with a little more courage than the previous afternoon and so always a little closer. Finally I must have been near enough so that the conductor spotted me out of the corner of his eye, because all at once he was lifting me into the air and putting me right down beside him. The fifteen or so players went right on playing while he put the baton —I remember how light it was!—in my hand, moved my arm up and down a few times, and then stepped off the cupola platform. I continued moving my arm, the band continued playing. It did not mean anything to me. My next clear memory is me scrambling down off the platform when the music stopped and running to my mother. It was only when I got to her and she was bending down and smiling that I heard the sound of people clapping. She explained that it was for me. I didn't understand what I had done, and I had no sense of what conducting was. But even now, remembering, I can feel again the warm flush of pleasure in sensing that I had been part of something larger than myself.

Somehow I am certain the signal will come in the night, so I have allowed myself to sleep in the daylight hours. The railroad car is warmer then, too. The most important thing is to be alert during the night. That has become easier now. In fact, I look forward to the descent of darkness because my senses come alive and places and people move out of the dimness and fill the hours. Right now the white glow of the railroad yard becomes the acres of frozen parks in St. Petersburg.

All winter long they were kept flooded, and the ice stretched in all directions. Skating through those parks was something we children did almost every weekend. Sometimes Mother and Father would even join us.

When such a specific memory comes, it is hard to think I will probably never go back again to that city, and even if I should return, my old life would not be there. I am sure that when I have more new experiences away from there it will be easier to look back and to accept the disappearance of that life. Even now the memories are not always fresh and detailed as they were only two years ago in Kislovodsk. Communications to and from Yalta were virtually nonexistent because of battle lines between the Red and White armies. But I had finally discovered that my mother and the children had not gone to Constantinople as planned but remained in Yalta, where my father's parents were. She wanted to keep as much of the family together as possible. I found this out only after they had all left Yalta, so I didn't know anyone's whereabouts for a long time.

My days in Kislovodsk were full of music and the comfort of having good friends. Yet I found myself allowing memories of Petrograd to fill my thoughts. I wanted to go back, to find the aunts and uncles who were left, to see if I might be able to continue my new career.

So I wrote to my aunt Sonia, who was married to Aleksey Tolstoy, a novelist and distant relation of Leo Tolstoy. I had developed a habit of circumspection so I didn't dare say outright in the letter that I wanted to return to Petrograd, but I told her I was working in the Kislovodsk opera and wanted to continue my career. Almost immediately I received a wire from her that showed she had read between the lines. She said she was glad to hear I was alive and why didn't I come north.

Aslanof was not receptive to my idea of leaving Kislovodsk, leaving the security of my job at the opera. Perhaps he thought to protect me by not giving the release paper I needed in order to travel to Petrograd, but it didn't stop me. I was determined to go.

Everybody in Kislovodsk seemed to be talking—whispering—

about the presence of a certain prominent member of the All-Russian Extraordinary Commission for the Suppression of Counterrevolution and Sabotage—the dreaded Cheka. This man had arrived in a private four-car train in the company of the novelist Aleksandra Kollontai. She was famous as one of the first women who had become prominent in the Soviet hierarchy. Currently she was "people's commissar for social welfare." The reputation of the Cheka officer was cause for the whispering, for supposedly he was already responsible for countless murders and the imprisonment of thousands of suspected counterrevolutionaries. Regardless of how he had used—and abused—others, he represented to me an authority figure of the new regime whom I might be able to use! I decided to enter the lion's den and present the only "papers" I had, the wire from my aunt.

He was sitting at a table when I entered. He had the short brush cut of the military tradition. Without getting up or looking at me, he asked what I wanted. I told him and gave him the wire. He told me he was leaving the next day for Petrograd and that I should come to the train at four and present my wire (on which he scribbled something as he spoke). The guards would let me through. That was all.

The remaining hours in Kislovodsk are compressed to no more than one in my mind. Except for Satik I didn't linger over my good-bys. There was too much to say, and I didn't know how. And even as Satik and I promised each other that we would somehow meet again, I knew the truth was we never would.

The only baggage I carried was a burlap bag and my fur coat. Whatever made me think to take it on that hot June afternoon I don't know, but in the months to come it was the best friend I had. My "pass" worked, and I was allowed onto a crowded fourth-class car. The train moved north all through that night and well into the next day. Slow and steady, just beginning to border on monotonous. And then all at once somebody on the train was yelling, "Fire!" There was a great commotion, and then it was discovered the fire was in our car. The next thing we knew the train had stopped and our car was summarily uncoupled. We found ourselves drifting along a siding in a field somewhere in the Ukraine, watching the rest of the train disappear into the hazes of heat rising off the steppe.

As soon as the car stopped, even before, we all scrambled off and went back to the main tracks. In the distance we could see the slow approach of a very long freight train loaded with coal. A few of the cars were closed; that is, they had roofs, and as they lumbered by, all of us, one by one, managed to climb up on top of one or another of them. Our long, slow trip north resumed, but this time there was more to keep us occupied. Just staying on, for one thing. And watching for low bridges, which seemed to occur with more frequency the farther we went. Nobody had challenged us. In fact, at the first stop we made, some soldiers even warned us about the bridges. We all managed to flatten ourselves just enough to clear them, but more than once I was convinced that I wouldn't make it underneath in less than two pieces!

Finally we were approaching Moscow. Without hesitation we all jumped off in the rail yard just outside the city—after all that, no one looked forward to an opportunity of relating his adventure to some stone-faced police or army official.

My document had worked once. I didn't have the nerve to test it again. I fully intended seeing the Kremlin—it would be the first time in my life—but I thought my wits would give me a better chance than some note with a signature no one could read anyway.

I walked into the city, dragging my coat and burlap bag. It must have been an odd-looking sight; the coat alone would have drawn attention. Yet not one person came near me, either on my tour around the Kremlin or on my way out of the city. I was too tired to try to hide or to slink along close to buildings to keep out of sight. And that is probably exactly why no one challenged me: whatever it was people thought I was doing looked legitimate simply because I was doing it so openly.

The Kremlin was worth my side trip. I saw as much as I could, but I did not want to linger too long. It took me awhile to find the right station for a train to Petrograd but I did, and I boarded it in the yard (by this time I was an experienced traveler). There were a few soldiers around, but nobody stopped me. I sank into a seat with my coat and my bag. And all the luck in the world.

The first thing I did when I got to Petrograd was go to Kara-vanaya Oolitza, number 2. As I approached our apartment building I saw that all the windows were broken. Inside, the elevators were not working. I climbed the stairs.

Nobody would be living there now. I knew that. My parents were gone, and my sisters and brother. They had left long before I had, and I myself had been away a year and a half. I knew that. So why wasn't I better prepared for the emptiness I found? There was no atmosphere of warmth and familiarity, no evidence at all that this was the only home I had ever known. Only when I looked out the windows at the circus across the square was I sure I'd come to the correct address.

I walked across the huge living room, and an awful yearning came over me. As if I'd reached a point where all I needed was comfort—not a way to get by, or a pass, or anything that would require my wits—just someone to take care of me for a while. It was a shock, so unexpected, this feeling. Up to this moment I had gotten through fine. I had been courageous, even, or at least dar-ing, and always things had worked out somehow. And in this empty room now a little scene passed before my eyes from not so long ago: Boris was four or five, and I was big brother, fifteen or so, making trenches for him with the Oriental carpets so that he could play at soldiers. . . .

It was the same when I entered the library. I noticed all the blank shelves—every beautiful book was gone. And suddenly I was six again, smelling smoke, and I saw the ashtray where Herr Blu-menthal, a business associate of my father's, had left a half-smoked cigar. No one was in the library, and I longed to know what smok-ing a cigar was like. I found matches, and I lit it, seeing in my mind's eye Herr Blumenthal holding the match close to the tip and closing and reclosing his lips over the end, like a hungry fish. It worked fine, and I smoked the half cigar down to a butt.

And now there was a problem: how to change that odor of cigar that clung around me and filled my mouth. My parents would smell it, and there would be trouble. I rushed into the kitchen, and there on the sink were some strawberries. Things now went from bad to disastrous very rapidly. I stuffed my mouth with strawberries; my parents suddenly stepped into the kitchen; I immediately threw up the strawberries. That was the summer of an awful cholera epidemic in the city. People thought that eating unwashed fruit would almost certainly be one's last voluntary act on earth. Even if I had been one of the unfortunate victims, I doubt the attack would have come quite that instantaneously, but in their first moments of alarm at what they saw, my poor parents didn't think of that. . . .

I wished Mother and Father would come into the empty library now. But there was something of them here after all. A packet of letters lying in a dusty corner on the floor, still tied with a ribbon. They were the courtship letters of my parents. I sank down onto the floor and devoured every word.

There were welcoming arms for me in Petrograd. A good number of relatives had remained in the city and were managing to get by. I visited all of them. My uncle Leo had a position with the Soviet government—everyone seemed to have "a position with the government"!—in charge of maintaining the wagons-lits for the state railroad. But a salaried job obviously wasn't everything. I was shocked at my aunt Ida's thinness, and their little son, Sascha, was so very white and small for his four years.

I ended up staying with my aunt Gusta, who had provided for some years a home for a young painter named Marc Chagall. And he would say to me, "I see in your blue eyes those of your dear aunt Gusta."

Up to now nothing in my experience had justified making plans for the future. The shorter the projection the better. My family's whereabouts were uncertain. I knew their ultimate goal was New York and that they had already taken the most dangerous step toward that goal, getting out of Russia. Somewhere inside me I was certain I would leave, too, but this was not the right moment. There would be time enough to make my plans once I heard they were safe.

My most immediate intention was to enter the St. Petersburg Conservatory. It was the best in Russia. Rimsky-Korsakov had taught composition there, and his student Aleksandr Glazunov was director for years.

The straightforward approach seemed to me the best, so I took a streetcar to the Conservatory. On my way there I indulged in a game: I added up the numbers on my ticket, and I saw that the two digits of the total guaranteed me tremendous luck for the whole day—according to the tradition of this superstition, anyway —for they equaled the first two digits of the ticket number.

I am not superstitious, but I clutched that ticket in spite of myself as I waited for someone to answer my knock. Finally the Conservatory caretaker opened the door. I quickly told him I wanted to take the entrance examination although I was very late for that. When he asked why I was so late I tried to sum up the reasons quickly. But toward the end of my narrative I noticed a kind of stunned look on the caretaker's face. And I realized it couldn't have been too often that he had heard such an astounding story offered as an excuse for lateness. He remained silent after I had finished, so there didn't seem to be any reason for me not to plunge on to a final incredulity: I asked if I might have an interview with Professor Glazunov. That seemed to startle him from his daze, and he agreed to see about it.

Not too much later I found myself in a room that was dominated by the presence of a very large man who turned out to be Glazunov. I had to repeat my hegira for him, and then, because I had asked to study composition, he told me to play something I had written. By this time I was in a daze myself. I went to the piano and played a short piece I had written in Kislovodsk. Afterward he called in a colleague about whom I remember only that he puffed continuously on a cigarette, and the two held a short conference underneath a thin, flat haze of smoke. Then: "Kostelanetz," Glazunov said, "you are admitted."

As I said, I am not superstitious—but if I were, I would say that streetcar ticket gave me way above and beyond my money's worth. The very next day, in response to an announcement in the newspaper, I presented myself at the Opera as a candidate for the job of accompanist-coach. I was not quite nineteen, but to my mind that was no reason to hesitate about taking such a bold step. My only thought was that it was imperative I have a job, and music was what I knew. Even before my experience as coach and assistant conductor in Kislovodsk I had discovered a strong instinct in myself for coaching singers. Shortly after my parents had left Petrograd I was at one of my uncles' for the evening. A military doctor and his wife, a singer, were among the guests, and she had brought music for Schubert's "Du Bist die Ruh" ("You Are Peace"). She knew I played the piano so she asked if I would accompany her. As she sang I realized that she was completely unaware of the emotional meaning of the piece. (I didn't put it exactly that way to myself at the time; I just knew there was something missing, and I felt I would have to say something.) Perhaps she wasn't too familiar with the German language, or maybe it was simply that no one had ever told her that part of good singing was conveying the mood of the music and the shades of meaning in the words.

I think I must have played particularly well because when I asked her if she would mind if I made a few suggestions about interpreting what she had just sung, she said not at all. And I worked with her for about an hour, examining each phrase and explaining how it should be expressed through shadings and so on. I had no idea then that coaching was what I was doing. My motivation was a desire to hear the full expression of emotion in the song, to be able to understand what it was about underneath the words. When we finished, "my pupil" told me I should coach singers because I had a deep understanding of music.

At the Opera I auditioned before the chief conductor, a very tall man who was Don Quixote incarnate, and the director. They kept putting the scores of various operas in front of me at the piano and asking that I play from them. Finally I just laid them all aside and played selections from all of them by heart—my job in Kislovodsk had prepared me well. After about ten minutes they stopped me. I could see that they were impressed, so I explained how I had come by such an apparently miraculous accomplishment. But one thing bothered the director: Didn't I think I was awfully young for this sort of job? (I was short and fair, and probably looked about fifteen.) How did I expect to have authority with all these professional singers? Could I tell a famous diva that she was singing off key or too fast? Don Quixote answered for me: "I started when I was fourteen!"

I began my new job the next day, and for as long as it lasted, one and a half years, I never missed coming—even when I had chicken pox and knew I could pass it along!

That streetcar ticket was made of very thin paper, so that it was not much more than shreds in my pocket before long.

The months passed quickly into winter, the season when shortages of food and fuel are most noticeable. Those were days when anything that burned was a great present. A log or two made a wonderful birthday gift. We were always cold. At some point in the day it might be possible to say you were less cold than you had been that morning or the night before, but never would you say you were warm.

I worked hard at the Opera, and because I was so busy most of my studies at the conservatory were arranged privately. My sessions with Professor Kalafati in composition remain most clearly in my mind, partly because of the great charm of the man and also because of the setting in which we worked. It was an unusually large room, and the professor had placed an iron stove right next to the piano. It had very thin walls and heated up quickly. The result was that the very warm halves of our bodies on the stove side took our minds off the very cold other halves. I am sure there was an advantage in all that coldness because it stimulated an amazing amount of physical and mental energy, although that comforting thought escaped me at the time.

My days were long and bulging with work in music. They were precious to me then, just as they are now in my memory, because they held an unending trove of discovery. My mind and soul were filling up with music. Those eighteen months were a perfect balance of study and work, designed, it seemed, especially for me.

Much of the time it was possible to ignore the larger, less benign reality within which my own existed. On my walk to the Opera each day I passed a beautiful stone cottage, right on the River Neva. It had been a gift of the czar to his mistress, Mathilde Kchessinska, a famous ballerina. When Lenin arrived in Petrograd the cottage was requisitioned for him. But the knowledge of its romantic purpose stayed stronger in my head. On occasion Lenin would be addressing a small crowd as I passed, and although I never made any effort to get close enough to hear everything he was saying, the contrast of this tableau made a lasting impression: the earnest, drab Communist revolutionary shouting party dogma from the balcony of the czar's mistress. Yet six months later this man had all of Russia in his pocket.

The happy busyness of my life made a fine natural defense against the workings of the new Soviet order and, for a time, the penetrations were small and sporadic. One night I came home to find that there had been a fire at Aunt Gusta's. We all lost everything. Aunt Gusta moved to another apartment, and I went to live with my uncle Leo and aunt Ida. In theory, the government insured against such losses; in practice, that meant a new shirt and a pair of socks.

The experience surely affected my life, but I was only a passive participant. My loss was only of material things, nothing really important. The next time I came up against that same disparity between Communist theory and practice it was much more serious, and I was not so lucky.

There was a period of experiment at the Opera when part of what Lenin must have been preaching from Kchessinska's balcony was put into practice. In the tradition of a true Communist state there would be no distinctions in salary, no matter what the worker's job was. Tenor or floor sweeper, the pay would be the same. It was also announced that the government had created cultural departments in the military and in the factories so that soldiers and workers could have the opportunity to learn something about art and music. Singers and coaches at the Opera, for instance, could go out to a regimental barracks or to a factory once a week and try to teach anyone who wanted to learn the rudiments of singing. Not a very serious enterprise, as it turned out, because most of those people were just not ready for it. And the attention they paid was based more in the idea that their instructors were from a remote, fantastical world unknown to them. But worse, it was not a very honest enterprise, either: for giving such instruction a person would receive the food ration of the worker or soldier he was teaching. Even so, when one of the singers came to me and suggested we both try it, I did not hesitate. I joined two such cultural departments, as he had, one army and one factory. And suddenly I was receiving extraordinary gifts—flour, bacon, whatever the ration happened to be that day—and I would have to bring a little sleigh to take it all home. . . .

It might seem a stroke of good fortune, but I cannot now look back to that situation and call myself lucky. The egalitarian experiment had broken down right at the start because the curtain raiser or the janitor could not teach anything. We all got the same salary but only some qualified for extras. And what of the workers and soldiers who had to give up their rations? These realizations were painful for me because I had to admit to involvement in a system I did not respect, had only tolerated because it did not reach into my life. Overnight my happy ignorance had changed to self-benefiting participation at the expense of others.

From then on I was painfully aware of what was really going on around me. Beyond my world there was no freedom of movement, little food, no joy, no place to hide. The Revolution—the fighting, at least—was over, but people were still dying because of it, arrested in the night and murdered before dawn. The lists were posted, sometimes as many as five hundred people. More than once I noticed names familiar to me in my childhood, friends of my parents. There was never anything further heard about them, no explanations given for their disappearance.

One day, in the late winter of 1922, I went to the Mariinsky as usual. There was a small piece of paper on the door: OPERA CLOSED FOR LACK OF FUEL. It struck me as such a paltry reason for this great tradition of the past two hundred years to just stop. All of us who had been working there had managed to live with the shortage. Coats and mittens were the standard uniform. The somewhat comical sight of steam emerging from singers' mouths had long since become a commonplace.

It seemed to me the last—the only—vestige of another time had finally ended. I stood still and read the notice several more times. And as I turned away I knew the time to leave Russia had come.

Illegal emigration from the Soviet Union (and there was no other kind) was a capital crime. As a deterrent it was a marked failure. The one function it served was to solidify the intention to leave.

By this time my immediate family had reached New York City. My father had gotten there first and then brought my mother and the children. He was able to send me an affidavit of his willingness and ability to support me should I be admitted to the United States. I would need it to present to the American consul when I applied for a visa. To do that I would have to somehow get to Warsaw, where the nearest consulate was.

The first question was what border point to choose for my crossing. The most convenient—between Russia and Finland—was also the most heavily guarded. No one considered that route any more. But the Polish-Lithuanian side was more laxly watched. Many had success crossing there. I decided on Minsk as the most logical city of departure. My biggest risk at this point was confiding my plan to a friend at the Conservatory whose family lived there. I shouldn't have worried, for he was completely sympathetic, and he managed to secretly communicate with his parents about it. As I found out later I was luckier than I realized, for they were part of a group of people in Minsk who were already quite practiced in arranging to help people leave the country. Almost immediately word came that my project could be arranged.

I was able to obtain a release from the Opera. It was a simple statement to the effect that I had worked there from July 15, 1920, to February 1, 1922. But good traveling papers—permission to leave Petrograd and a statement of destination and purpose—were impossible. At this point I didn't even want to try, for it might be an alert to the authorities. I would just have to slip away.

Uncle Leo's "position with the government" was the key to everything. One of the perquisites of being inspector of the wagons-lits was a much reduced risk of being challenged while traveling. He said he would take me to Minsk.

My last sight of Petrograd was through a window of this very wagon-lit I wait in now. All my relatives had come to the station, and we had a coffee together—I can still see the long million-ruble note which inflation dictated we pay for it. My baggage was exactly the same as it had been before: a burlap bag, which they had pulled through the snow on a small sleigh for me on our walk to the train. This time I could wear my fur coat. It was hard for me not to throw myself into their arms in that good-by, but we had to appear unsuspiciously casual.

My uncle and I were four days traveling to Minsk in the comfort of this car. Sometimes the train stopped for hours, but no one ever bothered us. It might have been because my youthful appearance gave the innocent impression of a young boy traveling with his father. And there were times during those four days when I wished that were exactly the situation so that I could have squeezed my "father's" hand and told him how much he meant to me.

My uncle had arranged for the wagon-lit to be held in the rail yards at Minsk—as an inspector, he would not be questioned about it—so I would be able to stay there without jeopardizing the parents of my Conservatory friend. We went to see them as soon as we arrived, and they told me the only thing I had to do was wait in the wagon-lit until someone came for me. They gave me some food, and my uncle and I went back to the rail yards. The tea man was still there, in his little compartment. He had never once spoken to us on the trip to Minsk, and he did not now.

It was time for the final good-by. I told my uncle I would send a message back to him if I crossed well: "4711." He stepped out of the car and made his way through the snow. I settled myself into the silence.

I am aboard the S.S. *Aquitania*. The ship is several days out of Cherbourg, sailing calm waters. A tremendous storm broke the rhythm of her progress for two days, but there is nothing now in her powerful plowing of the sea to suggest that. My visa is good only until September 30, and it is already near the end of the month. I can hardly believe that if the ship arrives later in New York I will be turned away.

Yet I do find myself imagining such a disaster—my parents and sisters and brother waiting on the dock, waving to me, and I bravely waving back but knowing I will have to tell them the impossible news. . . . I am not sure why I allow this painful fantasy to assert itself over and over again. My life of the past few months has been so filled with high suspense, unbelievable chance occurrences, that perhaps I have developed a habit of dramatically coloring my thoughts.

The door at the end of the wagon-lit was locked, so when the signal came I had to use the conductor's exit. It was on the fifth night that three soft taps on the window ended my days of sleep and my nights of reverie and watchfulness. There was nothing to do but blow out the candle and pick up my burlap sack. I crept silently past the *provodnik*'s compartment—although, considering his thorough lack of acknowledgment of my presence up till now, I probably could have shouted good-by without any risk of interference.

I opened the exit door and felt the frigid air surround me as I jumped down into the snow. My eyes were already accustomed to darkness so I had no trouble making out the figure of a man standing nearby. There were no introductions. All he said was, "Come with me." I didn't know whether to trust him or not, but I did not hesitate. There was no choice.

We walked a few yards to a tree where a horse was tethered. He was harnessed to a sleigh very simply constructed from a few planks. We climbed on, and the man took the reins. We started off through the snow. At first we moved in a series of circles, I supposed in order to cover our tracks, and then we drove out of Minsk and into the surrounding fields and woods. I sat still, not wanting to break the silence, and hugged the burlap bag against my chest. Through it I could feel the hardness of the loaf of bread, inside of which I had hidden some gold coins borrowed from my uncle. The inspiration for that had come from my childhood English lessons, that odd sentence in Mr. Scott's grammar that had stuck in my mind: "Bread is the most useful article of food."

We drove for the rest of the night and all the next day, stopping twice so the horse could rest. Sometimes there would be no road at all, and more than once the sleigh tipped over. The man never said a word, even when occasionally we would hear a single gunshot reverberate through the crisp air. I thought it might mean we were getting close to the border, that somebody had been caught trying to cross, but I took my cue from him and kept silent.

At sunset the dull gray daytime sky came alive with hot reds and orange. The next moment the brilliance was gone and the colors melted away into darkness. Almost at once I could see the lighted windows of what looked like a schoolhouse. As we got closer I thought it must be a makeshift army barracks. There were several soldiers outside, smoking, and I saw more through the windows. . . . And then it seemed very obvious to me—I was being double-crossed. This man was about to turn me in, receive his money, and be gone!

The guide motioned me out of the sleigh, and we began to walk to the door. Strangely, he didn't make any attempt to hold on to me, and we passed the soldiers seemingly unnoticed. Now I had a second revelation: bribes had bought their silence and turned their barracks into a virtual way station for illegal emigration. I must be in the hands of an underground ring that helped people escape.

I gave my guide a little money. He told me I must also give him my burlap satchel so that I would not look as if I were traveling. I handed over the bag, bread, gold coins, and all.

There I was, with what looked to be about thirty Soviet soldiers. Nothing was said to me. My guide brought me a glass of vodka. It was the first time I had ever tasted it. Suddenly I felt very comfortable, relaxed, warm. Sublime. My guide took me to another room with a couch in it, and I lay down. The soldiers began singing. So beautiful—it sounded like a professional choir. I drifted into sleep.

I awoke to complete silence and darkness. The house was empty. There didn't seem to be anything to do but wait. It wasn't long before a man appeared. The guide's role in my escape was apparently over, for this was someone I had not seen before. He gave me snowshoes and said we would leave right away. I knew this was it: we were about to cross the border.

The night was perfect for our purpose, absolutely black. The snowshoes kept us from having to wade through the deep drifts, yet our progress was slow. And then a figure stepped out of the darkness right ahead of us, a soldier with a gun. He let my guide pass, but he held up a hand in front of me and asked where I was going. I looked at him but didn't answer. It was now or never. I pushed around him and began to move as fast as possible. The snowshoes made it a clumsy effort. I seemed to be getting nowhere, exactly like the classic nightmare. I began to feel my temples throb with the tension of waiting for the gunshot. But it never came; nor was the soldier chasing me. I realized all he wanted was a little something extra for himself.

My guide was just a few yards away, and as I moved toward him I suddenly had an intuitive notion to destroy my Soviet passport, leave the pieces of my unwanted connection behind me in the snow. I knew that in Poland a person identified as a Soviet could be sent back, but what could they do if there was no evidence of identification? I might be able to pass myself off as a Pole who had lost his papers (although how I would convey that was still a mystery, since I knew no Polish).

Where exactly the border was I don't know, but before long we saw rows of small, neat houses. We were across, somewhere in Lithuania. The door to one house was open, and we stepped inside. No one was there. We went up to the second floor, and I couldn't resist falling onto a bed and immediately into sleep.

Once again, I awoke alone and in darkness. Male voices rose from the floor below. I went to the window just as the men were leaving and saw that they were soldiers. I went downstairs. My guide was there. He told me the next and final stage of the journey would be to Vilna (the Russian name for a city that was also called

Wilno by the Poles and Vilnius by the Lithuanians; at one time or another Vilna belonged to each of these three countries, although geographically and culturally it was Lithuanian. At the moment it was Polish Wilno).

We traveled by horse and sleigh, mostly at night. Our only real fear was that the wrong person might discover that I was neither Polish nor Lithuanian, so my guide asked me to keep quiet no matter what the circumstances. That worked very well—even when a Polish soldier decided he would hitch a ride with us for a while. Fortunately, he was not curious about the silent passenger.

By comparison with conditions in Russia, food was almost plentiful in Lithuania, and we stopped in several places to see people my guide knew and to eat with them. Once we stayed overnight, but even then he reminded me not to talk at all. Although he did not say, I was sure these people were all part of the underground.

We approached Wilno in the requisite circling pattern. It was arranged for me to stay briefly with the Kowarski family, who had made a successful escape from Petrograd earlier. This family happened also to be distantly related to my own—there had been several intermarriages—and the father, a banker, had been a business associate of my father's.

Just before I left for the Kowarskis' the guide and the Wilno contacts presented me with my burlap satchel. The precious "most useful article" was still inside.

Only four days had passed since I had handed it over at the military barracks, four days in which I had been ushered over an invisible border that nevertheless separated two complete worlds. Compared with other trips I had taken in the past few years, this journey was as quiet as a dream, but I know there could never be any as propitious or exciting or stirring in a lifetime of travels because it has brought me finally to where I am now, sailing to America.

I took a night train to Warsaw, but I did not sleep. Anticipation made it impossible. The final phase of my emigration was about to begin. I kept seeing myself in the American consul's office in Warsaw, actually being granted a visa, having everything made official.

. . . In Wilno I had obtained from the police for a little money a new "identity," a passport for a "citizen of the former Russian Empire." It would be something to present to the consul, something to be *stamped*.

The first thing my Warsaw contact family—curiously, also named Kovarsky, but a different spelling and no relation—told me was that a "citizen of the former Russian Empire" could remain in Warsaw only three days. Well, that simply meant I would go immediately to the consul's office and then be on my way. I did not confide this optimism to the Kovarskys, so I arrived at the consulate unwarned. . . .

My first impression was of a tremendous undulating swarm of humanity, so many people that it was impossible to distinguish them as separate individuals without hard concentration. I didn't know how many people I was looking at, but everyone was issued a ticket with a number; mine was 4,000. I asked how long it would take to obtain a visa. Three years. Three years to wait; three days to stay.

The Kovarskys were understandably sensitive about my remaining with them beyond the time limit—no one wanted to be noticed by the police—so I thought I would try to find a job, which would not only give me a little money but also allow me to stay in the city legally. I visited the musicians' union office and showed the man in charge of admissions my Petrograd opera papers. He said the Warsaw Philharmonic needed a pianist—would I be interested!

On my way back to the Kovarskys I stopped in a shop to get some shoes. The shopkeeper had a record player which at that moment was playing unusual, fascinating music. I pointed to the record to indicate I would like to know what it was. " 'Alexander's Ragtime Band,' " the man said in English, "by Irving Berlin." They were the first English words I had heard since my school days. I took it as a good omen.

Mischa Mischakoff, who is sailing with me now to New York, was the concertmaster for the Warsaw Philharmonic. He, too, had escaped Russia—leaving Moscow at the same time as a cellist named Gregor Piatigorsky—and we quickly became friends. I was doubly fortunate in this friendship; not only was he a grand companion, but it was a notion of his that launched us suddenly and finally out of Warsaw.

Mischa had decided to give a special Sunday afternoon recital that would feature solo performances by some of the orchestra players, and he asked me to accompany them on the piano. We gave the concert, and it went very well. Afterward, in a reception room just offstage, there was a small gathering of musicians and some members of the audience. Mischa spoke only Russian, so I stayed near him to help communications along by fitting in some German here, some French there. And it worked out pretty well. At one point a couple came up to us and introduced themselves as Monsieur et Madame Keena. Monsieur began to praise us, continuing in French, saying that we were wonderful musicians and had we ever thought of going to the United States, where great artists were much appreciated? I told him we would love to do just that, but unfortunately there would have to be a three-year wait for a visa. And now both Keenas smiled at me, and it was Fortune's smile. *"Je suis le consul américaine!"* M. Keena said. If we would come to the consulate the next morning, he would personally issue us our visas.

PART TWO

Discoveries

Overtures

I HAVE NEVER BEEN ABLE to think of trains as merely vehicles of travel convenience, because during several crucial years they carried me not so much to a given destination as to a new point of departure.

After the eight-day desert walk from the Caspian shore, at a depot I still cannot identify, there was a train waiting, one car made up for Kislovodsk. At Armavir, when I did not know whether my mother had got to Novorossiysk and if I should go there or return to Kislovodsk, there again was one train in the station, and it was going to Kislovodsk. A coal-train ride to Moscow gave me the taste of pleasure in unplanned adventure right in the midst of a struggle simply to survive the aftereffects of a civil war. These were the trains that rescued me from chaos and oblivion, and—literally and figuratively—forwarded my life. And there was my wagon-lit, which kept me still and safe, and whose darkness invited comforting visits from my past life. I don't believe this kind of coincidence is strong enough to be named a lifetime leitmotif, but trains then seemed to hold a magic—and the spell was not yet over.

I had been in the United States for a little over four years before I had my first transcontinental train trip. A prominent voice teacher named Lazar Samoiloff had hired me for a ten-week tour on the West Coast. He had organized teaching sessions by well-known figures in music, and I would act as accompanist. These so-called Master classes would be held in Seattle and Portland, Oregon, for two weeks each and in San Francisco and Los Angeles, California, for three weeks each. I was much taken with the idea. Not only would it mean working with some of the day's best singers, conductors, and players, it was also my first opportunity to see something of the American continent. My only stipulation to Samoiloff was that we travel by the northernmost route, the Canadian Pacific Railway, and he agreed. So we went to Montreal and boarded the transcontinental. We would be at least five days on the train, and it was May. I remember thinking—a bit romantically, I suppose—how stunning it would be to have so many views of nature waking up to spring.

Well, I was right. But how could I have been prepared for just how stunning it was? One of the stops was Lake Louise in Canada's Banff National Park. Clichés have their beginnings in such sights: it did take my breath away. There is a description of it in a Kipling poem, I think, or maybe in his *From Sea to Sea*—but it is so long ago that I read it I can't be sure—and one line remained in my mind: "We saw the wonder-working lake lying mute in its circle of forest—a lake carved out of pure jade." It was indeed a wonder-working lake, for it inspired me to compose! "Lake Louise" was published in 1928. I wrote it originally for solo harp and dedicated it to Annie Louise David, a harpist whom I was currently accompanying. Later I orchestrated it, and Deems Taylor conducted a performance on the Chesterfield program for which I played the harp part on the piano. "Lake Louise" is one of a very few pieces I have composed. The necessary compulsion has seldom been present, although I have sometimes pondered whether my response to the awesomeness of nature might not have been cultivated to the point of inspiration. In the end, though, I think the impetus to write music is dictated by some inner drive, or perhaps even in the genetic make-up. It is true that places have inspired many composers to write, but I doubt such inspirations were the *sine qua non*. It is the imagination that is the key—otherwise, how to explain the fact that Puccini wrote *Madame Butterfly* without ever having visited Japan? Or that E. Y. Harburg wrote the lyrics to "April in Paris" but had never been there?

One early evening, about halfway across Canada, Lazar and I

were in the dining car. It was fairly empty—there were relatively few passengers on the train. For that matter there were few people to be seen anywhere during the trip. The view from the windows made it easy to imagine ourselves the only intrepid travelers in some endless unexplored wilderness. Lazar remarked that we would be stopping in Roseburg, Oregon, before going to Portland and that he had to make a speech there at the national convention of Music Clubs of America . . . and could I help him with an outline. He was not specific about the topic, just so long as it pertained to music. I said I would be glad to try.

After dinner I went to the observation car at the end of the train. There was no one there. Pale streamers drifted in the western sky, left by the setting sun. It was such a flat terrain that even the last lingering evidence of the day was visible. I decided to settle down on the car's rear platform and think out a subject for the outline. As I expected, no one was there, either, just the endless plains flashing by, the rhythm of the clicking wheels accompanying. I let my gaze float on the sea of darkness beyond the windows. From time to time I would see a single small light that would quickly diminish to a pinpoint and then fade away as the train steadily lengthened the distance between us. After a while I imagined them as signals, beacons registering human existence on these vast prairies. People living out their lives in tremendous isolation, cut off from close communication with the rest of the world. I thought of the little crystal set I had recently bought back in New York, my first radio. I listened to it every chance I had, fascinated by how it transcended time and distance. Could that be the answer for so many millions of people just like these, the end of isolation? They would have music, news, a feeling of participation in the world. That would be a subject for Samoiloff to talk about.

I went back to my compartment and made a draft for him to consider. We were standing face to face with a new age, I wrote, the age of radio, which would diminish loneliness, open communication, end isolation. . . . When I finished, I realized I had found not only an answer for the speech but a new point of departure for myself as well.

At breakfast I read what I had written for Lazar. He was somewhat dubious: "My God! People will think I am crazy!" But he gave that speech, and it was published, too (under his name, of course), in a magazine called something like *Musical West*. There the matter stopped for him—but not for me.

The West Coast was a completely new experience with nature. I was not used to thinking of the outdoors as invitingly warm and lush. The California weather, of course, was balm, and the flowers, so rare in Russia, were literally everywhere you looked. I had enough time in between our assignments to travel to the great Yellowstone and Glacier National parks. How can mere words reveal the breath-taking drama of these natural wildernesses? I was bewitched by the shimmering lakes, by the waterfalls like liquid diamonds and emeralds, the dense evergreen forests, the mountains of heights I had only dreamed existed.

In those days few people had the impulse to visit the parks. During my stay I never saw or heard a single person. So the quiet was immense. It was a natural silence, though, not devoid of the sounds of nature, only of human noise. It was so awesome that I began to feel the minor proportion of my presence there. I would stand still and gaze around me for so long that my legs would get numb. It occurred to me that it would be the simplest and most natural thing in the world to stop here forever, to surrender to the magnitude of this beauty and be nourished in every corner of my mind and soul. I knew that it was not possible, not in me to do so. I disengaged myself and, as I'm sure many have before me, fixed these visions in my mind to be drawn upon for peace and solace throughout my life.

By the time we had been in Los Angeles for a week, the radio idea was firmly fixed in my head, and I had admitted to myself that it was what I wanted to pursue. I announced to Samoiloff that I was resigning and returning to New York immediately. His good-luck wishes were heavily laced with broad hints that I was completely insane.

That was not the first opportunity I had turned away from. The difference now was that I had a compelling reason for doing so, well beyond the notion of wanting to explore as many avenues as possible, which had pretty much governed my actions up to now. It seemed to me that radio was an ideal gamble in which to risk my chips. It held challenge and promise. The possibility of being able to bring music to millions of people—and many would be hearing it for the first time—excited me tremendously. I wanted to be part of that connection, part of that discovery.

Discoveries had highlighted my experience of America ever since that first September day I rejoined my family on the Hudson River pier. On top of the thrill of seeing them all again, of knowing we had managed to survive, was the excitement of the city. The sounds, the lights, the people on the streets everywhere. For me it was love at first sight. I surrendered immediately.

Our apartment was off Morningside Park in upper Manhattan. On our third or fourth evening together we took a long walk down Broadway, and I thought, what a fabulous street! In those days it was not so glaringly tawdry as it is now. I couldn't get over the freedom of movement, the display of lights, the aura of vitality. This was it! The glimpses I had had of Unter der Linden in Berlin and rue de la Paix in Paris, on my way to Cherbourg and the *Aquitania*, had hinted that a street needn't be just a street; it can have a flair, a style that distinguishes it from all others. It was a new idea to me. The streets of Petrograd were, many of them, beautiful but virtually devoid of life. Quiet, cold, forbidding. . . .

We were all so happy to be together, to be finally out of danger, that we did not miss our old life. There were differences. My father had lost all his money and was just beginning to establish himself in insurance, so there was very little income at first. Luckily, my mother had managed to bring some of her jewelry, and we were able to live from the sale of it for a while. There was no complaining; as far as I know none of us felt deprived, just very, very lucky.

I thought my first two projects should be learning English and getting a job. Fortunately, in music, the one does not hinge on the other. I was able to set myself up as a voice coach almost at once on a free-lance basis at two dollars an hour. As soon as I could, I took a separate apartment, first in the same building as my parents and eventually in a different house, nearer Morningside Park. I wanted to avoid having my pupils disturb my family, but there was another reason, too: I had grown used to independence, to the heady notion that I could, at least to some extent, control my life. In the past few years I had learned dramatically what it meant to be rescued by the kindness of friends and by the lucky strokes of fate—but those were hardly dependable elements, to be called up at will. In between those particular rescues, the only help I could expect had to come from me. By the time I reached New York and was safely reunited with my parents, my status as dependent son was well behind me, and I wanted to continue going my own way.

I never enrolled in a formal English class. My method of learning consisted of a strong belief in exposure. The English dictionary I had bought in Poland was always in my pocket. I made sure to read a newspaper every day—looking up virtually every word on some occasions. I asked people to speak in English whenever they would considerately try to devise some more elementary but surer way of communicating. My crystal set, the only radio I could afford and to me the most fascinating invention I had yet come across, turned out to be a great aid in familiarizing my ear to the cadence of spoken English.

My most immediate need was to learn musical terminology in English. Although opera singers usually have some knowledge of German or French, both of which I could fall back on, I was reluctant to rely on those "foreign" languages. A friend advised me to talk to Walter Damrosch, who was then conductor of the New York Symphony Society and whose brother Frank was head of the Institute for Musical Arts, which later became Juilliard. I went to see him (we spoke in German), and he recommended I attend an advanced class in music taught by a Professor Goetchius at the Institute. One day, after a session, eager to try my wings with this new language, I boldly turned to another student sitting next to me and said something in English. What I meant my message to be I have no idea now. More to the point, neither had he *then*. He said nothing, only looked at me a little strangely. Years later Richard Rodgers told me it was he who had nipped that conversation in the bud!

The public library was a great haven for me in my early linguistic studies. One thing I especially liked to do was select some poetry and try to work my way through it. It was not only good practice in learning a little bit more about the language, it also gave me some exposure to its more graceful expression. On one such occasion I had wanted to see what the poetry of O'Neill would be like—everyone was talking about him then. One or another of his plays was always in performance on Broadway. At that time it was *Anna Christie*, O'Neill's second Pulitzer Prize winner. Well, I asked at the library if I could look at some O'Neill poems and was given a slim volume of what turned out to be delightful poetry. Each poem was short and on a separate page, and most had no titles. They were so evocative and yet simple. And there were a few that particularly appealed to me, so much so that I thought I might write some music for them. Rather than take the book home with me, I copied out the poems, thinking that I could keep referring to them whenever I had time and eventually, perhaps, compose something.

A friend of mine told me to be sure to get permission to use the poems if I intended to publish them as lyrics with the music, so I wrote to Eugene O'Neill and, of course, included copies of the poems I wanted to use. I still remember the first line of his answer: "I share with you your admiration for these poems, but I didn't write them." The poet was George O'Neill, or possibly John O'Neill. I realized then what had happened—I had never bothered to say Eugene O'Neill; I had just assumed he was a poet as well as a playwright. But the story doesn't end there. Some years later, in 1928, Eugene O'Neill's third Pulitzer Prize–winning play appeared, and its title matched exactly the first two words of one of those poems: *Strange Interlude*.

In a relatively short time my father had quite an impressive string of clients in his newly adopted country and had gotten to know a good number of people in the arts. He smoothed the way to my first important job interview; it was with the principal conductor of the German repertoire of the Metropolitan Opera, Artur Bodanzky. Bodanzky was an extremely charming man. He talked to me kindly, and he offered me a coaching position—at $75 a week!—similar to the one I had had in the Petrograd opera. I thanked him and told him I would like to think about it, but on the way home I decided to turn it down. The idea of becoming a conductor was always in the back of my mind. In those days one did not study conducting formally. The usual route to that goal was to coach in an opera house, something I had done in Russia. The foundation in operatic repertoire that had afforded me was priceless, and the added responsibility of rehearsing an opera chorus, sometimes even conducting it from the wings during a performance, gave me practical experience in conducting. I was sure that coaching at the Met would only have repeated what I already knew. Besides, I wanted to conduct a concert orchestra, not opera. Where or how, I did not know.

In the meantime I continued coaching privately in Lazar Samoiloff's voice studio. In that way I was able to earn a living, keep myself exposed to music, and yet remain free of a commitment I might regret. I avoided the risk of becoming hypnotized into something I didn't really want by the security and prestige offered in a renowned organization like the Met. The only thing I was hypnotized by, and most willingly, was what I was seeing and hearing and feeling in America, in this eager, all-embracing New York City. At times I could barely believe I was here. Images of my life in Russia were being more persistently overshadowed every day by the contrasting realities of my new world. No residue of anguish left over from a perverted revolutionary ideal and an insane civil war. No echoing silences. No empty streets. No secrets. No fear. Instead—warmth, energy, inventiveness, bold smiles, and an unabashed but somehow forgivable certainty that this place was the center of the world. How could I not catch the fever of such an atmosphere? I wanted to explore this hopeful land, to find my place in it, and finally to contribute to it something of myself.

I have always loved poetry. To me it is language on the very border of music. And I think that stood me in good stead when I came to earn my living at coaching because what is needed there is an ability to feel the totality of the work. The clue is in the words, for they color how the music is expressed. Some singers have this gift, but many more do not. That is where coaching can help. Once the singer has learned the notes and the musical construction of the piece, it is time to begin capturing the meaning of the words and to translate that meaning through proper phrasing.

I found that nine-tenths of the singers who came to me had given little if any thought to the idea of conveying the mood or moods of what they were singing. For instance, Schubert's "An die Musik" is a beautiful song with a very spiritual mood almost always ignored. The singer would just not feel it—and so we would read the words together and talk about them. Eventually we would be able to grasp the meaning. And once that happened, it was as if a match had been struck. Actors are concerned with that very thing, too, and can often enlarge the dimension of their roles through the interpretive suggestions of the director. The achievement of the singer, though, is much more hardly won. The words must be more than correct; they must convey the appropriate emotion. And there is the additional necessity of simply staying on pitch.

I have always felt that sensitivity to the drama, the message, the "colors" of music, is the most important part of the orchestral conductor's responsibility, too, which is probably why voice coaching is such an ideal preparation. The composer's marks are often ambiguous, sometimes nonexistent. So the conductor must convey by his markings on the music and by his signals just what subtleties of color and phrasing he believes are in the score. The players in the orchestra rely on him for this because there has to be a unity of expression in the performance. If each player put out his own reading of the music, the effect might be quite uneven at best, chaotic at worst. And if a piece is a vocal work that has been arranged for orchestra alone, making the players aware of the lyrics can lend special sensitivity to the performance. In the Thirties and Forties, I often conducted orchestral arrangements of popular show tunes of the day. And I would make sure that each player had the words available in front of him.

Working in Samoiloff's voice studio so long ago was quite a revelation. His job consisted of developing the voice, those two tiny vocal cords, for strength and control. But he had an eye on the business side, too. Samoiloff wanted to keep as many students as possible coming on a steady basis. And he succeeded. The place was run like a dentist's office; every hour on the hour a student appeared. Samoiloff's secret to maintaining such a steady clientele was, I think, getting them to believe in their talent. A simple approach lay behind that achievement: a singer would finish a song and naturally look expectantly to the teacher for a reaction. Samoiloff was always ready: "Why," he would say, "there is no voice like yours at the Metropolitan!" The vast majority of pupils took it as the greatest of compliments, and, of course, he hadn't said anything that was untrue. . . .

Very soon after I had rejoined my family in New York I realized that my father had undergone a conversion. His attitude about music as a career changed totally. He had seen enough in this new world to realize that there were possibilities in every direction, including every kind of music, from which someone could make a worthy and rewarding career. And if one of those someones turned out to be his eldest son, so much the better. The longstanding disagreement between us dissolved, and I was touched, sometimes amused, by his efforts to introduce me to people he had met through his business who he thought might, directly or otherwise, help me on my way.

One of these visits was meant to encourage my desire to one day conduct, and even though quite the opposite intention was apparent in our host's remarks, the original object was achieved. It was, however unconsciously, an exercise in what today might be called reverse psychology.

Modeste Altschuler had immigrated to the United States from Russia as an already successful cellist and conductor. By the early

Mother, Rosalia Kostelanetz.

Father,
Nachman Kostelanetz.

At the "seashore" with baby sister Maria and big sister Mina. Our baby brother, Boris, had not yet made his appearance.

With Mina and Maria.

(Left) In my late teens. *(Below left)* First passport photo. *(Below)* Aboard the *Aquitania*, 1922. Mischa Mischakoff is on my right.

(Above) The People's Theater and the Opera, Petrograd. *(Below)* The Conservatory, where I studied music, Petrograd.

Mina and her husband, Alexei, their new baby daughter, Lily, my mother, proud Aunt Lily and Uncle Andre.

Maria's son, Bob, Boris and son, Richard, and me during a visit to Israel.

For the Pontiac program, c. 1931, we had our first studio audience, which gave rise to the idea of having a comic interlude during the commercials. Directly behind me are Alex Cores and, to his right, Nicolai Berezowsky, who were always ready to take over the baton at rehearsals so I could monitor what was coming through in the control room.

The Hudson Theater, one of the most acoustically superb broadcasting homes I knew in my radio career. We did the Chesterfield program three times a week in 1934, the first of its four years, with plenty of opportunity for musical innovations. Chester Hazlett, directly below the cigarette package, between the two music stands, was an imaginative contributor to new sounds with his invention of the sub-tone clarinet.

(*Above left*) Harry Freistadt, first trumpet for the classical selections we played on Chesterfield. Russ Case took over for the popular. (*Above right*) Three of the opera stars who appeared often on Chesterfield. Grete Stueckgold is seated next to Nino Martini, Rosa Ponselle stands next to our producer, Fred Bethel. The apartment is Rosa's. (*Below*) The Coca-Cola program was broadcast from this wonderful studio, Liederkranz Hall, in the old German Singing Society headquarters on Fifty-eight Street in Manhattan. During those five years, from 1938 to 1943, I also recorded quite a few records here. CBS later converted this acoustical miracle into a television studio, a decision that still mystifies me.

(*Above*) In 1936 I flew a total of 126,000 miles—mostly to the West Coast to visit Lily—a record, as I discovered the following year at the National Aviation Show. Mayor Fiorello LaGuardia presents me with the Number One air passenger trophy while Lily looks on knowingly. (*Below*) Lily and I were married in 1938 and flew to South America by clipper for a honeymoon. The clippers flew only in daylight, since they had to land and take off on water. The trip took six days.

Lily in costume for *Lakmé*, with her most ardent admirer.

Caught off guard.

In Hawaii.

I've always found it hard to resist an opportunity to try something new, particularly when it came to flying. In 1939, I became the first helicopter passenger to land on a rooftop. We flew from New York to Philadelphia and alighted on top of the post office. Exciting as that was, it didn't compare to my first USAF jet plane ride some 16 years later at Yokota Air Base in Japan.

(Above) In the early forties I commissioned Virgil Thomson *(right)* to do a musical portrait and he chose New York Mayor LaGuardia, who graciously allowed himself to be musically captured while on the job. *(Below)* When I approached Aaron Copland to compose a musical portrait, he selected Abraham Lincoln as his subject. The words of Lincoln and the music of Copland made one of the most enduring and inspiring examples of *melodeclamation* I have ever heard.

(*Above*) The resonoscope. Its capacity to make pitch visible was originally intended as a way of settling arguments among singers, but the machine wound up as a timely boost for those working to discover a way of locating enemy submarines in World War II. (*Below*) Varsity Arena, Toronto, was the setting for a wartime concert benefiting the Canadian Merchant Marine. It was before these 7,603 people that, due to a misunderstanding about the order of encores, I discovered to my amazement how one orchestra could begin a Sousa march and *Clair de Lune* at the same time!

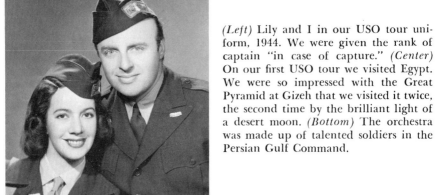

(Left) Lily and I in our USO tour uniform, 1944. We were given the rank of captain "in case of capture." *(Center)* On our first USO tour we visited Egypt. We were so impressed with the Great Pyramid at Gizeh that we visited it twice, the second time by the brilliant light of a desert moon. *(Bottom)* The orchestra was made up of talented soldiers in the Persian Gulf Command.

(Above) At this concert, for Soviet officials in Iran, Frank Versaci, flutist, accompanies Lily. Carolyn Gray is at the piano. They were part of our small personal entourage. (Below) Part of the truck convoy that took Persian Gulf Command instruments and players "on the road"—the same road used to route American supplies to Russia. (Inset) In our tent quarters with Carolyn Gray and Frank Versaci, who seemed to adapt readily to life in the Persian desert!

Outdoor theaters at night were the most desirable settings for the summer tour in Iran, where daytime temperatures were so high that wearing anything metal—like a belt buckle, for instance—had the effect of a white-hot branding iron.

This concert, in Teheran, was broadcast via short-wave to CBS in New York.

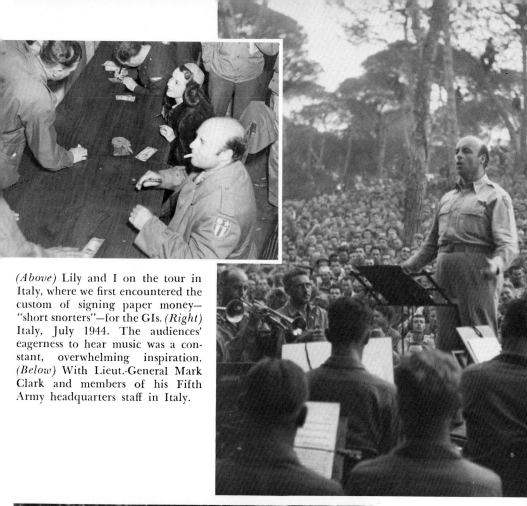

(Above) Lily and I on the tour in Italy, where we first encountered the custom of signing paper money—"short snorters"—for the GIs. *(Right)* Italy, July 1944. The audiences' eagerness to hear music was a constant, overwhelming inspiration. *(Below)* With Lieut.-General Mark Clark and members of his Fifth Army headquarters staff in Italy.

Lily and I began our second USO tour in India, December 1944. This first rehearsal, with an orchestra recruited from Army personnel, was held in a public park in Calcutta. Eventually the variety of traffic, including camels, donkeys and a funeral procession complete with drums, forced us to retreat to an indoor hall.

(*Left*) Second concert in India, Christmas Night. Someone managed to find cow bells, which we used as a background for "Jingle Bells," sung by the audience. (*Right*) Some of the India orchestra and one of three Liberator bombers that flew us and the instruments from Calcutta to the "up country"—East India and what is now Bangladesh. The lieutenant is Don Taylor, regular leader of the up-country band when he wasn't co-pilot on bombing missions.

Twenties he had formed the Russian Symphony Orchestra and toured with it all over the United States. He was well respected, and many composers—Rachmaninoff, among them—gave him the first performances of their new works.

The day my father and I visited him, Altschuler had just returned to New York from one of those tours. I couldn't help noticing the touch of glumness that frequently punctuated the narration of his travels with the orchestra, and finally it became clear that the tour had not been very successful financially. Having admitted that, he asked me why I wanted to be a conductor. I began to explain that I had studied music, coached in Russia, realized that conducting was what I wanted— "But," he said excitedly, "in my travels in this country I have seen that there is one profession that has a great need for people. . . . Why don't you become a dentist?" I thanked him kindly for his suggestion and said I would think about it.

Setbacks like that were not typical of his career, though. Many years later I met him for lunch in a restaurant in Los Angeles, where he was living in semiretirement. He must have been quite old by then, but he looked and sounded like a man with few regrets about his chosen profession. He was dressed with great chic and was in a reminiscing mood. I can see him now, gazing just over my shoulder and telling me all about his good friend Tchaikovsky. . . .

"You know," my father one day confided to me, "there is a whole new school of music here in America that we did not know in Russia." Sometime later I realized this music must have made as much of an impression on him as it was making on me (and had been ever since I heard Berlin's "Alexander's Ragtime Band" in a Warsaw shoe store), because he said that he thought I should meet a certain composer, the son of a man named Gershwin who had himself come from Petrograd. My father had put his finger right on the button.

Accordingly, one fall afternoon we went to George Gershwin's apartment on the upper West Side. Fathers and sons—George's brother Ira was there, too—shook hands all around, and then Mr. Gershwin suggested I ask George to play something. We went over to the piano and George began to play, one piece, then another and another, all the most wonderful tunes. I couldn't help noticing that his attitude about what he was doing was as alive and delightful as the music he was giving us. Clearly, he loved entertaining. Finally I asked what it all was, and he replied it was his latest musical, *Oh, Kay!* I asked how long it took him to compose one song. He said he sometimes wrote as many as twenty a day. I gasped.

"How is this possible?"

"Well," Gershwin replied, "that way I get the bad ones out of my system!"

On the grand piano there was a single photograph, inscribed "From George to George." Later I learned that Gershwin had enjoyed early and tremendous popularity in England—and that the first "George" in the inscription was King George V.

There were modern paintings everywhere—Picasso, Modigliani, Rouault, Chagall. (George painted, too, and he was as accomplished and prolific at it as he was in his music; by 1937, the year he died, he had completed over a hundred works, many of them portraits of people in music whom he admired. Many years later, in 1963, I would be very proud of the fact that for the inaugural series of Promenades Concerts at Lincoln Center—"an American gala"—we collected fifty-five of his paintings and drawings and put them on exhibition at the hall.)

Although I had not yet heard it, *Rhapsody in Blue* had premiered the previous year, in 1924, and the *Concerto in F* would be heard within a few months. An interesting fact illustrates the brilliant wedding of traditional and jazz forms of music that produced an extraordinary and original child, the *Rhapsody*. During World War II a recording of it was made available free to servicemen—a so-called V disk—and the performers reflected that time-tested marriage: Arturo Toscanini conducted; Oscar Levant played the piano solo; and Benny Goodman was featured clarinetist.

That fall afternoon was the beginning of a long association with

George and Ira Gershwin. With George it would be mostly through performing his music—and, after his death, through Ira—that I would come to feel I knew him well. My admiration was unabashed. I once asked him to give me a photograph of himself, and he did, adding a few bars of "I've Got Rhythm" to the inscription. When Ira told me that I was the only person George had ever done that for, my pleasure bordered on childlike glee.

George Gershwin was not yet out of his thirties when he died of a brain tumor. Yet his contributions to the musical treasury of this century were more than enough for a life twice as long. Even so, there are to this day many songs—at least forty, perhaps twice that—that were never published, never performed. I have kept in touch with Ira through the years and used to visit him in his villa whenever I was in Hollywood. On one of these occasions, some sixteen years ago, he told me about the fugitive pieces. Naturally I asked to see them. I became more and more excited as I read through the Gershwin notebooks. There were about fourteen I especially liked, and I suggested to Ira that they be copied out and I would send them to George Balanchine for consideration as music for a modern ballet. I did. Unhappily, nothing came of it. Ira, who composed the lyrics for many of George's songs, had never put words to any of those in the notebooks. He said he always needed to have a story in mind—a book for either a Broadway show or a movie—in order to add lyrics.

Actually, three songs that came to light at that same time fared better. At the urging of Billy Wilder and other friends, Ira consented to write lyrics for the musical score of Wilder's movie, *Kiss Me, Stupid*. He was told he could select any composer he wanted to do the music. (Ira does not play an instrument, nor does he read music, although he does have a remarkable talent for being able to hum a tune after hearing it once.) Well, quite naturally, Ira selected his brother as the composer and gave lyrics to three of those "secret" songs—"I'm a Poached Egg," "All the Livelong Day," and "Sophia."

That first meeting with the Gershwins echoes sweetly clear in my memory. I left their apartment intoxicated with what I had seen and heard. To me George's personality and his music were the America I had fallen in love with—rich in ideas, sparkling, original.

Around 1926 I met a pleasant, very musical man named Joshua Zuro. My association with him was interesting but very brief.

In those days the Broadway movie-house audience was treated to an orchestral interlude after the film was over. Zuro was a producer of such entertainment, and he asked me if I would like to try my hand at developing a fuller program, with dancers and singers. That was attractive and I agreed. My job was to take a piece, like "Song of India," for instance, and arrange the music so that it could be played, sung, and danced to. We set up a program for the Rivoli Theater, I think it was, and I enjoyed it tremendously. So did Zuro because after a very short time he asked if I would go to Hollywood with him and develop our ideas there as a team. It was tempting, but I declined. Somehow it was just not the right time to leave New York. Poor Zuro did go to the Coast, and one week later news came that he had been killed in a car accident.

The end of the job with Zuro marked the end of my free-lance period as well and, with a final, bizarre twist, seemed to confirm my desire to make New York my home and my "territory."

I began working on a steady basis for Arthur Judson—who has been described from time to time as "the czar of the music industry"—as accompanist and voice coach. Judson was something of a phenomenon on the business side of the classical music world. For a while he simultaneously managed the Philadelphia Orchestra and, with Bruno Zirato, the New York Philharmonic; with Frederick Schang he founded Columbia Artists Management, the largest concert agency in the world. In his words he was "grateful to be endowed with the love of music," and he spent his life demonstrating that—even, in 1927, forming a radio broadcasting network as a means for the classical musicians he represented to be heard. (It was bought in 1928 by William Paley, who formed the Columbia Broadcasting System the same year.)

Being in Judson's stable, I was naturally brought into contact with many other musicians and conductors he managed, among them Eugene Ormandy. For a time, before he became conductor of the Minneapolis Symphony Orchestra in 1931, Ormandy was conductor of the Capitol Theater Orchestra in New York City, and in that connection I would sometimes arrange music with him and play the piano for rehearsals.

I took quite a few informal lessons in conducting from him—approaches to certain rhythms, interpretation, and gestures. Sometimes we would practice in front of a mirror. To me he seemed a naturally gifted teacher—indeed, he must have been, for in 1914, at the age of fifteen, he joined the faculty of the Budapest Conservatory, from which he had just graduated!

We became close friends, always keeping in touch with each other despite the different directions our careers have taken us. Such was my respect and admiration for this man in those early days of our association that I got into the habit of holding his coat for him. Some years later we were both guests at a formal affair, the details of which escape me now, and true to old habit I found myself holding his coat.

He turned around, saying, "Andre, just like old times."

"Gene," I said, "it's the same coat!"

One of the singers for whom I was coach and accompanist was Helen Stanley. She was principal soprano with the Chicago Opera. It was with her that I made my first public appearance at the old Manhattan Opera House on Thirty-fourth Street. Her husband, Loudon Charlton, had arranged a recital for a violinist at that same auditorium. It was a January day in 1926, and in walked a boy—he couldn't have been more than ten years old—carrying a violin. He put it down and rubbed his hands to warm them. It was soon clear that this youth was the violinist about to perform. That was a very memorable day, the first time I heard Yehudi Menuhin.

There were other interesting surprises that marked my association with Helen Stanley. During a concert in Boston I had an opportunity to see what it was like to transpose a song on the spot; that is, during its performance. The song was Schubert's "Der Erlkönig." Just before we went on the stage Miss Stanley told me she realized her voice wasn't up to the key the score was written in, and she would have to sing it a tone lower. What this meant was that I would have to virtually rewrite the song while playing it. If you have the music in front of you, a pencil, and time, it is not an overwhelmingly difficult exercise. But doing it during a performance, a live performance, with a five-second advance notice is akin to a locomotive engineer who is trying to control a downhill runaway train and suddenly finds he has to lay track at the same time. I knew that most people in the audience would not be aware that anything was being altered—unless, of course, I played a couple of wrong notes. Happily, pumping adrenaline notwithstanding, it went well.

Another exciting—but, I confess, far more enjoyable—surprise occurred during that same engagement. A Russian musician and friend of mine, Nicolai Mednikoff, was also in Boston, as accompanist for Pablo Casals. I told Nicolai I would very much like to meet the famous cellist, and he said right then was as good a time as any. So we went to the hotel where they were staying. I don't remember that Nicolai introduced me when we entered Casals's room, because the maestro was quite disturbed over a nasty paper cut in one of the fingers of his left hand and wanted to rehearse to make certain it would not impair his playing. "Nicolai," he said, "let us try the sonata." It was a very small room. For my first Casals concert I was sitting only about three feet away from him! After the sonata he and Nicolai played Tchaikovsky's *Variations on a Rococo Theme*—and they played every note, not just a few bars. In the end they rehearsed the whole program.

Remembering Casals's concern over the paper cut makes me think of the confession he made to me one day many years later on one of my visits with him and his wife, Martita, in Puerto Rico. He was reminiscing about his first visit to San Francisco, in 1900, when he was about twenty-five. On a mountain-climbing adventure he slipped and hurt his hand quite seriously. Recalling the moment, this emperor of the cello, then at least in his eighties and still blessing the world with his genius, leaned toward me and confided the single thought in his mind when he realized his hand was hurt: "I had a hidden sense of joy because now I wouldn't have to practice the cello any more!"

In 1928 I became a United States citizen. To my amazement, the judge, in the midst of the formalities, suggested to me that it might be a very good time to change my name. Something simple like Jones or Smith, he said, because in this country those were the kinds of names people had. Kostelanetz was difficult to pronounce and to write. Well, I didn't think much of the idea then, and, all things considered, don't now.

Actually, the family had always been aware of the unusualness of the name. We were the only Kostelanetz group in St. Petersburg. My father and grandfather had a theory that the first Kostelanetzes had come to Russia from Spain, as exiles perhaps, where the name might have been Castellaños, a very common name there. That is as good an explanation as I have ever heard.

I have never regretted not changing it. For one thing, from time to time it has caused people to use their imagination when it came to spelling it. My favorite—in this case, lapse of imagination—appeared on a post card I received years ago: "To Maestro Kostel—et cetera." In the hands of a neighbor of mine when I lived on Fifty-seventh Street, the name was the inspiration for a bit of romantic intrigue. This neighbor, a Hungarian, had a similar name. At least it began the same way and had the same number of syllables. I would occasionally see letters meant for him, love letters mostly. I wondered if he was getting my bills but, beyond that, never thought of it. He did, though. And later he confessed his bachelor days' hijinks to me. When he realized that I had a Sunday afternoon broadcast, he allowed his Girl Friend Number Two to believe that he was me so that he would have the afternoon to spend with Girl Number One. Girl Number Two would call him after the broadcast and say how wonderful the music was, how inspired! Well, I suppose you could say he was inspired.

"Music Is Not What We Play but What People Hear"

THE FIRST TIME I ACTUALLY conducted on the air was a Sunday afternoon, a quartet of singers on something called, I believe, "The Ballad Hour." It was a modest debut; in fact, I confess that the main reason I remember it has to do not with the program itself but with the flurry of excitement after the broadcast. One of the horn players, Maurice von Prague, came up to me and, after kindly complimenting me, asked casually when I had joined the union. I said, "What union is that?"

He became very excited because the union law carries a fine for a nonunion person who conducts union players. It was about $500 then. I had no idea such a thing existed. When I had returned to New York after resigning from the West Coast tour to enter radio, I sought the advice of a friend, Bill Murray, and he sent me to the Atlantic Broadcasting Company. There I saw a slim and elegant elderly man named Collins who asked me what I could do. I said, "Everything!" He hired me at $30 a week. (On the Coast I had been making an incredible $200 a week, which seems evidence of my enthusiasm.) No mention of a union, then or later, until now.

"We'll keep it all quiet," von Prague was saying (I think he was warming up to a role as savior in this tiny bit of intrigue), "and just slip down to the Musicians' Union headquarters in the morning."

If he was expecting the drama to continue in miles of red tape and perhaps even a stern session with an unsympathetic interrogator, he was disappointed. Apparently because I was a relative newcomer to the States, there was no wait. I passed the examination, paid a $50 fee, and became a union member.

Things moved fast in the last years of those Roaring Twenties. The stock market was already teetering off balance and was about to take its drastic plunge, bringing the country to a despairing standstill. Yet, as far as the baby radio industry was concerned, the "roaring" kept right on into the Thirties. (My dear friend Lou Robbins, who is the New York Philharmonic's librarian now and whom I have known since he began at CBS in the early days of the Depression, has always appreciated the fact that he happened into one of the two legitimate industries of the period that were booming—apples and radio.)

It was in the early part of 1928 that I began at Atlantic Broadcasting, on the seventeenth floor of Steinway Hall on Fifty-seventh Street, and before the year was out William Paley had added it to other broadcasting acquisitions, all of which shortly became a coast-to-coast network, the Columbia Broadcasting System. The dream I'd had on the train across Canada was of entering radio and of one day working in what I was certain would become the world's largest concert hall. Unbelievably, both parts of that dream were materializing with stunning speed. At the time I was not aware of the precise details of the situation; I only sensed that this country was about to be introduced to itself on a far-reaching scale by a tiny, do-it-yourself device first known as a crystal set. In William Paley's memoirs decades later I find a few interesting statistics about that brief period just before the Thirties began. That concert hall then consisted of, in the CBS network, "forty-nine stations in forty-two cities," representing a likely radio range of eighty-seven percent of the country's population. Of course, not every home had a radio as yet—only perhaps thirty-three percent did—and, Paley says, "we were broadcasting only twenty-one hours a week."

By 1930, the year I became conductor of the CBS orchestra, the network had moved to its own home, four floors at 485 Madison Avenue, with six large studios. And that twenty-one hours a week increased steadily until finally it was virtually twenty-four hours a day. A good proportion of those was live music, because the union forbade the broadcasting of transcriptions. With that kind of work available it is small wonder the worst of the Depression was something that we in radio could only realize through empathy with others.

Nonetheless, the national pinch did squeeze us. At one point a notice came from "upstairs" that there would have to be a salary cut for everyone, either ten percent or fifteen percent. Everyone seemed to feel that wasn't much of a hardship—after all, we had the greatest of luxuries for those times, a job. But when my next pay check arrived it was for the same amount I had been receiving. I told the cashier it must have been a mistake, but she said word had come down that my salary wasn't to be altered. So far no one had come to tell me how I was doing, but I took this as a sign of approval.

Ironically, the Depression years, the end of hope and opportunity for so many, were for me—for all of us in the youthful period of broadcasting—the kind that make the fondest memories. Everything was new. Every day was an experiment, an adventure. For every problem solved, a new one presented itself. Happily, there was little time for complacency or smugness about what was achieved because, for one thing, we had to admit there was a good deal of luck involved in our successes and, for another, there was enough power and mystery about the new technical resources to keep us respectful, even a little humble.

The Chesterfield program, which debuted in April, 1934, was in several ways a first, and it was a culmination of trial-and-error programming efforts of the previous four years. There had not been a regularly scheduled commercial radio series with a large orchestra until Chesterfield, nor one that freely mixed classical and popular music. And there was the use of new microphone techniques, which was the result of our proud and surprising discovery that music was not what was played at all, but rather what people heard—that is, what went through the studio mike into the control room and out over the air.

The "laboratory" for our experiments was Studio One at 485

Madison Avenue. In the four years preceding Chesterfield, the discoveries we made came over the air on various half-hour music programs. There were cottonseed-oil half hours, and Buick and Pontiac, and one show, sponsored by O. N. T. Clark Thread, with a title that made up for its lack of wit with a double dollop of sincerity: *Threads of Happiness. Threads* was particularly notable because it was the first time I worked with a great classical music orchestrator, Amadeo de Filippi. Good orchestrators—and, later, arrangers, when we began to include popular music in our offerings—were essential to making broadcasts work because the one constant in preparing a thirty-minute show was the limitation on time. We didn't have a full thirty minutes for music on commercial programs; selling a product required a total of ten minutes out of those precious thirty, and we had to play the music for those commercials as well. So every second had to be planned in advance. A symphony is at least a half hour long. The choice was never just which one to play, but whether to attempt only one movement or an abbreviated version of the whole work, and that's where the orchestrator came in. Filippi and I would have to edit the work down, tailor it to fit exactly the time allowed. It was not something that was appealing to me—I don't think any conductor ever wants to be in that position. The response of the radio audience to our programs didn't reflect my concern; the letters were virtually all thank-yous for playing music. But I decided that since I had to do the trimming I would at least announce the fact. And I was criticized for it, by *Time* Magazine, for one. Later I asked the composer Deems Taylor about it—how he would feel if I changed one of his works. He gave a short and, I thought, perfect answer in terms of what I was trying to do in the first place, bring more music to more people: better some than none.

The criticism in the press came *after* I announced what I was doing, which made me wonder if their musical expertise was all it should have been. And after José Iturbi's confession to me, I concluded that it was not. Performers trim all the time, said the pianist. The only difference is they keep quiet about it!

Our laboratory experiments had to do mainly with microphone placement and the seating of the musicians—should the strings be in one line in the first row or grouped to one side? Where is the best spot for the flute? The horns? And so on. My assistant conductors in that early period were Charles Lichter and Nicolai Berezowsky—wonderful musicians and especially helpful at working out exactly how for a given piece of music the string players should do their bowings. I was fortunate in having such talented people with whom I could work out, for instance, whether one draw of the bow should strike one note or two or many, with heavy or light touch, a long bow or a short; and whether all the string players should begin by drawing their bows at the same time in the same direction—top to bottom or vice versa—or be free to decide themselves. I discovered that there were some conductors— Stokowski, for instance—who allowed free bowing, but I have always felt that uniformity was a good habit to get into, because there are some works where it is critical. But that is part of what makes a conductor's interpretative identity, gives his work its personal character.

Partway through a rehearsal one day, I decided to listen in the control room to see, or rather hear, just what happened to the music after it passed through the microphone. So I gave the baton to Berezowsky and asked him to go through a few phrases we had just done. It was immediately clear that a lot happened. I realized that equally important with the seating of musicians and with carefully marking scores for bowings and other subtleties of interpretation was the placement of the microphone. Some instruments were virtually lost; others came through several sizes too big, so to speak. One of the first corrections was to hang the mike above the whole group of musicians, not favoring any section.

But the more we worked the more we realized that each piece of music needed its own treatment. So we began using more than one microphone, sometimes two or three. Most often we put one near the strings, favoring them—and with little danger of their getting too dominant a role, because strings are aurally transparent: the sound they produce is distinct, but at the same time it allows other sounds to pass through it. Colors began to come through that were not there before, because certain instruments combined to make whole new sounds—the blending of flute and horn, for instance. We placed one mike near a trombone, to which a special mute had been attached, another close to an alto flute, and another next to a viola. I would have the trombone played very high and soft, and when the three sounds were mixed in the control room they became a new sonority. No one who wasn't in the studio could say what instrument or instruments they were listening to. Not even Arturo Toscanini. My Sunday broadcasts on CBS (called WABC back then) were right after Toscanini's weekly program when he was conducting the New York Philharmonic-Symphony on the same network. Often I would attend his rehearsals—an instruction, an entertainment (his well-known excitability over mistakes provided that), and, most of all, an inspiration all rolled together. I was one of millions of his admirers and, as admirers sometimes do, failed to think of him as human. It never occurred to me that he might listen to the radio like other folks or go to clubs for an evening of jazz. Then came the Monday morning when I received a phone call. The first sound I heard was a great chuckle. Then: "Kostelanetz!" said the unmistakable voice. "What was that instrument I heard on your broadcast yesterday afternoon?"

Chester Hazlett, who played lead alto saxophone and clarinet with Paul Whiteman's orchestra in the Twenties, came up with a microphone-inspired invention that is known as a sub-tone clarinet. I made frequent use of the technique, that is, bringing the clarinet very close to a mike and having it played soft and low. When the result was amplified in the control room you could not tell what the instrument was, only that it created a gorgeous "sub-tone" accompaniment for the rest of the orchestra.

Other of our innovations echo in my mind, still with the same frisson of surprise and delight they gave on first hearing. For "Clair de Lune" I asked that the orchestra play the beginning softly and more softly still. Then, in the control room, we gradually amplified it—and it was like listening to the breathing of angels! At another time someone suggested placing a microphone, closed, under the inside of a piano. The pianist then struck the C major chord. In the control room we opened the microphone and heard the chord resonating through all the strings of the piano. The opening and closing of mikes at particular times became one of my favorite techniques.

The advent of the microphone brought into play the principle of amplification and started music down the seemingly endless path of new sonorities, not creating new music—the original piece remains utterly recognizable—but, rather, enriching what already exists.

The microphone was and is only as good as the imagination and skill of those who use it. Accordingly, it can either undermine or enhance musical endeavors. Years of familiarity with it do not necessarily guarantee expertise and certainly not mastery because the microphone is a tool of the science, or perhaps art is a more apt term, of acoustics. This scientific art yields as much to whim and intuition as it does to the application of acoustical principles, a notion that was beautifully and unwittingly demonstrated to me almost fifty years ago by Rosa Ponselle, a magnificent soprano with the Metropolitan Opera. Her voice was extremely powerful, like Birgit Nilsson's, and very expressive, a perfect combination for the opera stage. When she first sang at rehearsal in the Hudson The-ater on Forty-fourth Street, our broadcasting studio until the end of the Chesterfield series in 1938, it was glorious to hear. Acousti-cally, the Hudson was exquisite—no matter what we played, it sounded good—and, of course, Rosa sounded fantastic anyway. The only problem was she was so loud I couldn't hear the orches-tra. I gave the baton to Alex Cores, my assistant, and went into the control room. Her voice was coming through so strong on the high notes that the needle, which should register ideally in the center of the meter, was all the way to the right. The engineer cut the volume way down. He controlled Rosa's voice in such a way that the louder she sang, the softer it came through, and vice versa. It was not clear who was in control. A classic example of that type of situation occurred at a broadcast rehearsal of Ravel's *Bolero*. The engineer found that the beginning of the work was coming through very softly—in fact, he could barely hear it; so, having no idea of the structure of the work, he increased the volume. Now the flute came through like a trombone, and as the composition went on there was so much sound that he had to bring it way down. By the time he was finished he had completely reversed the slow-working crescendo effect of the music!

Well, when I told our engineer how powerfully Rosa was heard in the hall, he suggested that she sing more softly. But I just couldn't imagine her voice, which was something close to a primitive force, having to be restrained. And I also did not feel justified in asking her to, in effect, reinterpret the whole piece just for the microphone. I decided it was the moment for an experiment: why not move the mike away from her and from the stage altogether, hang it out over the sixth or seventh row? An hour or so later we were set up. Alex took the baton, and I posted myself in the control room once more.

The effect was unbelievably beautiful. Rosa's voice was in all its glory, the orchestra was heard. And something else happened: the quality of the sound was immensely improved, the overtones were beautiful. We were all in a state of happy bewilderment that so simple a change, and one prompted by nothing more than a whim, could make such a significant difference.

Rosa finished singing, but I decided to remain where I was for the next selection, an orchestral work. Again, the most gorgeous sounds came through. And the engineer said he had forgotten to close that mike—what we came to call the "distant mike." All the instruments coalesced and sounded their best. The poet was right, distance does indeed lend enchantment.

After that, of course, we used the new "principle," and before long it was adopted by everybody in broadcasting. Sometimes we would use a booster mike—if, for instance, a flute had a special part and might otherwise be lost.

Every day we increased our skills and became better able to capture the richness, the intensity, the nuance in music, whether for the great voices of the day—Ponselle, Grace Moore, Lawrence Tibbett, Lily Pons, Grete Stueckgold, Ezio Pinza, Bidu Sayao,

Nino Martini—or for the instruments, solo or in the exciting range of combinations. The effects were dramatic; the possibilities endless.

The Thirties and Forties provided a luxury of riches in popular music; there was an abundance, and it was immensely attractive, uniquely American in its conception. Names like Kern, Gershwin, Porter, Berlin, Rodgers were on everybody's lips, and it seemed that everything these composers wrote was nothing less than irresistible. People hummed, whistled, and danced to their tunes—and they still do.

There is a tired phrase that can creep into a personal history, particularly one written by a man whose long life affords a long view: "What ever happened to . . . ?" I had hoped to avoid that cranky question, but it is almost impossible when I start to think about the glorious trove of songs of those decades. It is not what ever happened to the songs—they still live independently and as a nostalgic history of that time—but, rather, what ever happened to the impulse that created them? Melody and lyric combined to uplift, to distract from the humdrum, to comfort, to amuse. Of course, there have been great songs written since then, but what I miss in much popular music today is that poetic dimension that can remind us of what is best in ourselves and the world. It is easy enough to emphasize the grim view—the daily press reads like horror stories—but surely there are good things in life, and surely a need for our music to reflect them.

Much of that earlier music was written for the theater, and maybe the fact that a Jerome Kern or a Cole Porter knew he was addressing a finite number of people, an intimate audience, had something to do with the strong personal appeal and, ultimately, the sweeping acceptance of the music.

I did not make any effort to explain that phenomenon in those days, no philosophical excursions into the meaning of it all. (That's the kind of thing reserved for personal histories!) The only thing I knew then was that I wanted to make those songs part of our broadcasting repertoire. The radio-listening audience was growing all the time in number and variety, and I wanted to acknowledge that variety with a free mix of classical and popular music. So, in 1933, on a sustaining, or network-sponsored, program called *Andre Kostelanetz Presents*, we began introducing one or two popular ballads each week. It was a success, judging from listener response. The network was impressed, and the next thing we knew Chesterfield cigarettes had bought the idea.

But not everybody did. I suspect I had been under suspicion by the critics in the press ever since I had dared to trim the classics to meet the demand of limited broadcasting time. And this juxtaposing of classical and popular music proved to be the final straw! I confess, though, that once I had got over my initial hurt and annoyance I began to derive satisfaction from contemplating the critics' reactions. I did not, of course, plan a program deliberately to tease a response from them, but I did allow myself a silent chortle in anticipation of certain broadcasts. For example, the one that included a medley created out of themes from Tchaikovsky's Fourth Symphony and a popular song that had been around for a while, Charles Jackson's "I'm Alabama Bound." Having popular music on the same broadcast with classical was wicked enough, but mixing the two in one selection?

It was never clear to me exactly what the critics' objection was. At worst, experiments like these are "interesting"; at best, they are beautiful. What other criterion is there beyond beauty? Right versus wrong somehow has no application to music. Appropriateness? That is, should a conductor of classical music confine himself strictly to classical music? Apparently Toscanini didn't think so when he conducted a recording of Gershwin's *Rhapsody in Blue*, with Benny Goodman on clarinet, or when he orchestrated "Skaters Waltz." Nor did Jascha Heifetz when he transcribed another Gershwin breakthrough, *Porgy and Bess*, for violin and piano. Part of the wonder of music is that it can survive—and is often even improved by—being expressed in different forms and by different interpreters.

I have respect for the difficulty of sincerely trying to judge new music, however. Judgment is affected by the state of emotions in a particular individual at a particular moment. A new piece of music might or might not be just what a critic wants to hear;

nevertheless, where a tight deadline is involved, he must write intelligently and quickly about it. But so often, music has to be heard more than once before its effect can be truly felt and articulated. And there can be great pleasure in slow discovery, in letting the music work its spell. So quick and quixotic judgments are to be avoided. And yet, while I preach that, I haven't always practiced it.

Many years ago, in 1933 or '34, I went to see a new Jerome Kern musical, *Roberta*, with Bob Simon, who was a critic for *The New Yorker*. At one point the stage was bare except for the female lead, who sang "Smoke Gets in Your Eyes," accompanying herself on a guitar. When she finished I turned to Bob and said, "Why did Kern put that song in? It's terrible. It has no future!" And Simon agreed! (In our case I think the smoke was in our ears.)

About six years later Kern's *Very Warm for May* was still running on Broadway when I broadcast an orchestrated version on the Coca-Cola program. And Kern called me and asked what I thought the "big" song would be. " 'All the Things You Are,' " I said. (By that time I had learned something—probably that it's better to be lucky than right!) Well, Kern told me he didn't agree at all. He favored "In the Heart of the Dark"—which is exactly where the song remained. When he declared his candidate for popularity, I confessed what I had said about that other Kern song that had "no future"!

Such experience suggests the possibility that of all the arts music is the most unpredictable—and independent. Once a song is ready to fly and leaves the composer's nest, nobody can control the course or length of its flight. No composer or critic or conductor or musician can either destroy it or propel it into immortality. It becomes part of the music in the air, soaring or dropping on invisible currents.

The Chesterfield program was broadcast three times a week the first year. And suddenly there was more of everything: more music (two kinds now), more time, and more need for innovations.

With the opportunity to program popular music as well as classical came the problem of orchestra size and make-up. Of the fifty-five or so men I conducted, about half were CBS staff musicians and half were free lance. By using free lancers we could control the size of the orchestra according to the changing demands of the music and without overstepping the limitations of budget and space. More musicians were needed when we played classical selections than when we did popular, so those who were strictly classical would be dropped for the light numbers. Some musicians could play more than one instrument, and they were particularly valuable. The third-stand flute could switch to piccolo or saxophone or clarinet; the first oboe—who for several years was Mitch Miller—remained first oboe, but second oboe doubled on saxophone and clarinet. First trumpets were not interchangeable: Harry Freistadt did the classical and Russ Case took over for popular.

We used a "doubler" system with the instruments as well. French horns are essential for the classical orchestra but not for the popular, so we eliminated them from the orchestra make-up altogether. Whenever a score called for them, the parts were converted to brass—"written into" perhaps three trombones and a trumpet. Similarly, a clarinet or saxophone could be substituted for a flute part.

Essential for presenting popular music was expertise in arranging. Unlike a classical piece, which came to me as a full orchestral score with every instrument's part noted, a popular tune generally arrived as a sheet of piano music. There were usually orchestrations available because most of the popular songs we played had come from musicals, and those orchestrations were for the theater's pit orchestra. But they were conventional to the point of dullness, so we started fresh with the sheet music. First, the instruments to be used had to be decided on and then parts written for them, always with the idea of enriching the song, emphasizing its best qualities, giving it a fresh perspective.

There was a practical necessity for arranging, too. The average length of a popular song was only one or two minutes and the broadcast time allowed for four- or five-minute compositions. Suppose the chorus of a given song was thirty-two bars, which might equal fifteen seconds. To make the song into a four-minute selection you might choose to repeat the chorus, but it would have to be a little different the second time, and preferably longer. The key can be changed, perhaps from major to minor, or the registration, or the style of the accompaniment if it is a vocal arrangement. Repositioning the players can also be a useful device. Once, for an instrumental arrangement of Richard Rodgers and Lorenz Hart's "My Funny Valentine," I placed two violins, a viola, and a cello right in front of me, with a microphone above. The rest of the strings were in the background. (And, as usual, I made sure the musicians had Hart's words in front of them so that they could "play" the lyric.)

Arranging was brand-new to me in those early days, but I worked at it. I had two advantages: I knew the instruments, and I was blessed with a very gifted arranger, Carroll Huxley, who had begun to work with me around 1933. His great admiration for the music of Ravel was often reflected in his work, particularly in some magnificent harmonic progressions. There were others throughout those four years of Chesterfield and, after that, the five years of Coca-Cola programs, each with his special talents: Nathan Van Cleave, later a film-score composer, and George Bassman, who came in as a very young man with little knowledge of harmony but great imagination and fresh ideas. He composed the Tommy Dorsey theme song, "I'm Getting Sentimental Over You."

The arrangers would bring their work to me, and I would go over it, making suggestions and refinements. The only real problem we had was selecting material—there was so much to draw from.

Jerome Kern and Oscar Hammerstein II had presented *Show Boat* to the world in 1927. It was one of the longest-running musicals of the Twenties, and its music—songs like "Ol' Man River," "You Are Love," "After the Ball," "Make Believe"—is with us still. It is probably impossible to exaggerate the quality of the songs that cascaded out of the musical theater season after season. All through the Depression and the years of World War II that followed, this music worked its charm: it comforted, it suggested there was reason to hope that humor, grace, and romance would one day be restored to our lives. Echoes of humanity's better visions were in those songs. They hadn't the power to convert those visions into reality, but they did keep the imagination alive. Long after the shows that gave them life had closed, songs like these were heard again and again, wherever there was a radio or phonograph: "With a Song in My Heart," "Where or When" (Richard Rodgers and Lorenz Hart); "Dancing in the Dark," "You and the Night and the Music" (Arthur Schwartz and Howard Dietz); "I've Got You Under My Skin," "Begin the Beguine," "All Through the Night," "I Get a Kick Out of You," "Ev'ry Time We Say Goodbye" (Cole Porter); "This Is the Army, Mr. Jones" (Irving Berlin); "Oh, What a Beautiful Mornin'," "People Will Say We're in Love" (Richard Rodgers and Oscar Hammerstein II). . . .

"You and the Night and the Music" and another particularly beautiful song, "If There Is Someone Lovelier Than You," are part of a Schwartz and Dietz score for a show called *Revenge with Music* that was the first Broadway show we arranged for broadcast.

Kay Thompson and the Rhythm Singers appeared with us often, as did Frank Parker and Ray Heatherton. Even though there were times when I might include a classical work in a medley of popular songs, I did not make what I consider the mistake of having opera-scale singers interpret popular songs, where the "message" is very often intimate, personal, subtle. ("Ev'ry Time We Say Goodbye" as done by Frank Sinatra, for instance—he has it to perfection.) There was a great variety of talent, and we drew from it—mixed-voice choruses, male quartets, variety singers.

It was hard to go wrong with such music available and the performing and arranging talent to present it. And the truth is, in the next ten or twelve years there were very few wrong times. Not only did the listening public respond but composers did, too. Cole Porter's thank-you for "Begin the Beguine," which we broadcast in 1935, really belongs to Carroll Huxley, who did the arrangement. My only contribution was to change the ending a little by having one of the players whistle into a mike.

There is no question that records are one of the miracles of the age. No one would argue seriously that they have the thrilling immediacy of live music—although constantly improving equip-

WESTERN UNION (28)

R. B. WHITE
PRESIDENT

NEWCOMB CARLTON
CHAIRMAN OF THE BOARD

J. C. WILLEVER
FIRST VICE-PRESIDENT

The filing time as shown in the date line on full-rate telegrams and day letters, and the time of receipt at destination as shown on all messages, is STANDARD TIME.

Received at

1935 OCT 16 PM 10 2

NB189 13=WA NEWYORK NY 16 1016P

ANDRE KOSTELANETZ, COLUMBIA BROADCASTING SYSTEM=

MINUTES IN TRANSIT	
FULL-RATE	DAY LETTER

:485 MADISON AVE=

I JUST HEARD THE BEGIN THE BEGUINE FOR THE FIRST TIME THANK
YOU=
COLE PORTER

WESTERN UNION (00)

R. B. WHITE
PRESIDENT

NEWCOMB CARLTON
CHAIRMAN OF THE BOARD

J. C. WILLEVER
FIRST VICE-PRESIDENT

The filing time shown in the date line on telegrams and day letters is STANDARD TIME at point of origin. Time of receipt is STANDARD TIME at point of destination.

Received at 203 West 52nd Street, New York

1936 NOV 13 PM 11 00

NAK113 35 VIA HO=WA NEWYORK NY 13 848P

ANDRE KOSTELANETZ=
1687 BROADWAY CHESTERFIELD HOUR STATION WABC=

EVERYTIME YOU PLAY ONE OF MY TUNES I/GET A NEW LEASE ON
LIFE STOP I JUST HEARD YOUR BROADCAST OF IVE GOT YOU UNDER
MY SKIN AND IM THREE YEARS OLD MANY MANY THANKS=
COLE PORTER

Postal Telegraph
THE INTERNATIONAL SYSTEM

Commercial Cables   All America Cables

Mackay   Radio

SA 431 17 NL=BL BEVERLYHILLS CALIF 30   37 JUL 1 AM 12 32

ANDRE KOSTELANETZ, COLUMBIA BROADCASTING SYSTEM=

:52 ST AND MADISON AVE NYC=

MAYBE MY MUSIC HAS BEEN PLAYED BETTER BUT WHO KNOWS WHERE OR
WHEN MANY THANKS YOU'RE WONDERFUL=

     DICK RODGERS.

WESTERN UNION
(18)   1201

WAD209 12 SC=LOSANGELES CALIF   E42 MAR 3 PM 10 48

ANDRE KOSTELANETZ=

     COLUMBIA BROADCASTING CO MADISON AVE=

IF I WERE A WRITER OF SONNETS I'D WRITE ONE FOR
KOSTELANETZ=

     ARTHUR SCHWARTZ.

ment and techniques bring them closer—but they do allow people to hear more music more often even than radio. Perhaps listening to a recording as opposed to attending a concert is—as my friend Dr. Albert Sabin once remarked—like receiving a kiss over the telephone. But isn't that in itself a kind of miracle? Those are my feelings now, but I wasn't always so enlightened.

Periodically, as my broadcasting career developed, I would be asked to make a record. But I was against it. Radio was my métier; music went out to people live, on the spot. Recordings lacked that immediacy of contact and, too, faithfulness of reproduction was then largely a matter of luck. However, the person I kept saying no to was a great believer in the miracle, and he persisted. In fact, Edward Wallerstein might say to me over a sumptuous meal at Barbetta's, you could count your broadcast as a rehearsal and simply record it the next morning. That way the music would be getting to even more people—think of all those who might miss the program! And besides, you can write your own contract.

Very persuasive. I capitulated. Wallerstein was a man of great charm and patience when it came to pursuing what he thought was a good idea. When I signed my first recording contract with him, in 1934, he was at RCA Victor Records and very interested in finding a way of developing the commercial possibilities of the long-playing record. It proved impractical then, but he never let go of the notion. In 1939, a year after moving over to Columbia Records, he became president and board chairman of that division. Nine years later Columbia introduced the "LP" to the public.

I made only two recordings for RCA. The studio was an unimposing upstairs room in the home of the old German Singing Society, Liederkranz Hall on Fifty-eighth Street. To have played there is to be spoiled forever as far as acoustical standards are concerned. It was all wood, which is the best material for good acoustics. One mike picked up everything. I was lucky not only to record in the Liederkranz studio but to do the Coca-Cola program there for five years, beginning in 1938. My ear became so sensitive to the acoustical perfection of the room that after a while I could tell just by how the orchestra sounded on a given morning whether the floor had been swept the night before. When CBS decided, in the mid-Forties, to turn it into a TV studio I was frantic; I tried to change Paley's mind but to no avail. I believe the building is gone altogether now, a loss that even today's most sophisticated technical equipment cannot make up for.

The first recording I made was *Revenge with Music*, at Arthur Schwartz's suggestion. We used three small choirs. Because of other commitments the musicians would come in at around 1:00 A.M. and we'd work until about 5:00. That recording had some lovely things on it.

A gratifying rapport developed between "my" musicians and me, partly because we had worked our way through many experiments in our "laboratory" at CBS and partly because they were just extremely professional and responsive players. Officially, they were not my orchestra, any more than any group I've been associated with. I have always felt that whatever orchestra I was currently conducting was mine, though. Sometimes there were long associations, as with CBS and later with the New York Philharmonic, and for recording work many of the same musicians would come again and again to work with me. In that sense there is a validity in the ". . . and his orchestra" that often appears on my record albums.

The second, and final, album I made for RCA was *Andre Kostelanetz Presents*, which mixed classical and popular music just as the radio program had done. It was released in 1936, I believe, and I don't remember very much about what was on it except there was an emphasis on Latin songs, which were arranged by Alan Small. One of them underwent a slight title change. In "Chant of the Weed" an *s* was added to Weed, apparently to avoid an implication that it was meant as a celebration of marijuana!

My first royalty check was something in the neighborhood of $18,000. I had to admit that this recording business was something one could not casually ignore!

Once I began doing concert tours on a large scale some years later, I realized that, contrary to what I had thought in my early radio days, records do form an extraordinary bridge between performer and listener. It was obvious that my records accounted for the tremendous audiences on those tours; they preceded me, were in effect my letters of introduction. I have always thought a conductor's role was not only to lead an orchestra through a piece of music but also to literally conduct that music to the audience. Records were another means of doing that.

In 1940 Wallerstein, who was now at Columbia Records, signed me up again. The first recording I made there was "Clair de Lune," and it had a special role I never knew about until many years after World War II. Wallerstein, who was with the wartime Office of Strategic Services, told me that "Clair de Lune" disks had been used to send messages to American prisoners of war. The device was simple and played on the fact that the quality of recordings in those days was not all it should have been: a Morse code message would be scratched onto a disk, which would then be sent to a Red Cross station, where it was played on the air. The prisoners would know that it contained a coded message and listen for it, but to anyone else it seemed like just another record with bad surface noise.

Lily

In 1931 A PETITE YOUNG Frenchwoman named Lily Pons made a spectacular debut at the Metropolitan Opera. There were sixteen curtain calls!

Fate was asserting herself. Just the year before, a serious throat ailment had forced into retirement the reigning coloratura soprano Amelita Galli-Curci. Now, people said, here was her operatic heir. In the few hours it took to sing the role of Lucia di Lammermoor in Donizetti's opera, Lily Pons became a star. Part of the excitement of the evening was the fact that she sang the "Mad Scene" in the key of F, a tone higher than the original score. Her range was high, even for a coloratura.

I did not hear her sing that night, that season, or even for the next three seasons. It is probably fortunate for me that I did not, because I would most likely have fallen in love with her from afar—as I'm sure hundreds of other young men did—and my modest position in the world then would not have helped me to advance the situation in my favor.

But toward the end of 1934, with the success of the Chesterfield program, good things began to happen to me and pretty fast. "Mr. Chesterfield" was actually a charming white-haired gentleman named Carmichael who had a taste for classical music—and a belief that it could, if presented by great stars, sell cigarettes. Great stars like Lily Pons.

So when her agent, Frederick Schang, called me I was not surprised. Schang was a founding father of Columbia Concerts Corporation, which later became the huge Columbia Artists Management, and the only agent Lily had for her entire singing career. There would be an immediate demand for Lily by the radio audience, Schang told me, if she could be heard just once on the air. I said fine. He arranged a meeting for the three of us so that we could decide what she would sing.

Schang and I went to her apartment one late evening. She greeted us charmingly, in an amusing mixture of French and English. (Despite the fact that Lily spent virtually all her adult life in the United States—she became a citizen in 1940—French was "nevaire" absent from her speech. I think she sensed how delightful a grace note to her personality it was.) Within a very few minutes I was quietly dazzled and having a little trouble remembering the purpose of the meeting.

The first piece Lily wanted to sing was Gilda's *bel canto* aria from Verdi's *Rigoletto*, "Caro Nome." I sat down at the piano and she began. She sang right through to the end, which is E above high C. What I'd heard was so contrary to what I'd expected! Her voice was shockingly out of tune and there was a wobble in it, two symptoms of fatigue frequently due to a combination of too much work and too exacting a repertoire. A dramatic soprano can sometimes get away with making extra demands of her vocal cords, because they are thicker and can take it, but coloratura is the highest ranging of the soprano voices, and the delicate vocal cords must not be abused, forced. There are only a few operas—*Lakmé*, *The Barber of Seville*, *Rigoletto*, *Daughter of the Regiment*, for example—that perfectly suit such a voice. I didn't know what Lily's repertoire had been, but her voice sounded as if she had asked far too much of it.

I asked her to sing something else while I tried to figure out how to handle the situation. As a conductor I had an obligation to keep her from showing herself poorly, but how was I going to approach her with this problem? She finished the old English song, "Lo, Hear the Gentle Lark," which had gone no better.

We exchanged a few pleasant remarks. I don't remember going to the extreme of complimenting her; I let it go at saying how good it was to meet her, hear her sing. But as Schang and I went down in the elevator, I asked him how we could let her sing like this, and on a coast-to-coast network.

I wondered if Lily herself had noticed the deterioration. Singers are not always able to hear their own voices; they rely on the response of the coach or teacher, or the audience. Perhaps there had been times when Lily sensed that something was not quite right—she may even have seen the occasional signals in the press— but simply put it down to her extreme "nervosity," something she suffered from before every performance all her life. And, of course, by the time the trouble became noticeable she was in the very top rank of opera stars, a nice place to be—for everybody. There must have been some among the many people who benefited from her success who knew something was wrong but were unwilling to give up their profitable participation in her career. And there were probably nights when she sounded better, which made it easier for those people to rationalize their silence. No, it was not difficult to imagine how the situation had developed. The problem was what to do about it. How would Lily take it?

Schang knew there was something wrong, of course, and when I suggested that time be found for her to rest and to resume study with a good teacher, he did not resist. The next day I telephoned Lily and asked if I could see her. We met and talked. She was very approachable, which encouraged me to be direct: did she have a voice teacher? A somewhat nervy thing to ask someone already at the top. But she was absolutely open. She did, although she hadn't seen him for quite some time. It was Alberti di Gorostiaga, who had been her teacher for some years in France. I confessed what my true reaction had been to her singing the night before. To my relief she accepted what I said and agreed that something had to be done.

We sent for Alberti—and what an absolutely delightful man he was! A *Basquais*, slim, mustached, very excitable, and—a priceless quality for the job before him—very frank. If Lily sang a wrong note, he would clap his hand on the piano to accent his "No! No! No!" But if it was good, he would literally jump into the air.

I convinced Schang that Lily should perform as little as possible for a while, and she and Alberti began to work. It was a slow and tedious process. Alberti played fa, Lily sang "Fa," and so on. She did get tired and discouraged, but she realized it had to be got through.

Alberti was perfect for her. He understood exactly what her voice could do and what it could not. He believed the mouth cavity, as well as the vocal cords, was part of the whole instrument. And he trained Lily to sing the very high notes not with her mouth wide open—as if she were gargling—but instead with a smaller aperture, almost like a smile. It was Alberti's idea and a very attractive one, I thought. (The complete, perhaps fascinating, but irrelevant details of a suddenly revealed oral cavity can often seriously distract from the beauty of a song, even ruin it altogether, something the photographic intimacy of television has demonstrated!)

Alberti and I conspired to keep Lily's spirits up, to keep her sure of herself. And her confidence was strengthened. She realized she didn't have to sing so often just to prove herself. Or worry about being drowned by the orchestra—"I will be heard again," she would say.

The work went on for almost a year. By the end of that time two things were clear: her voice was on its way back to its full glory, and we were in love with each other.

Our courtship was a whirlwind in one real sense because it kept me in the air a good deal; on the other hand, it lasted four years, much longer than any whirlwind. Lily had been signed to appear in a film called *I Dream Too Much,* for which Jerome Kern had written the score. As usual, all the music was to be prerecorded. The problem with recording the voice is that it must be absolutely note perfect; a mistake is easily noticed and there is no excuse for allowing imperfections onto a record or tape anyway, because the equipment is there to make it right. Lily's voice at that time was still not in the condition to deliver a perfect performance—Alberti had gone with her to California so they could continue working.

I recorded the arias and the motion-picture conductor Max Steiner took care of recording the Kern songs.

We began with the "Bell Song" from *Lakmé*. The problems were apparent right away; one note would be flat, another sharp, and so on. Fortunately, by that time tape was available, which meant that recording could be done in sections. I asked an accompanist I knew, Caroline Gray, to help. The plan was to have Lily sing a song section by section, doing six takes for each. Caroline was in the control room with the score. Her job was to select the perfect notes in each take and mark them with a little cross. At the end we put it all together, note by note. We congratulated Lily on the perfection of the final result, but we never told her how she achieved it.

She made another film, *That Girl from Paris*, I think it was, and so I was flying cross-country virtually every week for almost two years. I never minded the flying; in fact, I enjoyed it tremendously. On one flight a fellow passenger, bound for Tucson and very nervous about flying, I guessed, judging from his talkativeness, asked me if I had heard of this crazy conductor who flew to California every week and actually loved doing it! I told him he was sitting right in front of that conductor. I'm sure his embarrassment took his mind off the fear for a while at least.

I find planes are wonderful places to spend time. The view is staggering. The drone helps induce rest. And you can get a lot of work done—if you know how to establish your wish not to be disturbed. About ten years later, when Lily and I spent a lot of time in our house in Palm Beach, I had to fly back and forth quite often, and I would always notice a man wearing a beret. Finally it turned out that he lived very near us in Florida with his rather large family. His name was Joseph Kennedy, and he explained about the beret. A man wearing a beret in America, he advised me, is most often taken for a foreigner who probably doesn't speak English. If you have work to do, wear a beret. No one will talk to you. I once told this story to Admiral Nimitz as I was leaving San Francisco after a visit with him. And he said, "Wait a minute." He went to another room and got an English-Chinese newspaper.

"Now," he said, "if you wear your beret and read this paper, you will really be guaranteeing complete isolation!" I thanked him and took the paper. When my plane stopped in Chicago I decided to send him a wire, not all of which was quite true: "Dear Admiral: Everything worked fine. Until Chicago. Three Chinese came aboard and sat down with me. All wearing berets."

In the mid-Thirties transcontinental flight took about eighteen hours. I would leave from Newark about 11:00 P.M., fly through the night and most of the next day. When I first started flying, the planes were quite intimate, carrying about fourteen people. Then came the DC-3, which held twenty-one passengers, and finally the DC-4 with four engines, fifty seats, and, best of all, sleeping berths. Whatever I flew, the plane seemed to stop everywhere. Kansas City was always the midpoint and, on the way out, the place to get a morning shave. The plane would land, and when the door was opened there would be the barber ready to freshen you up for a new day. Then up in the air again. The next person to greet me would usually be Lily, who met me at the airport in Los Angeles in her huge Hispano-Suiza roadster.

Those weekly flights were not the beginning of my long years of fascination with being in the air. When I first started the Chesterfield program, with the three programs a week and all the rehearsals, I began to feel the need for another dimension in my life, something that would take me out of doors. One day I noticed an ad in the paper that claimed a person could learn to fly in ten one-hour lessons. It sounded just right, so I rented a car and drove out to Roosevelt Field on Long Island to inquire if it was really possible to learn in ten hours. I was assured it was. Of course, said the pilot, some people took longer. (I verified that, twenty-four hours of lessons later.)

Every Sunday I drove out to Roosevelt and had a flying lesson. Each time we took off I had the same glorious feeling of a completely new adventure. Whenever there was snow on the ground the plane took off and landed on skis instead of wheels.

One day in April my instructor and I went up as usual. After we landed he said, "You are ready now," and got out of the plane.

This was it—wasn't it? For an instant my impulse to jump out too was very strong, but I had come to fly, so I did not hesitate to push the throttle forward and begin the run. Before long I was up. Alone. Solo! I hardly remember anything before or since that has been quite that thrilling. For the first solo minutes it was as if every cell of my being had been electrically connected to three sensations at once: freedom, beauty, and fear. . . .

After that I went out to the field every morning about seven. It was to me the most perfect way to begin the day. There was no traffic, and it was quiet and cool. And then the hypnotic pleasure of flying. On my way back to the city I felt completely rested yet alert and ready for the day.

One warm May morning I went out to the field as usual. The instructor got in the plane with me so that he could show me a few rudiments of aerial acrobatics. We began the run. I did everything exactly as I always had, but, although the plane picked up speed, I couldn't get it to lift off the ground. The hangars were suddenly right in front of us, and that is when the instructor took over and managed to fly us sideways between two of them. He explained that the warm-air breeze that day created a downdraft, and the plane hadn't the power to get through it. I took the controls again and we did go up, but I was shaken. After that I flew less frequently alone.

The newspapers made much of the flying romance. Lily's career and mine, and concert appearances, kept us traveling a good deal. And the fact that we did so openly, and lived together openly, seemed to attract a lot of attention. The big question seemed to be: when would we be married? Our friends wondered, too. The only people who weren't concerned were Lily and I. In fact, I think we were a little hesitant to disturb the situation. Marriage shouldn't change anything, at least not for the worse. Yet I had observed that it often seemed to do just that, as if it were some sort of signal for trouble to start. In any case, we were content to let things slide, until the summer of 1938. By then I think our friends were as surprised as we were to find us married. We told no one except Lily's Metropolitan colleague Geraldine Farrar, who was a stand-in mother for Lily at the small ceremony. As far as the world knew we were simply having a party for some friends at Lily's house in Silvermine, Connecticut.

Our honeymoon turned out to be a semiworking tour in South America. And, of course, we flew. In those days, before World War II made the distinction obsolete, there were two categories of planes: those that flew over land and those that flew transocean. The latter were so-called flying boats, which took off and landed on water and for that reason had to fly only in daylight. On the first day of a six-day trip, Lily and I took one of those "boats," a Pan Am Clipper to Puerto Rico, with a stop in Havana. We left at 6:00 A.M. The plane seated thirty-four, very comfortably, too. Flying speed was about 160 mph and the flight was at low altitude, so everything was beautifully visible below.

Our first stop in South America was Paramaribo, the capital of what is now called Surinam but was then Dutch Guiana. From there we went to Rio de Janeiro and then down to Buenos Aires. It was winter there—June and July—and the middle of the music season. Lily sang a number of operas, and I gave concerts. We fell in love with those incredibly beautiful cities.

On the return trip, when we stopped at Paramaribo again, we decided to give a concert for the *libérés* from Devil's Island, the French Guiana penal colony which was then drawing worldwide attention because a fugitive from the colony had written a book exposing the cruel conditions the prisoners, who were mostly political offenders, had to endure there. Feeling was very high because of Belbenois's book. Even Eleanor Roosevelt had taken up the cause of these *libérés*, who were not really free at all; while they were no longer serving time in the prison colony, they still could not leave French Guiana.

We knew there was a fairly large number of *libérés* just across the Moroni River, which separates the two Guianas. Lily and I asked permission to enter French Guiana, but the governor refused, so we thought that in order to come as close to the internees as possible, we would give the concert on a river barge. It was just Lily and I and a piano, and, of course, some men to steady the barge and keep it under control. In the twilight we could make out a small group of people who had gathered to listen. I'm sure, to anyone who might not have known the circumstances of our river concert, we created a rather comic picture. But we wanted to do something simply to show our sympathy and support. A small gesture then, smaller still in light of the long struggle to do away with Devil's Island altogether. Thirteen years passed before the penal colony system was completely phased out.

The theme of the World's Fair of 1939 was "The World of Tomorrow," and the perisphere building contained the Futurama exhibition, which offered views of America as it might look by 1960—sleek car and train models, intricate road- and rail-travel systems, fabulous buildings. It was surrounded by a circular moving aisle that had chairs for the viewing audience. There was a backdrop of motion-picture film which showed men and women walking, presumably into the future, and a narration that had been recorded on tape by a respected newscaster of the day, H. V. Kaltenborn. Also on tape was the sound of all those men and women walking, marching feet. Finally, there was *Music for the Perisphere*, composed for the occasion by William Grant Still, which I was asked to conduct for the recording that would be repeated for each revolution of the circular aisle. It seemed a simple enough job, a matter of timing the revolution and then conducting the music within that time allowance. Then I was told that I would also have to coordinate the two "click-tracks," the marching-feet tape and the Kaltenborn narration, with the music. Considering the time it took and the drain on my patience, it is odd that I can't remember the exact time one revolution took, something more than two minutes but less than eight. Well, I timed each element carefully and conducted the music at the tempo of the marching feet, fitting it all together finally.

I was not in New York for the opening of the Fair. When I got to it some months later, the perisphere was naturally the first exhibit I wanted to see. I stepped onto the moving aisle and was immediately taken in by the display and was sorry when the little circular trip was over—or was it? The music was still playing! Obviously someone had decided to increase the speed of the walkway so that more people could get in to see the exhibit, but no one bothered to correct the tape.

On the day in 1939 that the Russians, fresh from signing a pact with Nazi Germany, claimed control of Finland, a touching gesture took place at the Fair. As evening darkened the sky, the tremendous fountain in the center of the International Pavilion displayed in lights the colors of the Finnish flag, and over the loudspeakers people were suddenly hearing Jean Sibelius's *Finlandia*. There were probably some who had not heard the news and could not identify the colors or the music or know its significance, but soon everyone at the restaurants and cafés was standing. For some moments after the last note of music there was silence. A soundless echo touched with prophecy.

The Fair ran through 1940, a year longer than expected. Countries all over the globe had sent their best ideas, their finest expressions of cultural and scientific achievement, to be displayed and admired. They sent, too, their dreams of the future, and thousands of people came to see it all, to be inspired, to dream, to hope for a better world of tomorrow.

Now the dreams were ended. The nightmare of war was upon us.

PART THREE

"The World of Tomorrow"

THAT WORLD OF TOMORROW WAS formed seemingly overnight, and it remained for seven years in darkness. Neither the Germans nor the Japanese penetrated the Western Hemisphere in force. The United States was not an Austria to be "annexed" or a Malaya to be invaded or a France to be forced into surrender. The sun still lighted our days, but in much of the world tanks and guns, grenades and fire bombs provided the light. Before the Second World War was over, thirty-five years ago, this country—my country—experienced that darkness, too. Our soil was not stained but our blood was spilled on other soils.

It may be true that time puts an order to horrific events, lends a cooling perspective. But I can't say that is true about war. Visions of war haunt me still. Their power to stir emotional memories remains undiminished. In 1919, caught in the street fighting in Kislovodsk and trying not to stumble over the corpses as I ran for a hiding place. . . . In 1944, standing beside the hospital bed of a soldier in Naples, wondering what in God's name to say to a man who had lost his legs in battle.

There have been millions of words inspired by war—poems, novels, plays, histories. Yet I doubt the last word will ever be written. There is a timeless fascination with what war reveals about the human soul, and that display of human character is on a scale larger than life as it is otherwise encountered. For those who take a stand in war, commitment implies sacrifice—of personal interests, of comforts, of life itself if necessary. There are no ordinary days, no empty hours, no irrelevant acts.

President Roosevelt's fateful announcement came after a joint session of Congress, December 8, 1941. Lily and I were in the midst of a musicians' fund concert at the Waldorf-Astoria Hotel. We stopped at the appointed time, and a radio was brought into the room so everyone would hear those words:

> Yesterday, December 7, 1941—a date which will live in infamy —the United States of America was suddenly and deliberately attacked by naval and air forces of the Empire of Japan. . . .
> Hostilities exist. There is no blinking at the fact that our people, our territory, and our interests are in grave danger.
> With confidence in our armed forces—with the unbounded determination of our people—we will gain the inevitable triumph —so help us God.
> I ask that the Congress declare that since the unprovoked and dastardly attack by Japan on Sunday, December seventh, a state of war has existed between the United States and the Japanese Empire.

In some ways the war had begun for us even before that day. American men, and lads who would shortly become men, joined the Canadian Air Force to serve in England and France, where the battle against the Nazis had raged for two years; our government created the Lend-Lease program, which made money and supplies available to the Allies; and Bundles for Britain campaigns were initiated. By that Sunday morning of December 7, when the Japanese bombed Pearl Harbor, the dreams had been laid aside; the determination to fight had found expression.

To the question, what should my contribution to the war effort be, the answer was obvious: make as much music as I could in as many places and as often as possible. I was conducting the Coca-Cola program every Sunday in Liederkranz Hall and making recordings, but there were plenty of opportunities to go beyond that, even very early on.

The first request to make a personal appearance came in 1940. Canada was already in the fight and had begun a war-bond drive. Two men paid me a visit—I still remember their names: Herbert, of the Canadian Treasury, and Taggert, from the Canadian

Broadcasting Corporation. They wanted to know if I'd lead a coast-to-coast broadcast to sell bonds. I said yes. They said, "In Toronto, and the train leaves at 11:59 tonight." And if I wanted to bring some people, they would arrange everything.

My first thought was to play popular music—and why not a straight Rodgers and Hart concert? It certainly seemed to be one way of pleasing everybody, and it saved me the time it would take to select a well-balanced new program from the very large repertoire that all those weekly broadcasts had built up. I phoned two singers who had appeared regularly with me, Mary Martin and Judy Garland. And Rodgers and Hart. I was lucky. All four said yes. Within seven hours everything was arranged, and everybody was on the train to Toronto.

The concert was a success, and it was because of the high spirits and instant readiness of everyone involved to do whatever had to be done. I was to witness this overwhelming generosity of heart and mind over and over again in the ensuing five years. It was part of a new and benign contagion, an invisible network of moral vitality that connected all who fought the war with weapons other than guns.

Once the United States had entered the war I determined to make my services available to the men on the fighting fronts. Early in 1942, Oscar Levant and I decided to form a pianist-conductor unit for the United Service Organizations. Eagerly—and, I think now, somewhat naïvely—Oscar and I took the train to the capital and made an appointment to see the Secretary of War.

My traveling companion was a Broadway and film composer and a fine pianist. He had a special fondness for George Gershwin and had given many concerts of his music. As a panelist on the radio show *Information Please* he was known for his wit, which could be quite acerbic. Oscar's special charm was an ability to provoke you one minute and endear himself the next. "You can't always take him," S. N. Behrman remarked, "and you can never leave him."

The train to Washington was crowded, and the dining car was dense with people. We had to wait a good while for a table and then wait some more for the services of the harried waiter. I was privately waiting, too, for some sort of explosion from Oscar—instantaneous and unmistakably candid reactions were his specialty. So, when he leaned across the table, I braced myself, which was a good idea because what he said, although not the fireworks I had expected, was startling just the same: "You know, we are living in such an extraordinary time that we must take things as they come!"

Secretary Stimson told us we were a little too early with our plan, that the USO had not yet been fully organized. We left on the next train back, having to be content with at least registering our availability—and, amazingly, feeling no chagrin at taking the time of one of the busiest men in the land.

Part of the musical culture I had been schooled in during my youth was something called *melodeclamation*—music with the spoken word. It can be a dramatic and emotionally powerful combination, given the right music and words.

In my opinion, American music had not given enough attention to the idea of *melodeclamation*, but it was not until after the war had begun that I thought to do something about that. I decided to commission music that would reflect the spirit of this country as expressed in the ideas of some of its great historical figures. One of the composers I asked to contribute to the project was Aaron Copland. I was not alone, either in my intention or in my choice of Copland, who had something of a reputation as an agitator for American music. The early war years were inspiring a good deal of patriotic fervor in the music world. Eugene Goossens—then conductor of the Cincinnati Symphony Orchestra—had invited Copland and seventeen other composers to create short fanfares that would contribute to strengthening morale for the war effort. The most enduring result was the extraordinary *Fanfare for the Common Man*.

I spoke to Copland just after I returned from Washington. His first thought was to compose a musical portrait of the poet Walt Whitman, but I felt that the atmosphere of war made a statesman the more appropriate choice. I mentioned Abraham Lincoln. Aaron took to the idea.

The composer began the work right away, selecting the narrative material from letters and speeches of Lincoln. The portrait was finished in April, 1942. It was more than I had hoped for. All the gentle passion, the integrity, the simplicity of Lincoln's wisdom were there. In addition to his own music Copland made freestyle use of the American folk song "Camptown Races" and of a ballad, also American, called "Springfield Mountain." It was just right.

Nineteen forty-two was probably the year when morale was lowest. The Nazi aggression in Europe, Russia, and Africa was matched in fervor and even more in extent by the Japanese in China, Indochina, Thailand, Malaya, Burma, Indonesia, and the Pacific Islands. Until the Battle of Midway, in June, the prospect of a Japanese attack on the U.S. West Coast was a fearsome possibility. That spring seemed a good time for the *Lincoln Portrait*. I arranged for the performance to be given in the nation's capital on a barge in the Potomac with the Lincoln Memorial in the background. Carl Sandburg agreed to speak.

I had already premiered the work in Cincinnati, so I had some idea of its power to move an audience. Well, we did it in Washington. Sandburg was, to my mind, the perfect narrator of the words of a man he had studied and written volumes about. He used his voice as an instrument, augmenting or tempering the somberness and power of the message:

> We of this Congress and administration will be remembered in spite of ourselves. . . . We hold the power and bear the responsibility. . . . We must disenthrall ourselves and then we shall save our country. . . .

We finished the piece. And there was only silence. No applause. After a while the audience began moving away.

"We were a flop," Carl said on the way to the dressing room. But I didn't think so. Those words must have seemed written for this night, for these people in these times, I told him. Besides, I reminded Lincoln's biographer, it wasn't the first time Lincoln's words were greeted by profound silence. The President himself had heard no applause after delivering his Gettysburg Address.

Lily and I did not begin our overseas tours until 1944, but we did make many national appearances, either together or alone. In the intervening time I never lost my determination to get to the fighting front. And, in a sense, I did get into the ocean war, if not actually overseas, some time before 1944—although I would not know that for thirty-seven years!

In 1940 I went alone to conduct a concert in Miami for the Officers Training School, and I met a friend of mine, a Navy man. Over drinks he told me he was attached to the antisubmarine school nearby. This was at the time when German submarines were wreaking havoc on Allied shipping. Some had come very close to American shores—the beach right there at Miami was then covered with oil from a torpedoed British tanker. In the antisub school the American Navy was helping the British in a search for a way of measuring sound underwater so that the presence and location of enemy submarines could be ascertained. I was curious about the actual procedures in this so-called echo-sounding work, and I asked my friend about it. He told me as much as security allowed.

At the moment, he said, they were focusing on the idea of determining submarine locations by listening to the echo of a *ping*, a sound emitted from, say, a patrolling destroyer. They would take a sub to sea and send out this *ping*; if it made contact with the surface of any object more dense than water, there would be an echo, which the detection/listening device picked up. If the object was moving, the echo changed pitch, according to whether the object was approaching or receding—the Doppler effect.

So far the work was very discouraging. They had brought in a pianist—Eddie Duchin—and a clarinetist—Artie Shaw—on the theory that musicians would be especially skilled at pitch identification. That was true, but, as I told him, some would be more so than others, depending on their instruments. String players would have been much better equipped for this job, since they deal continuously with subtle differences in pitch—even the most infinitesimal change in the finger's position on a violin string alters the pitch. But pianists, for instance, do not have this problem because pianos have a specific number of keys, each of which corresponds to a specific pitch. The player knows the note he wants and what key will produce it—there are no surprises. . . .

And then it dawned on me. Four or five months earlier a man had appeared at Liederkranz Hall with a machine that, he assured me, was designed to *show* the exact pitch of any given sound—and could thus settle any argument that might arise over whether someone had played or sung off pitch. It had twelve little windows with needles visible. One was the basic A, tuned and responsive only to 440 vibrations per second, the international pitch. The rest represented all the other half and whole tones of the octave. It cost $500. I couldn't see any immediate need for such a machine— we did not have very many arguments!—but I bought it anyway. And now I wondered if such a visible-sound device might be the beginning of an answer to the sub-detection problem.

I told my Navy friend what I was thinking. He expressed interest, in a quiet sort of way—but the speed of subsequent events told me just how important he and his colleagues thought it might be. The next thing I knew I was at the Massachusetts Institute of Technology, with the machine, getting fingerprinted and photographed. I was then escorted to a guarded room where I was asked to demonstrate to about twelve men how pitch could be made visible. Afterward they wanted to know if I would leave the machine with them. I said of course.

A day or two later I received a telegram in New York from the research group asking if the machine was for sale. I wired back that they could keep it without paying. Another telegram: they must buy. A friend of mine explained that to protect themselves legally they had to buy it, so I agreed to a modest sum. I had one last communication; the group wondered if there would be any objection if the device was used for another very important wartime matter, not connected with submarines. (I had not expected they would tell me what their intention was.) I told them to do what they wanted; I knew better than to try to find out what finally happened.

Time went by. It was July 4, 1977, thirty-seven years later, and I was in Bermuda. At the home of friends I met Bill Stevenson. I was delighted; I had just finished reading his *A Man Called Intrepid* on the plane going there. We got to talking about Sir William Stephenson, who, as "Intrepid," had organized and directed a huge espionage network in World War II. It so happened that Stephenson lived in Bermuda, too, and so I asked Bill if he thought Sir William would know something about what role the visible-pitch machine had played in wartime submarine detection. Bill offered to find out.

Shortly thereafter I received a statement from Sir William. There are no words for the exhilaration it gives me:

```
To Andre Kostelanetz
who contributed to the development
of the fiequency meter for
measuring electronic signals
to establish exact pitch.
This instrument helped win the
Battle of the Atlantic in 1941
turning the tide of war which
had threatened to destroy Britain.
You made pitch visible and enabled
a layman to distinguish between
friendly and enemy submarines.
```

You initiated it!

William Stephenson

Bermuda

July '77

There was tremendous activity everywhere on the home front— people collected money and tin and silk and rubber, staffed USO centers for the comfort and entertainment of soldiers on leave, organized air-raid warning systems, and planted Victory gardens. There was an intensity of purpose behind every act. Many of the ordinary activities of daily life were raised into something meaningful for the shared cause. I had what I thought was a pretty good idea along those lines, but it ended up having all the impact of a feather crashing into a bowl of Jell-O.

I conducted the Coca-Cola program at 4:30 on Sunday, and just after it finished Winston Churchill was broadcast live from London—at 9:00 P.M. their time. And that gave me an idea: as a salute to the Prime Minister, why not close the program with his favorite song? The chances were he would hear it.

It wasn't difficult finding out what the song was. I simply cabled Ed Murrow, the CBS war correspondent in London, who obliged with an immediate answer: "The Harrow School Song." At that point things slowed down to a crawl. The CBS librarian produced four volumes of English school songs. The Harrow school song wasn't called the Harrow school song, so it took us quite a while to finally find "Forty Years On." Step three was to arrange it for orchestra, since the music in the book was for choir.

At the end of the program the following Sunday, I announced our intention of greeting Churchill with his favorite song. And then we played it.

I never heard from the Prime Minister. I hope he heard me.

There was one musician, however, who did catch Churchill's undivided attention—Irving Berlin.

His musical *This Is the Army* was extremely popular during the war, not just here but all over Europe, especially in England. The composer used to travel with the show, and on this occasion he happened to be in England. Now, his name was far more widely known in most circles than that of another Berlin, Isaiah. Sir Isaiah, as he is known today, is a philosopher, political theorist, and writer; during the war he was serving at the British Embassy in Washington. One of his duties was to keep Churchill informed in detail on what was happening in our capital. The diplomat was very good at his job, so good that the Prime Minister took favorable notice. In fact, he told an aide to invite Berlin to lunch the next time he was in London.

The aide happened to know—along with at least three-quarters of the population—that Berlin was in London at that very moment, but he thought better of possibly embarrassing his boss by pointing that out. Instead, he immediately put in a call to Berlin's hotel. Naturally, Irving accepted right away. It was not every day one had an invitation to lunch with the Prime Minister, right in his office no less!

The appointed hour arrived, and the working lunch got under way.

"And," said Churchill, "what is your opinion of the new Sherman tanks the Americans are making—how effective do you think they will be against the Germans?"

An unexpected question, but Berlin hesitated only a moment.

"Well, I think they are pretty good."

The Prime Minister went on.

"Who do you think will be the next president? Will Roosevelt continue?"

If Irving felt the lure of flattery beneath this sudden interest in his opinion on matters of state, the modest simplicity of his answer showed he had certainly risen above temptation:

"Who knows?"

At this point Churchill rose abruptly and stormed into the outer office, shouting, "Who is this damn fool lunching with me?" He was told.

The Prime Minister returned to his luncheon guest, doubtless with higher-than-usual color in his cheeks.

Some years ago I came across an observation of Mark Twain's: "The secret source of Humor itself is not joy but sorrow. There is no humor in heaven." It was one of those declarations I've encountered from time to time that seem to carry the ring of absolute truth because they correspond instantly to my own experience. During the war I marveled at the number of funny stories in continuous mass circulation. Instinctively people turned to humor for comfort, for relief from the daily assault on their sensibilities. You had only to look, and humor was there. The most seriously motivated endeavors would almost inevitably be punctuated with a humorous exclamation point—and another anecdote was lovingly added to the trove.

I had never thought of conductors as magnets for high comedy, but there were incidents, like two I recall, that caused me to wonder if perhaps a rich seedbed of joviality had been overlooked!

Early in the 1940s the New York Philharmonic was scheduled for a concert in White Plains, about thirty minutes north of New York City. The last train home was 11:00 P.M. If you missed that, you would have to wait hours for the first morning train. So, thought Maestro Artur Rodzinski, instead of playing "The Star-Spangled Banner" first (the rule in those days was that all concerts were begun with the national anthem), it had better be put at the end of the program. That way the orchestra could pack up immediately afterward, without having to acknowledge applause—since anthems are never applauded—or worry about playing encores and missing the train.

Rodzinski saw no need to announce his intention to the audience. He simply raised his baton to begin the evening's opening selection, Beethoven's *Egmont* Overture. It just so happens that the overture's first note is F, the same as that of the national anthem, but held longer, and when that note sounded, six thousand people rose to their feet. Rodzinski didn't know whether he had forgotten to put on his trousers or what!

Sooner or later it had to be my turn. I don't remember being overcome with laughter in this situation, although I was possibly the only one of thousands who wasn't. Now, in the hindsight of advanced maturity, it strikes me as hilarious.

I was guest-conducting the Toronto Philharmonic Orchestra in that city's Varsity Arena for the benefit of the Canadian Merchant Marine. The exact attendance figure was 7,603—virtually every available space on the four sides of the arena was filled. I had decided on "Clair de Lune," from Debussy's *Suite Bergamasque*, and then "The Stars and Stripes Forever" as encores. We had rehearsed them, of course, but exactly 4.5 seconds into "Clair de

Lune" I realized that only half the orchestra was clear on the order of those encores, because *only* half was playing the Debussy—the other half had launched themselves into the Sousa march! And I was not alone in this realization. In "live" quadrophonic stereo the giggles and guffaws rolled in from every side.

Now that I think of it, that Toronto concert included the first performance of a work I commissioned, Paul Creston's *Frontiers*. And, early the following year, once in March, 1944, and again in April, it was part of the program I conducted on an occasion that was equally memorable, though not for a comic reason.

The concerts were given in Sanders Theatre, Harvard University, and the orchestra was the Boston Symphony. Lily sang at the second concert, and I was guest conductor at the invitation of Serge Koussevitzky. He had had his own orchestra in Russia for eight years and had been leading the Boston since 1924, making it, in my opinion, one of the greatest orchestras in the world.

Koussevitzky was one of two conductors I most admired, the other being Toscanini, so I was understandably thrilled. Alas, neither conductor would be thrilled at seeing his name here, in the same sentence with the other's! In what was actually a kind of backhanded tribute, the two greats were very jealous of each other. Neither ever used his counterpart's name. Koussevitzky's instrument was the double bass, convenient for Toscanini, who could—and unfailingly did—refer to the Russian as "that bass player!" "And why," Koussevitzky would ask in innocent astonishment, "does that old man want to conduct?"

The Boston's conductor was devoted to his orchestra and often exhausted himself polishing it to the sheen it has even today. Although Koussevitzky is long gone, the glow he imparted still adheres.

There is a little story, somewhat reminiscent of Chekhov, revolving around the fact that the master drove himself very hard. One day, after going through a first movement at rehearsal, he was heard to say, "I am sick." The next day the same thing happened. Now, the concertmaster of the second violins, a Frenchman who had been playing in the orchestra for many years, heard the remark differently—"You are sick." And he worried himself into such a state that he became convinced it was Koussevitzky's way of telling him he no longer played well enough and was about to be fired. So he went to him and said, "Maestro, after twenty years I don't deserve to be let out in this fashion."

"I never said anything like that!" the maestro told him.

"But, yes," said the violinist. "More than once, on different days, you said, 'You are sick.' "

"No! What I said was, 'I am sick.' "

"Oh, that's different," said the Frenchman, happy now.

Then Koussevitzky was offended. "Oh, so now you are glad that I am sick . . . !"

And so on and on. Enough to make them sick.

I always thought of Koussevitzky as a sort of *grand seigneur*; he had an air of elegant authoritativeness, in his conducting especially. His way of beginning something soft was wonderful—he would give a slow, deliberate downbeat, not an easy signal for an unknowing orchestra to respond to. But his Boston players had it all figured out. How did they know exactly when to begin? Simple: when his hand passed the third button on his vest!

In 1944 what I had been hoping for at last happened: Lily and I were asked to make two tours overseas under the auspices of the USO. The first would be during the spring and summer, the second would run from December into April of the following year. I thought it best to resign from the Coca-Cola program.

Only God and the War Department knew in advance exactly where we were being sent, but there were clues: among the necessary inoculations was a yellow-fever shot, which meant at least one stop would be somewhere near the equator, and we were to purchase uniforms for both hot and cold weather. We would be traveling as noncombatants, with the "equivalent" rank of captain in case of capture.

I kept a diary of our second tour—which I sent home, day by day, as letters to my brother, Boris—but not of the first. Immediately after the Persian Gulf Command series of concerts—the first leg of the first tour—I did write down the highlights of those weeks, but stringent security regulations prohibited the taking of on-the-spot notes. For the second leg of that tour, principally Italy, the rules were relaxed somewhat, and I did manage to record my immediate impressions from time to time.

The Persian Gulf Command series meant spending six weeks in Iran. At the beginning of the war Iran had a rapprochement with Germany and, because of that, Great Britain and Russia invaded and occupied the country in 1941. The Shah abdicated in favor of his son, and Iran's independence then came under the guarantee of Great Britain, Russia, and the United States. After that she cooperated with the Allied effort. From her northern sector American troops delivered supplies to Russia. Iran could then be called friend.

American hostages are being held by Iranians as I write this, and two countries who were united against a common enemy are now themselves enemies. I have always counted my experiences there as part of a treasured memory, but the harshness of the present reality makes it painful to recall those other days. If I hadn't composed these notes so many years ago, I doubt I could give words to the memory now.

The Persian Gulf Command,
May–July, 1944

WE FLEW FROM MIAMI TO Brazil, and then on to Ascension Island, part of the British St. Helena colony in the South Atlantic. The first thing I heard as the doors of the plane opened was my recording of Grofé's *Grand Canyon Suite*—the soldiers' way of greeting us. The island was volcanic, rocky and dry, but vegetables were chemically grown, without soil. Very impressive.

Next stop was West Africa. We landed in Accra, the Gold Coast. Enormous billboard advised: Do Not Stand Still! A precaution against sleeping sickness, which is carried by mosquitoes. The idea is to make it difficult for them to settle and bite by creating a moving target. Flew east the next day to a town near Lake Chad. From the air the African *paysage* seemed to be covered in a white blanket. It was humidity. We saw Khartoum, at the confluence of the two Niles, the Blue and the White.

In the morning we followed the Nile—it looked just like a highway from the air—up to Cairo. We were billeted right at the airfield. Constant air traffic, of course, as Cairo is a crossroads between Europe and the greater part of continental Africa. We had no concerts scheduled for Cairo at that time. It was an extended stopover point before going on to the Persian Gulf.

Lily and I went to Gizeh, near Cairo, to see the pyramids and were immediately surrounded by several dragomans, interpreter-guides, who insisted we needed their help. One was particularly insistent, so I decided to stop him cold with what I thought was a clever proposition. "Listen," I said to him, "I will let you go with us, but you must sell us these pyramids." From his silence and the look on his face I was sure that was the end of it. Lily and I began to walk away. We had gone only a few steps when I felt a hand on my shoulder, and I turned to face the dragoman. "I will sell them to you," he said confidentially, "if you sell me the Brooklyn Bridge!"

Our next visit to the pyramids was by full moon. We had transferred to Shepheard's Hotel in Cairo by then. On its famous terrace you could meet just about anybody at cocktail time, and we found ourselves talking with the American consul. In the course of conversation he admitted to having been in Cairo for a year without seeing the sights at Gizeh. I found this amazing and immediately proposed we make up for that by not only seeing the pyramids but in the most dramatic and magical of settings. And it was magnificent.

The Egyptian flies are justly famous for persistence. When they land on you, you actually have to push them off. Especially annoying in the morning at sunrise, which is when they wake. I found an answer to the problem. Since the windows had jalousies, I decided to try leaving a small opening in them at night. It worked like a charm. The sun rose and so did the flies, and in about two minutes they had all flown outside, seeking the light.

From Cairo we flew to Teheran, with a brief stop at Damascus, arriving in the evening at the Amerabad Airport. There was quite a large welcoming crowd, among them the officer in charge of organizing the Persian Gulf Command orchestra—the PGC orchestra, as we came to call it.

By prearrangement the War Department would provide me with my "instrument"'—the group of musicians that made up an orchestra. If the theater of operations we were in had a band, that became the core of the orchestra, with strings added by a pickup method from attached-service string players. Since every soldier has an ID card it was not too difficult to locate the musicians I needed. Example: for the PGC orchestra a double-bass player was found in the south of Persia, attached to a communications unit. He was from the Cleveland Symphony and invaluable, naturally. If the theater did not have a band, then the whole orchestra was put together via attached service.

I assembled the orchestra in a large hall for the first real rehearsal. There were gaps still to be filled, but it was a workable nucleus. Since we were far away from the strictures of a union, we could rehearse as often as we wanted without worry of going way over budget. What a luxury! And the musicians loved it. The double-bass player was so enthusiastic about playing again that before a half hour had gone by the fingers of his fret hand began to bleed because they did not have the protective calluses that constant practice provides.

After one week of rehearsals we had close to a professional-sounding complement of musicians. Lily joined us for a dress rehearsal, and I must say everything sounded wonderful.

Ever since our arrival I had been constantly aware of the Russian presence. The cement hut which was our home in the command compound was in full view of the Russian flags, and Russian officers and soldiers seemed to be everywhere. It was the first time I had been confronted with such a large group of my former countrymen since I had left Russia more than twenty years ago, and I began to feel somewhat uncomfortable. The more I saw of them the more intense my unease became. I was convinced they knew who I was, where I had come from and how. Would they react and, if so, how? I told myself I was overdramatizing the situation by so immodestly assuming that my identity and personal history were of any importance to them. But I didn't believe it; paranoia had taken hold of my reason.

I said nothing about my sense of foreboding to Lily, not wanting to upset her, or to anyone else. But something had to be done. I decided to present my problem to General Donald Connolly, commanding officer of the U.S. forces in Iran. When I told him I had left the U.S.S.R. "without saying good-by" and that I wouldn't want to embarrass him vis-à-vis the Russians, he immediately called in his aide, Colonel Pantuhof. He was apparently some sort of liaison officer, judging from his name and the fact that he spoke perfect Russian, and he assured me there would be no problem. The U.S. and Russia were allies, after all, and under the Lend-Lease Act we were supplying them with military equipment. Of course, that was not something ever acknowledged with thanks on the part of the Russians, the general interjected, but then we never said anything about the thousands of Russian dead at Stalingrad, either. Just before I left General Connolly suggested it might be a good idea if I announced the concert programs in Russian as well as in English. That should please the Russians and settle my problem by simple confrontation of it.

Our first concert was in Kazvin, north of Teheran. In 1941, during the British and Russian invasion of Iran, Kazvin had been bombed by Russia. I thought of this as we drove through the city gate, which was adorned with huge letters: U.S.S.R., as if it were still Soviet-occupied territory—even though Iran's independence had been guaranteed by the Teheran Declaration in 1943.

The first row of seats at the concert that evening was completely occupied by Russian generals. The rest of the audience was made up of American, British, and Russian troops. I could hardly take my eyes off that first row as I came out to announce the program, in Russian and English—it was packed so tight with the well-fed generals that there was no space between any two sets of shoulders, and the enormous shimmering epaulettes on those shoulders created a glistening river of silver. Their greeting was minimal, but as we progressed through the program I could feel enthusiasm growing. Lily sang like an angel, and they loved her. The concert was a great success, judging from the applause and the kind remarks afterward.

Lily has made an amazing discovery: she is not nervous singing for the troops. For the first time in her entire career the "nervosity" that has so plagued her before every performance has completely disappeared. She thinks it might be the absence of critical scrutiny. She is singing for audiences who are there only to enjoy the music, not analyze her technique or compare her, possibly unfavorably, to someone else.

One concert we gave in Teheran is particularly memorable because of the way it began. Since we performed for Iranians, British, Americans, and Russians, we always had to play their national anthems first. The day before this concert General Connolly called me to say that the Russian national anthem had just been changed —was there time to rehearse the new one? I looked over the music, which wasn't difficult—just pompous. It had been written at Stalin's request—he apparently thought the old anthem, the *"Internationale,"* was not Russian enough. And, of course, it wasn't. It wasn't even a Russian composition, but a French one. The new song, by Boris Alexandrov, could not be faulted there, as its name suggests: "Anthem of the Bolshevik Party." Well, we rehearsed enough to play it quite stirringly, in spite of itself! But when the time came and we began the piece, there was a problem: no reaction of any kind from that front-row river of silver—it remained at low tide! No one had told the Russians they had a new anthem.

Seconds passed. Every time I threw a quick glance around, there was the immobile row of seated patriots. Finally I noticed some movement, a nudge here and there, questioning looks (perhaps they noticed my distracted conducting), and then all at once the river rose.

Our mode of travel varied in the course of the thousands of miles we covered in touring Iran. Depending on the topography and on what transport was available we found ourselves carried by amphibious truck, train, or the prime minister's private limousine. For the trip to Abadan in western Iran and the port town of Bandar-e Shahpur nearby, we traveled part of the way by caravan. We made several stops, one at Hamadan, at the foot of Mount Alvand. The town is 6,000 feet above sea level and has a Jewish colony. Mordecai and Esther are reportedly buried there. We passed through Isfahan, another link to the Bible, for it was from that area, or so legend has it, that the Three Wise Men set out to follow the Star of Bethlehem.

The road we traveled began to descend gradually, and before long we were in a desert with the hottest temperatures I hope I will ever experience—between 120 and 150 degrees. The sand was gray, the air was gray—the haze almost obscured the sun. We were literally looking at heat. Everyone warned us against wearing anything metal, such as a belt buckle, which would become like a branding iron. In one place we stopped, known as the "city of the blind," the affluent lived three floors below the ground in order to stay cool. It was amazing what a contrast in temperature it was. We found ourselves shivering from cold as intense as the heat had been. The people who couldn't afford to have such luxurious living conditions had to make do with huts at ground level.

We drove mostly at night. Once in a while lights would appear in the distance. It was not a village—Iran had no electricity—but a convoy of lend-lease trucks. They were driven by Iranians, who must not have been very good drivers because we often passed overturned trucks.

We returned to Teheran by Trans-Iranian Railroad. The train was hot and slow, so I decided to ride part of the way on the cowcatcher—well, it seemed like a good idea at the time—quite a dramatic experience. One minute in the total—and cool—darkness of a tunnel, the next assaulted by the double impact of a spectacular mountain view and the terrific heat.

General Connolly greeted us at the compound with a special request to play three concerts, one each at the British and Russian embassies and one at the Shah's palace. We were entitled to three days of rest at this point but decided to do the concerts anyway.

The evening at the British embassy went without incident, very pleasant. The concert for the Russians went well, and there was a reception afterward. Despite the gracious tone set by the array of food and drink (I've never seen so much caviar in one place in my life!), things became a little uncomfortable for me. I found myself alone at one point, watching Lily dance with one of the Russian generals, and a woman came over to me. She was a general's wife—at least, I assumed she was, judging from the five huge men who were suddenly hovering close by like bodyguards. The lady began without small talk. "Why did you have to leave Russia?" she asked in Russian. "You could have made just as big a career in Russia."

In a sense I suppose this was the kind of question I had been waiting for ever since we had arrived in the Persian Gulf, yet I had no answer prepared beyond one simple fact. So I stated it: "Because I wanted to go to America." That was it. Everybody disappeared.

The concert at the palace was given in the midst of incredible Middle East luxury. Gorgeous carpets and objets d'art everywhere. (After the concert Lily and I were presented with one of those carpets.) The Shah introduced his family to us. His wife was the sister of King Farouk of Egypt. I was rather taken aback by her first question: Did I think Deanna Durbin had a voice? Our conversation did not really go much deeper than that.

We played for a very small audience, for security reasons, I suspect—no one but the Shah and his family and a few courtiers. At one point all the lights went out. Pitch-darkness. I couldn't help thinking it was a perfect setting for an assassination. Nobody said a word. Finally I felt I had to do something. The piano was very near me so I moved toward it, lowered myself to the bench, and began playing "Clair de Lune." I hoped it would have a relaxing effect. (It did for me, anyway!) Torches were brought and soon the lights went on and so did the concert.

The entire orchestra was then invited to a magnificent banquet. There was a tremendous quantity of Iranian food specialties, many of them raw. It looked very attractive, but Lily and I had been thoroughly warned to avoid strange foods in far-off countries. We asked for a simple rice pilaf. It came with a thick egg crust and, most important, very hot. Absolutely delicious. The next day half the orchestra was in the hospital.

By now we had been in Iran for six weeks. Before the second part of the tour there was time for a rest, in Tel Aviv. We flew to Cairo—incredible sunrise as the plane landed—and changed planes for the flight to Tel Aviv. (For some reason we flew with the loading door open.) Instead of staying at a military camp nearby, we chose a small hotel in the city. Suddenly everything was sparkling clean, hygienic, and we could eat vegetables, raw fruit, anything.

On July 4 we drove to Jerusalem and were escorted around this fantastic city by Consul General Pinkerton. After lunch I excused myself and went off to have a walk, with the secondary purpose of finding a jewelry shop that could repair my watch, which had stopped. When I did find one and stepped inside to ask what could be done, the watchmaker—a very old Jew—just looked at me with absolutely no expression, no response.

It took me a moment to gauge the situation. There was tremendous conflict in Palestine at that time between the Zionists and the

British. Great Britain, with Arab help, gained control of the region in World War I and hasn't yet been able to implement a plan to establish a Jewish homeland while preserving peace with Arabs who claim territory in the Holy Land. World War II has frozen all activity, but the resentments are very much alive. I realized that the combination of my speaking English and the uniform must have convinced the old fellow I was another British officer, and he was treating me accordingly. And then it dawned on me that right in front of me at last was an opportunity to put to use all those Hebrew lessons Father had insisted my sister Mina and I have so long ago. So, in not very good accents, I'm sure, I explained about the watch. The Hebrew our teacher Solodouho had taught us was that of the Ashkenazim, the German Jews, but in Jerusalem it is Sephardic Hebrew, originally from the Jews of Spain and Portugal, that is spoken. Still, it did not seem to matter. The watch was ready in an hour.

North Africa, Italy,
July–August, 1944

THE WEATHER IN NAPLES IS extraordinarily beautiful. We will leave this area soon for a tour of North African cities and then return to Italy. The USO asks urgently that all entertainment personnel everywhere visit hospitals whenever possible. Even if there is no possibility of playing we are to visit anyway, just to talk. We have gone to many, particularly in Naples, performing first if we can and then visiting with the men. All ambulatory patients wear lavender robes and sit in the front rows at the concerts. Patients who cannot walk are wheeled out into the courtyard to listen.

Talking to these young men who have been damaged in the war is not easy. When you face a man who has lost a limb perhaps, or worse, all you want to do is tell him how much his sacrifice means to you and to the whole world. It is a message that is virtually impossible to convey in words. There is too much emotion to manage without sounding glib or else breaking down. So you just try to talk about things you think they want to hear. And they often help you by asking about the States. The question is almost always: is it the same as when they left?

The grimmest thing is that some of these men will have to spend the rest of their lives in a hospital, just as some of the wounded veterans of the First World War are still confined, forgotten men. . . .

July 14, Bastille Day. Concert in Algiers, General de Gaulle attending. He creates a distinct impression even at a distance: a little stiff, but definitely aware of who he is.

This North African cities tour is going very quickly. For a concert in El Alamein we had an orchestra of professional musicians, British. (A British general has made me a life member of El Alamein Club!)

In Cairo, with this same British orchestra, there were four anthems to play—American, French, English, and Egyptian. When we got to the British, "God Save the King," there was suddenly cacophony—the orchestra had split, playing two different keys. A British officer rushed onto the stage and said: "Gentlemen, the king always in F!" We corrected that amazingly fast.

In combat areas we fly in bombers of all types, our favorite being the B-25, which is very fast. On the takeoffs we stand behind the pilots. During the flights we stack blankets for makeshift seats. The pilots are always very pleasant. Some let us sit in the cockpit. Once I was even permitted to help fly the ship.

Very early on in this tour, before takeoff for a flight over water, we were briefed for ditching—what to do in case the plane is forced into the "drink." Minute instructions on how to use the Mae West were given on the plane by a Britisher. We all—soldiers, generals, diplomats, artists—sat in rapt attention. If there was trouble, we were to pull two small cords, which would allow a chemical compound to immediately inflate the life jacket. If by chance that didn't work, we could unscrew a little rubber tube on our shoulder and blow it up. "And if this doesn't work," said our cheerful instructor, "a happy trip to you all!"

In Naples and Rome we can use the civilian orchestras attached to theaters—run by either the British or American army—like the San Carlo Opera in Naples and the Royal in Rome, and we have a place to play at the same time. Otherwise I organize an orchestra by putting together small military bands. The Army Special Services have built camp theaters, sometimes overnight, using whatever scraps of wood they could find. They accommodate thousands of men. Those who cannot fit inside hear through loudspeakers outside.

Band members also serve as litter bearers and ammunition carriers and as such are very often casualties. Having a chance to play music means a great deal to them. One night, just a few minutes before a performance was to begin, a British soldier, all begrimed and carrying a violin case, rushed up to me and gasped that he had just hitchhiked fifty miles and would like very much to play that night. His name was Farthington, and he was a former member of the London Philharmonic. He played with us, and the orchestra gave him a big hand.

Usually after a concert a table is set out and soldiers and officers line up for autographs, first come, first served. G.I.'s are great collectors, and instead of using paper they use money. (This surely derives from the aviation "short snorter" tradition whereby people who fly long range collect dated signatures on a dollar bill.) In Italy it is mostly our invasion money, 100-lire bills (equivalent to $1.00) and, considering there can be from 300 to 500 soldiers asking for autographs, this runs into quite a bit of money. Someone remarked that this is a very good control on inflation, since these bills are withdrawn from circulation.

We chat with the men, and they often ask us to get in touch with their families in the States by letter or phone when we return. We are keeping a list. I wish we could keep a list of all the memorable quips we hear everywhere. One fellow told Lily: "In Hollywood I had to pay four dollars and forty cents to hear you sing, and here at the front I can enjoy listening to you for nothing!"

The G.I.'s often present us with souvenirs of battles—cartridges, parts of parachutes, even guns. We have discovered that American soldiers are great souvenir hunters and very often pay prices far in excess of the value of the articles. They eagerly display their "bargains"—a "genuine" ruby, for instance, that cost only $10 or $15— and, rather than dampen their enthusiasm, we tell them that the man who really got gypped was the one who sold it to them. I remember a visit with a soldier in a hospital in Iran. He told me he had collected rubies for his wife, and he took out a matchbox with about twenty red stones in it, rather nice-looking. I asked how much he paid for them, and he said a dollar apiece. I knew he had been fooled, but I said nothing. If he believed they were rubies he would be bringing his wife—well, then they *were*.

We take many of our meals in enlisted men's mess halls. The food is good, but sometimes getting a full meal is difficult—albeit very pleasant—because of the signing of autographs. When the soldiers sit down to eat the standard question is: "What is it?" The standard answer is: "Don't ask." The food is almost always a form of pasta, but in some places the chefs are highly skilled in making unusual sauces. Once we had a delicious spaghetti meal and asked who had made it. The cook came out of the kitchen, and it turned out that she had been Ciano's cook and now was very glad to be working for the U.S. Army. This was the same Ciano—Mussolini's son-in-law—whose villa on Capri was requisitioned as a rest-and-recuperation station for the Air Force. We spent some time there ourselves when we first arrived in Naples.

On every table in every mess hall we have seen there are three bottles: Atabrine (an antimalarial drug), vitamins, and salt tablets. I overheard a story about the King of England's visit to the front. He asked General Harold Alexander, then field marshal and Allied commander in chief in the Mediterranean, about the vitamins—were they any good? "All my officers take them," the general replied. "Usually when they take one pill they jump—it seems to have such a vitalizing effect upon them." The king asked what happened when they took two pills. "They are immediately placed in protective custody, sir."

Often we can see dogfights in the evening from a mess hall. They are very high up, so the planes are not discernible, but we can follow their course by the streams of vapor that float behind them.

In Bari, southern Italy, on the Adriatic. There is not only a civilian orchestra available but an Army band. Yesterday I called for a friendly contest: each group had to play "Begin the Beguine." The G.I.'s won. Each unit cheered and applauded the other.

In the afternoon, as Lily and I were taking a walk in the city, we noticed an Army sergeant stopping every Yugoslav soldier he saw and giving each some of his cigarettes. We introduced ourselves— he said he was John Sullivan from New York—and then asked why he was giving away his rations to the Yugoslavs. He said that he didn't smoke, and anyway the Yugoslavs were wonderful to our men. If they were downed in Nazi-occupied Yugoslavian territory, they were rescued and carried to safety whenever possible—and at great risk. This was the sergeant's way of thanking the Yugoslavs.

In several places where we have given concerts, but chiefly in Italy, we have noticed young boys of about seven to thirteen sitting in the front row with the soldiers. They are dressed in cut-down U.S. Army uniforms, without insignia, of course, and are usually homeless orphans. The Army has made them mascots. They seem to learn English quickly and assist the G.I.'s in all sorts of chores. Here in Foggia, one such mascot has proved to be the cleverest little singer. He is about twelve and has lost his father and mother in the bombardment. He can imitate the ocarina amazingly well, and he is singing with us. The "orchestra" is made up of thirty-six musicians from the six six-piece dance bands that were available here.

At the hospital while visiting one of the musicians we saw one of our Connecticut neighbors, Madeleine Carroll. She was carrying a big bundle of laundry. I offered to assist her, but she very firmly declined. Madeleine is working for the Red Cross in strict anonymity. She is on hand at probably the most difficult moments for American fliers who have been severely wounded—burned or mutilated—to help carry them through the first shock of adjustment. She is so busy she could see us for only a few moments.

Of course, the soldiers have many pets—dogs, as a rule. Every regiment has a few puppies. Lily loves animals and is always quick to draw my attention to them. In Rome we saw a Jeep proceeding down the street with two puppies perched on the radiator, and the fellow sitting next to the driver was far more interested in watching them than in seeing the sights of the city. G.I.'s bring their pets to the concerts, and they are well behaved, for the most part.

Once when I walked to the podium I found a dog waiting for me. I petted him, and he stayed for a while and then was on his way to investigate the rest of the band. Perhaps he decided I would never throw the stick I was waving.

When we visited General Mark Clark, commander of the Fifth Army, at his headquarters, we found that he, too, had a mascot, a cocker spaniel called Pal. (Lily is going to send him a "necklace" after we get home.) Pal was very playful and everyone's favorite. He had his own short snorter, just like the general, and we had to sign it. The general signed ours, but we had to take for granted that Pal wanted to but was too busy.

We gave concerts for the Fifth Army troops—those who had survived Anzio and Monte Cassino. Those horrific battles took place only weeks ago, and Rome has fallen to the Allies as a result. The nightmare of those days shows in the terrible sadness of General Clark's eyes.

The Morans told us one of those awful ironic stories of war. Monsignor Francis Spellman celebrated Mass on a huge field, recently a battleground. The following day we gave a concert there, and the next night Pat and Patsy Moran did a show in the same spot. All such areas are still heavily mined, and safe pathways, from two to six feet wide, are marked off. Pat came back after his performance badly shaken. Two lieutenants in the audience had come up afterward just to talk awhile, and they offered to show Pat and Patsy an airplane that had been shot down, which necessitated a walk of about fifty feet. After they all looked the plane over, the officers suggested going a bit farther to see another plane, but the Morans decided to return instead. The two lieutenants continued on anyway, and two minutes later there was a shattering explosion—a land mine had gone off, and they were killed.

At breakfast our first morning in Rome we were reading *Stars and Stripes*—in which I was highly flattered to find myself listed as "Arturo" Kostelanetz!—when a swarthy waiter in white approached and said, "Sunny side up?" For a moment we thought we were in the States. He proved to be one of the Italian noncombatants. They are former war prisoners who now work for the U.S. forces of occupation. Incidentally, instead of tips American-brand cigarettes are preferred, and also autographs. All over the city, even next to the thousands-of-years-old Colosseum, there were posters and placards announcing our concert.

The entire Villa Borghese has been turned over to the Red Cross. What fascinated us most was that inside of ten minutes perhaps twenty fellows walked in and were each given a package of cigarettes and whatever information they needed in order to send a wire to their folks, look for somebody from another outfit, or get medical assistance. The efficiency of the place is amazing.

No mail for fifty days. Now we know firsthand what news from home means to the fighting man. It is surprising to find in talking to soldiers that they sometimes worry more about some trivial thing, like the rear tire of Dad's car finally blowing out, than they do about the dangers they constantly face. Or maybe that is not surprising.

This Italian summer is very hot and dry. Lily wears Western boots under her evening gowns because of the heavy dust, and when some Texans in the audience let out a few *yippees!* to show their appreciation of her singing, she took the microphone and gave an answering cowboy shout. I think those boots must have inspired her.

Right after that concert the Army asked for official pictures to be taken. In the momentary quiet, the photographer called out: "Miss Pons, will you please pretend you are singing?" She did better than that, with the first few bars of "Shoo Shoo Baby," which brought down the house.

G.I.'s seem to have developed an enormous interest in opera. Every seat for every performance in the Italian opera houses is filled. They are most enthusiastic. At the San Carlo in Naples the sergeant in charge of the house asked if I wanted to be seated in the imperial box, but I preferred to sit nearer the stage (imperial boxes are always located as far from the stage as possible). The no-encore rule for grand opera was broken that night, at the G.I.s' insistence, when Lily sang *Rigoletto*.

We have just returned from a concert behind the front at the Volturno River. They have told us there were 22,000 American soldiers in one audience alone. As we left a cake was presented with the inscription: "Goodbye Lily and Andre—Thank You Very Much." The cake was put into the bomb bay, since that was thought to be the coolest spot for it in flight. When we arrived at our destination the copilot, not realizing it was there, opened the bomb-bay doors, and, of course, the cake fell to the ground. But it did not go to waste—there were plenty of desperately hungry people who scooped it up and ate it, dirt and all. You are not here one day before you realize that the suffering and humiliation of war reach into every life everywhere. Yet each time we are reminded of that by such a pathetic sight, it is like the shock and pain of seeing it for the very first time.

About ten years ago I was in San Francisco for a conducting engagement. The day of the concert I received a phone call from a woman who spoke to me in Russian: "I don't know if you will remember me, but perhaps if I say 'Busia' it will help. . . ."

She had used my childhood nickname, which I had not heard in fifty years. This was the woman to whose home Dr. Roichel brought me one evening in Kislovodsk. That was the first of so many comforting times of laughter and music. After dinner Roichel took his violin and I sat down at the piano, and we would play well into the night. . . . Unbelievably, all these years later, here was that kind, wonderful woman in San Francisco.

We met for lunch and talked all the afternoon. After her entire family was lost, except for one daughter, she managed to get out of Russia and wound up in Germany, where she married an American Army captain. They live in Carmel now.

This was a woman whose seventy-odd years had been broken apart by the insanity of war and who had survived by literally starting a completely new life. And she is only one of millions who have suffered in those times when the world has gone temporarily mad. Everyone pays for that madness, if not the ultimate price, then the agony of its images, which stay somewhere inside you for the rest of your life.

As I read these notes I set down thirty-five years ago in Europe and the East, I think of her and of the many others like her whose similar stories I have heard. And even as I curse the injustice of innocents suffering I marvel all over again at the degree of strength the human being can bring to bear when the simple right to live is at stake.

In those USO tour days of late 1944 and early 1945 I felt a yearning to be involved in the struggle in the deepest possible way. But, while I have experienced war in my life, I have not been *of* it—not down in the mud pulling the pin on a grenade or in the gun turret of a bomber, not part of the total commitment. So that yearning was right behind me, like a shadow, all through those months. And I could never satisfy it. Even when we did finally play at front lines, with the smoke and smell and noise of war in our midst, it did not leave me. When I saw a soldier lying immobile under bandages in a hospital, for an instant I wanted to *be* that man, wanted to feel the relief of knowing I had taken the ultimate risk for life's most precious gift, itself.

I don't remember articulating this to myself at the time, but it is now clear to me that it was the yearning that made me persist in trying always to arrange for appearances at the front—the Volturno River; the bases around Kunming; Chungking (which we never did get to because of bad flying conditions); Krefeld; Cologne.

And I think it must have been also why I chose to write down as much as I could, every day if possible. It was a way of reassuring myself that, having cursed the darkness, I could at least try to light a candle.

India, Burma, China,
the European theater,
December, 1944–March, 1945

December 10, 1944. Last U.S. broadcast. Off the air 5:00 P.M. Home afterward and farewells. Lily and I drive to Queens and the airport through dark dismal Sunday streets. We pass two movie houses. One marquee says *Road to Morocco* and the other *Dangerous Journey!* We take off. Good-by New York. As we cross the Hudson we open the "sealed orders" envelopes—India, China, Burma, Belgium, France, Germany. The first autograph of this trip is asked for by a woman sitting across the aisle, and to our surprise it is a blank check!

December 11. Sunrise arrival at Miami. Getting Army identification papers takes one day. A little time to relax after strenuous weeks of preparation for the tour plus concerts, broadcasts, movies, recordings. Met "Joe Palooka" creator, Ham Fisher. We are all slightly blasé, since this is our second overseas tour. Because Lily and I are now "veterans," briefing for us is omitted.

Again, as on our first overseas tour, Lily and I are given rooms on different floors in this hotel, the Floridian, the only hotel in the world where it is considered necessary to keep wives and husbands apart. In fairness to the establishment, I must say that Captain George Stinchfield (in charge of this last outpost of American living) promised us a suite on the tenth floor decorated by Lord & Taylor and reserved for VIPs if we decide to go overseas again!

December 12. Delay in departure. Sense of expectancy increased. Everyone listens eagerly to loudspeaker announcements, calling individual soldiers and officers for immediate overseas departure. A tough-looking Captain X drinking an enormous malted, probably the last for some time to come. Suddenly the bark of the loudspeaker: "Captain———, report to desk immediately!" Reply comes in a perfect Henry Aldrich voice: "Yes, dear!"

December 13. We leave the shores of the United States at 1:45 P.M. Bucket seats greet us once again. The plane is a powerful C-54, and the meteorologist says we will have strong tailwinds. He is right. By the time we approach Bermuda we are traveling at 300 miles an hour with a better than 70-mile-an-hour tailwind, establishing a near-record time of 4 hours and 15 minutes.

We drive by Jeep with Major Bob Rados to the Bermuda weather station. Next hop, to the Azores, is second longest overwater flight, so the meteorologists who make out flight schedules are listened to with a great deal of attention and respect. The room is lined with maps. The report is a "cold front" with the dreaded "icing conditions." Everyone works quietly and confidently. A young captain points to a spot on a map: "That is where the famed naturalist Lucius Beebe descended in the bathysphere." Of course, he meant Charles William Beebe. Good old Lucius would certainly have gone down in tails and top hat!

In Bermuda, as in Ascension Island, the men get very little entertainment because most of the performers are rushing on to their designated war theaters. Islands are lonely outposts. Special Services officer asks whether we could drop into a movie—they would stop the picture if we would say a word to the soldiers. But at that moment we are called to board the plane. "Flight 741 to the Azores," booms the loudspeaker.

We taxi ponderously to takeoff position. The plane seems loaded to capacity, and the gas tanks are full for the big hop. With a mighty pull we leave the ground. It is night, and everyone makes himself as comfortable as possible on the floor. For the most part it is either too cold or else the heaters are too active and it gets quite hot. Lily is in her sleeping bag at the front of the plane.

December 14. Orange and green sunrise. Mt. Pico in the Azores, 7,500 feet, towers above the cloud blanket. We are about 70 miles from Casablanca, our next stop. "Will you take the controls?" asked Captain Tom Turner, with whom we flew on the first overseas trip, so he knew I used to pilot. We go through tips of cumulous clouds at 7,000 feet. Ice forms on the windshield wipers but disappears quickly. We land in Casablanca. Meet Colonel Fred Kelly, wing surgeon, Air Transport Command, North African Division, who gave me inoculations before the first overseas trip. His schoolmate, Pat O'Brien, just passed through on his way to New York from the China-Burma-India theater. He and Jinx Falkenburg were the first entertainers to reach CBI after the "round-up" call.

Casablanca in December not as pleasant as in August. Cold, somewhat dismal. With the overcast sky even the bright colors of Morocco look drab. We stay at the Hotel Anfa, where the Casablanca conference took place.

December 15. Leave early for the airport (Lily lost her valise in Casablanca). Our C-46 Army cargo plane has inscription on its nose: "Easy to Love." We discover we are VIPs.

Land in Tripoli for a short dinner and have time for a quick talk to the G.I.'s, who give us warm reception.

December 16. Arrive in Cairo at 2:00 A.M. Met by many friends. Since we last visited Paine Field a new cottage has been built. We are exhausted and retire quickly.

It is the Moslem New Year, the 1364th anniversary of the flight of Mohammed from Mecca to Medina after more than twelve years of persecution by the people of Mecca.

In late morning our plane taxis a short distance but has to go back—motor trouble. Take off in a new plane for stopover in Iran. Jerusalem below, then the Dead Sea. Beautiful sunset over the Holy Land. Our pilots haven't flown this route from Egypt to the Persian Gulf in a long time. They use the gyrocompass, an invention that permits automatic steering, thereby obviating necessity of navigating by landmark. (In case of emergency mightn't this lack of knowledge prove embarrassing?)

Many of the soldiers recognize us and thank us for the concerts we gave there a few months ago. Suddenly over the loudspeaker come the strains of one of my V disks.

December 17. By 6:00 A.M. we are flying due east over the Indian Ocean. The sky is full of gold. Sunrise. Hilly coastline below and Karachi.

Trip from Casablanca to Karachi, a total flying time of about forty-eight hours, extremely strenuous—C-46 was packed with passengers, 34, and cargo, which was crowded between the bucket seats and in the center aisle. Impossible to lie down or stretch out. Lily under a ventilator in the roof. At night the heaters went out of commission, and the high-altitude cold air blew on her.

Just before landing we notice our war-painted planes and, nearby, the Parsees' "towers of silence," several of them, about twenty feet high and surrounding a courtyard. The Parsees leave their dead on the tower roofs, where they are devoured by vultures.

Driven to the Hotel Killarney (not a very authentic-sounding name for a hotel in India) and sleep the rest of the day.

At 9:00 in the evening I decide to go out for my first real glimpse of India. I feel it is best to get acquainted with the Orient at night. The mystery and glamour are better retained without the revealing midday sun. I ask to be taken to the railway station so I can see as many different people as possible from all over India. I am not disappointed. It is overflowing with people and color and sound. Trains are jammed with passengers. Everybody seems to be speaking a different tongue. It all makes me think of the second act of *Lakmé*, without benefit of the stage manager. Outside, men, women, and children lie asleep on the sidewalks. Beggars surround me, asking for baksheesh.

In time we are ten and a half hours ahead of New York—day is night and vice versa. Surprisingly, for a country this size, there is only one time zone.

December 18. Hotel Killarney. Indian servants are called bearers and about half a dozen attend each hotel guest. Tips, one or two annas—one anna is about two cents. Each bearer does a separate task, dictated by the distinctions of caste. A floor sweeper is an untouchable, for instance, and the other bearers would not do that job. Their energy seems to be at a low ebb.

Very cold at night, warm in the daytime. The hotel has been built with an eye to the torrid summers and monsoon seasons—stone floors and walls. Pigeons fly in through the windows and alight on our bathtub.

Lunch with C.O. General Warden, and his staff. First curry in

India and we enjoy it. When I comment on that, the general says to his aide, "Now you can relax. You thought your guests would want steak." We ride through the town. In the marketplace people bargain amid filth and flies. We leave in the evening on Trans-India flight.

December 19. Early morning—still dark—we arrive in Calcutta. Damp and cold there. Major Melvyn Douglas, Special Services, meets us. "Sorry, there's no brass here to greet you," he says. I replied, "It is not the brass I am interested in—how many *strings* have you got?"

I begin immediate preparation for rehearsals, then learn that the orchestra is not fully assembled yet—no strings. Meeting in the afternoon with Brigadier General R. R. Neylon, football coach of University of Tennessee. Big man with a hearty laugh. He promises to help get string players, which will permit us to do the most interesting arrangements, to give the soldiers exposure to a concert orchestra instead of the regular military bands they hear so much, and to play a wider variety of music.

Kipling's description of Calcutta still fits perfectly:

> Chance directed, chance erected,
> Laid and built on the silt—
> Palace, mire, hovel, poverty and pride side by side,
> And above the packed and pestilential town,
> Death looked down.

Melvyn Douglas says: "China is closed. No civilians can go there." Great disappointment. We volunteered for the China-Burma-India theater because we knew that in China especially there is little entertainment. Hope the tactical situation will improve—we are very anxious to play to our men over the "Hump." [The Hump refers to the 24,000-foot-high Great Himalayas, beyond which is China. It was over the Hump that supplies for China and for the Allied troops there had to be flown. Those flights originated in Chabua, in upper Assam, which is also where the land route for supplies began, the Burma Road.]

December 20. First rehearsal. Picked up at hotel by Jeep, which to my surprise takes me to a beautiful park on the Hooghly River, the Maidan (*maidan* means "open space"). About twenty musicians are already there, ready to rehearse, so we begin—despite traffic noise, staring Indians, camels, donkeys, Indian funeral procession (complete with drums). Finally it is impossible to hear our music at all! I insist on transferring the rehearsal to a quiet indoor hall and ask for more violin players.

Afternoon rehearsal in a Red Cross rest camp. Men from combat zones attend. Many questions about the States. Hall gradually fills up with servicemen listening to us rehearse. At one point the Special Services officer asks our sergeant-pianist how the piano is. He tries it out and finds it about half a tone flat, so he tells the officer it is too low. "Well," says the lieutenant, "block it up, block it up!"

Lily and I are staying at the Great Eastern Hotel, and in the dining room are about 200 waiters, constantly rushing around. They are all dressed in dark red robes and white turbans.

Lily is *mem-sahib*, I am *sahib*. After a good tip—baksheesh—I become *Burra-Sahib*. In Hindustani *thik hi* is "okay," which is satisfactory response to Indian sentries' challenge we sometimes encounter when we are out after dark.

Talk to some pilots and ask about flying conditions in China. Their response: "Combination of zero-zero weather and Zeroes." That means ceiling zero, visibility zero, and Japanese fighters known as Zeroes.

Visit an American Expeditionary Force radio station in Calcutta, one of many throughout the world that provide entertainment and relaxation for our troops and give a reasonable replica of listening to a radio at home—naturally with commercials deleted.

December 21–22. Rehearsals, preparations for the concerts and the CBI theater tour.

Hear a local orchestra at the races in Calcutta. Maharajahs luxuriously dressed. Hindu women in colorful saris. *Everyone* bets on the horses.

Visit American residents in Calcutta whom I have known for the last fifteen years. When I remark that they seem to have no "servant problem" (considering the number of servants I see in their house), they reply that there is an acute problem. Some do not handle meat of one kind or another; Hindus and Moslems in the same house create difficulties; and the untouchables versus higher-caste people make even some simple tasks a problem.

December 23. The demand for admission to the opening concert is growing hourly. We planned this tour so that our first concert would be on Christmas Eve and we would continue to play for the rest of the holiday week for the servicemen stationed in and around Calcutta. The orchestra is improving with each rehearsal, and I am notified that we can have some additional strings from the Calcutta Symphony Orchestra. We decide to play indoors since ten thousand soldiers are expected. The dress rehearsal is called at the Eden Gardens. It's a hot and windy morning. Lily rehearses with us, and we try out the speaker system. She has a cold, but we hope by tomorrow it will clear up.

December 24. The big field in the Eden Gardens where we are to play is taken all day for the British cricket matches. Our concert is scheduled for five o'clock. Thousands of soldiers arrive at the Gardens early in the afternoon.

A great disappointment—Lily's cold did not get better, and she is unable to sing. It's announced over the air that the concert will take place without her. I ask Corporal Larry Malfatty of Philadelphia to join us and sing some of the Christmas carols. A record-breaking crowd of over ten thousand Allied troops. On the far fringes of the field we see Hindus in colorful attire and turbans. Concert is broadcast over All-India Radio and American Expeditionary stations. "Holy Night" under Indian sky. The sun sets quickly, and Captain Sherman, Special Services, asks me whether we can finish the concert before the rapidly settling darkness makes the music invisible to the musicians—"Can you play some of the music faster," he pleads, "because the power generator is out of order and we have no lights." I couldn't help thinking of the time that Walter Damrosch had to play the last movement of Tchaikovsky's *Pathétique allegro furioso* in order to catch a train.

It was a beautiful sunset, and as the dark blue-green of the Indian sky deepened, the stars shone ever more brightly. On the triumphant note of "Adeste Fideles" the concert came to a close in almost total darkness, which was filled with the cheers of thousands of soldiers.

Later that evening we drive through blackened Calcutta on the "wrong" side of the street, visiting Red Cross establishments, U.S. canteens, making a few speeches and exchanging holiday greetings with the soldiers, some of whom somehow procured a few evergreens for Christmas decorations.

December 25. Lily is no better. Doctor has diagnosed bronchitis and insisted she stay in bed.

Christmas concert this afternoon in Barrackpur, about an hour's ride from Calcutta. Preconcert lunch with General William Tunner at Hastings Mills, just across the river from Barrackpur. Corporal Leonard Pinnario, excellent pianist, joined us, and I exacted a promise that he will play with orchestra.

Simple, delicious Christmas lunch with very interesting view: the wide Hooghly in front of the house—river traffic included red-sailed junks with occasional U.S. motorboat darting in between them. On the opposite riverbank, Hindu temples. The general is much interested in providing good musical entertainment for his men. On one wall a drawing of him—Christmas gift from his Air Transport Command staff—with inscription: "Mahatma of the Hump."

After lunch we all crossed the river by barge to the concert area. Event coincides with opening of a servicemen's club. Great anticipation. When we arrive, about 4,000 listeners are already seated on benches in the broiling Indian sun. Snappy wind helps a bit, until a group of planes begin revving their motors on the windward side. Before long, orchestra and audience can scarcely see or hear for the dust and noise. This does not create much discomfiture—everyone realizes the planes are going on missions that will be sure to shorten the war.

The Christmas carols were greeted with much enthusiasm. The local Special Services officer supplied jingle bells (where ever did he get them?). Considerable *oohing* and *aahing* over announcement of *Rhapsody in Blue* and the *Ave Maria*, which is, so far, the most often requested song on both tours.

Much autographing after the concert, usually of paper money.

G.I.'s prefer to have it on money instead of anything else. In some countries, where there is considerable inflation and the money is not worth anything, they usually remark, "Now it's worth something!" after we have signed the bank note.

Driving home through Indian villages I notice banners in the shape of sails, with white and blue predominant. This is the Pakistan Moslem banner, emblem of a Moslem state which they hope to achieve. Another banner was also in evidence—the red flag with hammer and sickle of the Communist Party.

Lily and I have Christmas dinner in our hotel room in the evening. The stone floors make the room damp and chilly.

Can't help thinking about all the terrible hunger in this city. Ironically, in many cases the hunger is a result of people's unwillingness to accept any food that they are not accustomed to—or that their religion forbids.

December 26. Before third concert a surprise meeting with Lieutenant Colonel Frey. He is a doctor from Philadelphia, and the last time I saw him was in June in Teheran where he was in charge of the hospital. Our conversation revolves around the 150-degree heat of Persia and the 24-hour-a-day monsoons that occur for many months of the year in India. He is a veteran of both of these acute weather phenomena, so I ask him to take his pick. He selects the monsoons. Since I am constantly searching for string players I ask Colonel Frey if he knows of any. "You can have two of my men," he tells me, "and they will not be any trouble because they played in your Persian Gulf Command orchestra." Very welcome news!

It was good to see again my two violinists who traversed Iran with me, north to south and back again, on the previous tour. Other attempts were not always so successful. When I tried to enlist a violinist recently, a splendid player, too, he was utterly unavailable. Explanation: he was a specialist in Japanese code.

Our third concert takes place outside a rather formal building named Home for Aged and Infirm Cows. The cow is holy to the Hindus. As a result there are a lot of cattle but hardly any milk in India. The dairy industry barely exists.

Several times on the way back from the concert our progress is halted by thousands of Moslems in a religious frenzy doing something known as the "stick dance." Everyone is armed with large poles, which are waved in the air. A lot of cracking sounds as poles hit one another. The leaders of this procession brandish enormous swords. All the while countless drums are played in a rather disorganized fashion. A few Moslems carry Pakistan flags. When our crawling car approaches the wild dancers they make us a little alley and we pass through.

The average life expectancy of an Indian is about 26 years, which means that one out of five people on earth lives that long.

It was late evening as we drove through the outskirts of Calcutta, and the air was thick with smoke and haze. The smoke issued from native huts, which are made of bamboo and have no chimney or stovepipe. The smoke filters through every crack, giving the impression that the hut is afire. A few hundred thousand of these smoking hovels plus the fog of the Hooghly River provide the dense atmosphere. Dried cow dung is used as fuel, since there is not much wood available.

December 27. Army physician still insists that Lily must not leave the room. I am sure the long flight in a cold plane and the city air have combined to give her a cough—and Calcutta is not a good place to get rid of it.

Driving by Jeep to concert number four, at the Bengal Air Depot, we have to cross a railroad track. An enormous U.S.-made locomotive, pulling a load of lend-lease goods to the Hump, has stopped right at the crossing. The Indian engineer, in a turban, peers out at us. We wait for the locomotive to proceed, but after a little while we motion that we wish to cross the tracks. The Indian shakes his head sideways. We wait. He keeps shaking his head sideways—and suddenly we realize that that means yes.

Betel nut is chewed by many people here and accounts for their red teeth. The sidewalk merchant prepares it on a leaf, which he slices neatly to half size and spreads with some white chalky glue. He then adds two or three different colors and folds the leaf. It has a narcotic effect.

December 28. Concert in Dumdum, where the lead-nose bullet of the same name was first used, in the nineteenth century. They spread on impact. [Their use was prohibited by the Hague Conference in 1899.] Lunch is in the enlisted men's mess. The cook has two pets, seven-month-old leopards from the jungle. The cook is also the pet of the leopards, and they keep trying to get back to the kitchen.

With the idea of having the servicemen be an integral part of the show, I ask the Special Services officer, who has a fine baritone voice, to sing. He selects "On the Road to Mandalay," geographically fitting. He tells us that the countryside abounds in snakes, the most deadly being the krait, a small, aggressive snake. There is no antivenin for this snake or for the cobra, and anyone bitten by either usually dies in about ten minutes.

December 29. Day of rest. Visit to the burning ghats, the Nimtalla, where the poet and philosopher Tagore was cremated. Six pyres are burning, and a swami with long hair squats on the ground, surrounded by a group of disciples. The funeral pyres are made with sticks of wood on which the body is placed. The poor are not able to afford enough wood and usually burn only part of the corpse; the rest is thrown into the river. Dead babies are also thrown into the river, with the idea of having the turtles consume them.

Later, we visit the Jain Temple. This sect of Hindus believes in cleanliness and in not killing any living thing, no matter how small, like mosquitoes, flies, etc.

December 30. Before concert in Camp Angus, visit to France! Actually, the town of Chandernagor, on the Hooghly, not far from Calcutta. It was founded by the French in 1686 and is very much in contrast to its surroundings. The tricolor still flies on the town gate. I was sorry Lily could not see it.

Met a young Americanized maharajah today, and I asked him why his subjects sleep on the bare ground. "Because they are tired," he replied. (Serves me right!)

Concert was especially for men going home to the States. Grand enthusiasm.

We are getting ready "to go upcountry," a common expression for leaving civilization behind. [The upcountry in this case was the Bengal region, East India and what is now Bangladesh.]

December 31. Although Lily still has a cough she rejoins us and sings her first concert in India. In the middle of the "Caro Nome" she has a fit of coughing and has to stop. She receives an enormous ovation and resumes singing.

I ask General Stratemeyer to permit the two WACs in my orchestra to go on tour with us upcountry. (WACs are unknown in the part of the world where we are going.) Permission is granted. Corporal Madeline Stone of Cleveland, Ohio, and Private Eloise Hirschbein of Teaneck, New Jersey, are very happy at the prospect of the trip.

Everyone asks us to remain for the New Year's Eve party in Hastings Mills, but we decide to return to Calcutta. Lily, on doctor's order, wears a mask on ride home, to protect her throat from the fog and smoke.

Tomorrow another concert, and Lily is still coughing.

January 1, 1945. Letter from a G.I. in China includes question: "Why do you let us down and omit China from your schedule?" For some days now we have been trying to investigate all possibilities for getting into China. It is a great disappointment to us to be told that China is closed. We volunteered for the CBI theater, and to be so near to China and not be able to get there seems inconceivable. The tactical situation is precarious, and civilians are not permitted to enter—just the opposite, they are being evacuated from China. But now we have additional ammunition—this soldier has put the issue at our door. Of course, the schedules are made up by the Special Services of the theater, and nine times out of ten the artist goes to places that he has never heard of before. We ask for a meeting with General Neyland. He tells us that our admission to China depends on the China commander. He agrees to send a wire himself. We also send a wire. There is considerable suspense in this waiting.

New Year's Day concert at a hospital in Calcutta, in an open square. Some patients sit in wheelchairs outside; others listen from windows. Major Gillis, who is treating Lily's cold, is the hero of the day since he has just about cured her, making it possible for her to sing today. To close the concert I conduct *"Auld Lang Syne"* and the chief doctor motions for all those who can stand up to do so. I turn and conduct the audience. Lily and I are close to tears. It is not the first time. There is something about concerts in hospitals that sets them apart.

January 2. Leaving Calcutta airport for the upcountry, the co-pilot of our ship, Lieutenant Don Taylor (blond Hollywood type) tells me: "I am the regular leader of the band upcountry. Between combats I conduct it. I have one more mission and then I go home!" We set the whole program right there in the cockpit of the plane. In flight we get message that the second bomber is late in leaving the field—natives and soldiers have been trying to get the piano into the bomb bay for the past few hours, without success. It is a regular G.I. piano, a very good one, and it has to be loaded from below the belly of the ship. We keep radioing the field about the fate of the piano. These ships flew fourteen hours yesterday to bomb Bangkok. Our plane is carrying the "flying strings," twelve soldiers, and our two WACs. I am going to add them to the band of Lieutenant Taylor.

At Ramgarh we are met by cheerful, effervescent General Frederick McCabe. This place totally different from the "pestilential town" on the Hooghly River. Hilly—about 2,000 feet up—clear mountain air. Our first sight of Chinese inscriptions, the colorful Chinese flag. Chinese troops are healthy-looking and splendidly trained by our men.

I'm told one of the difficulties in the training was overcoming Chinese mistrust. They didn't quite understand why all this effort to train them. Suspicion of ulterior motives. They don't believe books or people are honest.

The piano finally arrives about five o'clock, during rehearsal which I have been holding since three. Lieutenant Taylor's band was also delayed en route, so only at 5:00 P.M. did we begin a full rehearsal, the shortest we have had on the tour.

Concert at 7:30 P.M. It is extremely cold—charcoal open grills backstage. The air is crisp like it is in our Rockies. Audience all-American, whistling and stamping—most enthusiastic. As the concert progresses it gets windier. An old Hindu tells me, "The wind is blowing tonight from the Himalayas."

Lily sang very well, though still bothered by fits of coughing.

January 3. Lily will remain at Ramgarh. Her cold is much worse, and her back muscles are stiff. I took her over to the hospital before trip to Pandaveswar.

Orchestra flies in formation, in three Liberators, four-engine B-24's in full battle attire—ten .5-inch Browning machine guns. Piano is in one of the bomb bays—replacing the usual "cargo," 5,000 pounds of bombs—hoisted there by the musicians themselves. One day the ships fly us, the next they go on fourteen- or fifteen-hour missions. I am in center ship, with the other two enormous bombers flanking. On this flight the navigator is my drummer. Most of the personnel of the orchestra are combat pilots, copilots, navigators, and gunners, with hundreds of combat hours—a great group of men with amazing tales to tell of danger and hairbreadth escapes.

Show without Lily. Extra orchestral numbers added. I introduce the two WACs, who are received with enormous acclaim. The men tell us they haven't heard American music performed in person for more than a year.

I ask the C.O. to take me to see a bombing mission land. I saw one at Foggia, Italy, in daytime. This one is at night, about eleven o'clock. Starry sky, but soon it seems as if some stars are moving. Then I discern the red and green lights, and the slanting, powerful twin landing lights. The enormous bird rushes into the alley of ground lamps. There is a thrilling casualness about it all. I chat with some of the men—relaxed fatigue after fourteen very busy hours in the air. I invite them to our show for the next night. Front rows are usually reserved for men who come from the latest mission.

At night I am awakened by the wail of numberless coyotes. This "concert" compares to a mixture of a baby's wail, a woman's hysterics, and a madman's laughter.

January 4. Driving to the concert we pass primitive collieries where mostly women work. They are paid a few cents a day, out of which something must be given to the contractor. Reflect on the familiar analysis of Middle and Far East: between 90 and 95 percent (1) are illiterate, (2) are unable to determine what is really best for them, and (3) think in terms of their village and immediate neighborhood and are not able to grasp interests of national scope. Famine in Bengal. Rice is the staple food. Wheat and other grains are declined, and various meats are out due either to custom or religious taboos—while there is unquestionably a real famine, some people possibly could be saved. . . .

Wonderful audience. Glider airborne troops, British commandos. Orde Charles Wingate and "Flip" Cochrane were former leaders of this great group of men. A young, sharp-eyed (long-distance look) lieutenant colonel now the third to command this group. From an airborne soldier I find out more about the fascinating Wingate. He was a British general who trained a group of guerrillas and led them into Japanese-held Burma. These "Chindits" kept up their raids for seven months. He had already gained fame as an ardent Zionist in Palestine, where he first used guerrilla tactics. He was killed recently, not in battle but in an airplane accident.

After the concert, autograph signing, visits with enlisted men, noncoms, and officers. Many of the Red Cross clubs and canteens are replicas of small night clubs at home. Drinks of different types are served, mostly local products, and a fine spirit of friendliness prevails. One of the enlisted men knew Commander Gillespie, formerly of the Roosevelt Flying School on Long Island where I learned to fly, and he asked me how my technique was. Immediate "pro" acceptance by the rest of the glider pilots!

January 5. Tonight's concert sent by phone to Calcutta and broadcast from there all over India. Late reports are that it was heard as far as China. I say a few words to Lily, who is some hundred miles away recuperating. There are no cheers like the cheers of G.I.'s coming over the air for a performance they like, and it inspires us endlessly. The value of the remote broadcasts is particularly great for hospitals and for outposts which for one reason or another cannot be reached.

Today the first rains since the beginning of October. A real deluge all night till noon. Some instruments got wet from the *chata* ("small monsoon"), but the piano is none the worse for the ducking. Everyone speaks about the monsoons—from May to October the moisture of the Bengal Bay blows against the Himalayas, condensing into hundreds of inches of rain. It is an extremely trying climate—24-hour saturation humidity—heat, mosquitoes, bugs of all types, and reptiles in profusion.

My drummer, Lieutenant Newton Hamfeld of Irvington, New Jersey—330 combat hours—tells me of his parachuting over China in bad weather. Plane out of gas in zero weather. Everyone jumped out. He hit some very hard rocks on landing but luckily didn't move an inch. Lay there in the fog all night. With the first rays of the sun he realized he was lying on the very edge of a thousand-foot precipice. It took him some time to walk out to a U.S. base.

My bearer in this upcountry place is a gnarled little old man, Del Mohammed Kahn. He acted as a bearer to Douglas Fairbanks, Sr., on his hunts through India. He told me today that he is getting married next week. At first I thought it was a way of raising the ante of the baksheesh, but the officers told me it is true. It is his first marriage. "The bride is fourteen years of age," he said. When I asked him how old he was, he said, "Sixty," without blinking an eye. He has never seen her or spoken to her. She is in purdah (which is strict Mohammedan seclusion). Everyone calls him "Babu."

Tonight, steak for dinner—the first in India. I thought it was very good. Later I was told it was wild boar.

January 6. Chata at half-past six. Air is cooler after the downpour of warm rain. The great vertical rush of water makes a theatrical noise. I suggest to the Special Services officer that we move the show indoors. He replies, "There are too many soldiers to hear the concert for our small recreation hall." I tell him I am sure no one will show up. When I arrived at the field there were about a thousand Americans, cold, wet, uncomfortable. They sat through the concert and cheered us with the greatest of gusto. The orchestra never played better, as if trying to show their appreciation of this situation which is one of the highlights of my career.

The C.O. had an enormous cake baked in our honor, and I cut it for the whole assemblage—which took some time. Most of these men left the United States before Pearl Harbor.

Lieutenant Taylor is out on a mission, and I hope he will be back, mainly for his sake but also because we need him for to-morrow's show. He jokingly said, "There must be an easier way to make four hundred dollars per month."

January 7. The Red Cross women are doing a great job. Their attention to each and every person and their unfailingly good spirits are an enormous help for the men who have been away for so long.

A very cold evening. Part of the music misplaced. Fuses blown out. Concert is postponed one hour while we try to remedy the situation. (I suggest that movie shorts be shown in the meantime.) Finally everything is arranged, with the exception of the speaker system. We go ahead, and the enthusiasm of the audience makes us feel that they fully realize the predicaments we had to face to put on this concert.

January 8. Lily is well and flies in from Ramgarh. I meet her at the Ondal airport at 3:00 P.M., and we take off immediately for Gushkara. Concert by a revetment. G.I.'s sitting on all sides. Lily's cold is gone, but she faces the difficulty of singing to this enormous audience, spread on all four sides, without the mike (a power failure).

We are told we must land in Calcutta before dark. Immediate takeoff after the concert—the pilot did not even warm the motors. Lieutenant Taylor's band leaves immediately for their home base, in the other direction. The strings go with us. I radio my farewell and appreciation to them.

Back to civilization in Calcutta. Hot bath, etc. Cold wave at night—coldest in forty years. The half-naked Hindus look frozen.

January 9. We meet Mrs. Nancy Love, great flier and organizer. She can fly anything with wings. We were told later that she piloted a giant C-54 over the Hump. When she called the control tower in Kunming, they were incredulous hearing a woman's voice nonchalantly asking for landing instructions.

This is a day of rest, and we are still working on our clearance for China. We meet Leonard Pinnario again, and he plays for us magnificently.

January 10. Flying to 20th Bomber Command base at Kharag-pur. Another great group of fliers and an inspiring concert. These are the men who fly the huge B-29's on long-distance bombing missions, the men who make Japan very unhappy. From a dark, unfinished tower we watch a mission leave after midnight. The giants thunder by at two-minute intervals with full loads of bombs and gas. The whole earth shakes. Everyone is moved by the courage of these young fellows because everyone knows what happens if you have to bail out into the hands of the Japanese. Back to our bungalow, much moved by what we saw.

January 11. Two bombers missing. At lunch officers tense but no mention is made of friends lost. According to the flight surgeon, not talking about it is tradition.

Arrive at field for four-thirty rehearsal. About fifty soldiers already sitting there on the benches, which are made of landing strips—perforated metal to even out pocked or rocky terrain. There is an enormous canvas stretch that acts as a windbreaker. By 6:00 an almost full field and by 8:00, when the show begins, it is completely jammed.

Concert gets terrific reception. Afterward, to the Red Cross and the Officers' Mess. We sit at tables and sign for hundreds of fellows. Later, back to airport to autograph a 500-pound bomb with inscription: "Greetings to Japan from Lily Pons and Andre Kostelanetz." Talks with pilots and a look inside the enormous bomb bay.

January 12. Visit to the hospital. The rest hall attached to it is called Thik Hi ["Okay"] Haven. Impossible to visit one patient, a gunner who has lost an eye and sustained shrapnel in one shoulder. Doctor says he is too uncomfortable. Some soldiers here were hit Christmas Eve. One says he listened to our broadcast from Calcutta and a few hours later he found himself in the hospital. He was just one of many that night. Coincidentally, just before going to the hospital I read a review of Moss Hart's movie *Winged Victory* in *The New Yorker* magazine: "I would be grateful if just once Mr. Hart could overlook a chance to rearrange life in the shape of art. . . ." There were other critics, too, who felt the story was melodramatic, unlike real life. One scene often referred to is a group of Japanese bombers sweeping down on some soldiers singing carols on Christmas Eve. From what I have seen and heard so far on these tours, I would say there is virtually no situation that a writer could imagine that does not have a correspondence in fact. . . .

Soldier being wheeled to the operating room smiles. Another example of how courage seems to increase in direct proportion to hardship in these times.

January 13. Arrival of Lieutenant General Curtis LeMay, commander of 20th Bomber Group, and Brigadier General Rainey. LeMay is tall and a bit stocky, very soft-spoken. He has just made the trip—the first ever—from Saipan to India and tells me he is thus a super short snorter. That is a very dangerous trip, over enemy territory.

In the evening we are driven to a theater for our concert. There is a large stage, and the lighting is excellent. Lily's dressing room has murals on the walls made by soldiers—much attention is being lavished on us by Special Services. Lieutenant Commander Jim McReynolds, son-in-law of Admiral King, drove us to the show and back. He says his illustrious father-in-law is less of a disciplinarian than his stern face leads one to think.

Tomorrow we are to be flown thirty miles from Kharagpur for next concert.

January 14. Breakfast with Generals LeMay and Rainey. Officers' Mess is a reconstructed political prison. LeMay says quietly: "An accident occurred where you are going to play today—a B-29 blew up on the field." My whole orchestra left about an hour ago by plane, and I am concerned as to their fate. Details are lacking, and at first there is some doubt as to whether the concert will take place. Then decision is made to go on. We drive to the airport and take off.

Circling low over the field, we see a gray-black corner of it is littered with parts of planes. We circle the field a few times and land. Flags at half-mast. My orchestra landed about five minutes before the accident and was at the other end of the field when it occurred. Most of those killed were soldiers, mainly firemen who rushed to the exploding plane and tried to save their buddies and control the conflagration. Bombs started to explode, and these courageous fellows didn't have time to turn back. A miraculous escape was recorded by a soldier on top of the B-29 who was thrown off by the power of the explosion and landed with minor scratches. I offered to go to the hospital in the afternoon to play for the survivors, who number over a hundred. The relatively small hospital is taxed to capacity by this emergency, and the doctor tells us it would be impossible.

Meet a Red Cross worker, Katy Harris of Baltimore, Maryland. This spry little woman organized a choir of enlisted men and officers on Christmas Eve. Could I use them in our concert? Of course. This is completely in accord with our having servicemen as part of the show. Fifteen of the forty choir members are out on a mission. We rehearse "Smoke Gets in Your Eyes" and "Bells of St. Mary's." They sing very well.

The outdoor theater is called Cactus Bowl. It is a large theater and has some splendid lighting.

After the rehearsal Colonel Blanchard drives me over to a B-29 that is being retired and flown back to the United States. Camels (insignia for the Hump trips) and bombs painted on the side of the big ship almost cover the nose. In the evening thousands of G.I.'s greet us with mighty yells and whistles as we drive up for the concert. The field is crowded with soldiers, and the concert is warmly cheered. Colonel Blanchard strides onto the stage at the finish and puts leis on our shoulders.

The Colonel asks us to go with him to the hospital to visit the victims. We jump into his Jeep and drive across the airfield, past the spot where the accident occurred. Suddenly crash trucks, ambulances, etc., are racing onto the field. We are on one of the runways, and we can see a plane with landing lights on. "What a day!" said our C.O. "He has only one wheel down and is coming in for a crash-landing." It is a B-29. We wonder whether he is loaded with bombs. Our Jeep races off the runway. The plane is coming in at great speed. Tremendous clouds of dust as he lands. For a minute it looks like fire—the plane landed on the one wheel, and as it slowed down the wing tipped and the crash was on. In a few seconds it was all over—enormous dust in the air, but luckily no one was hurt. No bombs. We go on to the hospital. Driving through dense jungle, the Colonel says that he saw a wild elephant there last week.

The small hospital is overwhelmed with disaster. Bloody clothing is on the floor, nurses and doctors cheerfully businesslike. Everyone thanks us for coming. One sad-eyed patient says, "It sure is a pity." "Hard day," says another. We lean over to hear them talk. "I recognize you, Miss Pons. They spoil me here," says one to Lily. Some are obviously too far gone for medical help. Some ambulating patients who were at the concert thank us warmly.

Finally, back to the airport. At the approach to the runway the big red tower light flashes at us. More trouble? A Liberator puts his lights on and lands safely. We are rushed past him to our B-25, which immediately revs and taxis to auxiliary runway—the main one is obstructed by the crash of the B-29. It is the roughest taxiing I have ever experienced. Obviously the strip had not been used for a long time. Colonel Blanchard waves good-by. The B-25 is taking off when the runway lights suddenly go out. We stop abruptly and wonder whether this is the last problem of the day. Lights flash on a few minutes later, and we take off with a mighty pull. It is past midnight. Behind us an arc of blue-gray flames from the exhaust of the B-25's motors. We land smoothly at our home base—and silence! Mac, our driver, is at the door with smiles and a "Welcome back." What a day!

January 15. We leave our 20th Bomber Command base today. Our bearer, Ali, is sorry to see us go. He says, "Before American came, jungle, leopard, panther, cobras. American came—all clear!" A C-45 is ready at the field. A Jeep drives up, and to our surprise we see Generals LeMay and Rainey. They say they are going to the concert and they will fly us there.

Smooth flight. When we land, General LeMay says, "I'm a half-good pilot, and Rainey is a half-good pilot, but together we are all right."

Unforgettable stay with the 20th Bomber Command. The men give us a great send-off, and the generals thank us. We leave for Calcutta immediately following the concert.

January 16. A day of rest in Calcutta. Visit a gem dealer from

Jaipur. "Your Ladyship, may I amuse you with some stones?" he says to Lily. Rubies from Burma—slightly violet tinge—light-colored emeralds, pearls, and diamonds of every hue and size.

We say farewell to our friends and associates in Calcutta. The bearers at the Great Eastern Hotel line up for tips. A dinner is given us by Special Services officers at Club 300. They have a Russian orchestra there that plays only jazz.

January 17. We leave Calcutta by air in the morning. The enormous city sprawling on the banks of the Hooghly gives way to rolling countryside. Our next assignment is to play the Bengal-Assam Railroad, which had such an enormous role in bringing men and supplies up to the Hump from Calcutta.

On landing we are driven to the railroad station—our first train trip on either tour. Accommodations are in some ways primitive—mosquito nets, special drinking water, washing water of dubious origin—but Lily and I do have an entire baggage car to ourselves, entirely refitted for comfortable travel, including a large bed. Our convoying officer brings us our *chota hazri* (morning tea and fruit). "No New York *Times?*" I say to him.

Rehearsal with American railroad units' musicians. They are first rate and their leader, Sergeant Scotty Grant, is a very good trumpeter. Outdoor theater was constructed with the excellent acoustical idea of using corrugated iron as a sounding board. It is interesting to note how inventive and different is the construction of theaters that we have played in all over the world. The men on this railroad do an amazing transportation job, especially for the amount and type of loads that they have to carry. The jungle, the roadbed, and the climate are not conducive to successful operation. When I returned from the rehearsal I had to look for quite a while for our car. Finally found it at the roundhouse. Locomotives puffing soft coal. When I climbed into our car Lily told me that she was unable to shut the windows, and there was no one around to do it for her. Though she was coughing, we rushed over to the concert.

Great enthusiasm again. After the show we met soldiers from Norwalk, Connecticut, which is very near our house in Silvermine.

January 19. We are getting farther into the jungle, traveling slowly. From the train window elephants, monkeys, and crocodiles are on view. The monsoon left quantities of puddles and small lakes. Snakes are everywhere. Dinner with General Yount, 37 years of age, who runs this great supply road. We missed him by five days at Teheran, on our first overseas trip, where he did a great job on the Iranian railroad.

Luxuriant foliage, egrets, rice paddies. Kanchenjunga, in Himalayas, is visible. It is third-highest peak in world. Train is carried across the Brahmaputra on old-fashioned barges, which take quite a few hours. Impossible to build a bridge due to monsoon rains.

We are getting into Assam. The British tea-plantation word for siesta here is "lay-back," one hour each afternoon.

Joint U.S.-British audiences that night. The British applaud "Stars and Stripes Forever" vociferously. That day there was a news flash of the capture of Warsaw, and I made an appropriate announcement before we played the *Warsaw Concerto*, which was greeted very warmly.

January 20. We are delighted—a wire just came in from the deputy commander in China theater, asking us to come for 25 days!

Playing for the smallest audience of our overseas career, 300 or so. A theater of the Gay Nineties type—all wood, with enormous overhanging balcony. Deafening enthusiasm. A few miles from this place there is a camp with many more soldiers, and we are wondering why they are being by-passed. It is getting rougher in every sense. "Rough" is one of the most often used words overseas.

Sacred cows on track, slowing up train. Hundreds of acres of tea plants with large trees providing shade. Many snake charmers, their pipes looking like narghiles and sounding like bagpipes. They put scorpions on their hands and arms while playing the pipe and getting the cobra to do its act. Baksheesh up to five rupees ($1.50)—inflation!

January 21. My orchestra sends a delegation each afternoon asking me to come and teach them to play a new number. The concerts that began with one hour and a half are now two hours.

Today we are playing to one of our largest audiences (not the one we missed yesterday).

We receive a wire from General Cheves, the deputy commander in China, asking us to stay with him in Kunming.

Tea planters' bungalows (Indian word) built like English Norman cottages but on stilts on account of monsoons, animals, snakes, etc. Naga Hills headhunter tribesmen much cleaner than average Hindu. Am told that they are very honest.

Letter by courier from General Neyland thanking us for our concerts in India—twenty-seven in twenty-nine days.

I notice that on some railroad cars the "B & A" has been expanded to read "Boston and Albany." A few days ago one of our admirers printed on our car "Lily Pons and Andre Kostelanetz." We played a special number for him.

We hear the first news of supplies starting overland to China via the Ledo Road.

January 22. Our closing concert in India broadcast over wide AES network. Farewell to this splendid orchestra, one of the best I had with G.I. personnel. Ice cream and special cake party for my players. They remain here for a twenty-four-hour rest, which will possibly give me a chance to arrange for the excellent string section to come over the Hump with us to China.

We leave the train with the minimum of regrets in favor of Frank S. Gregory's tea plantation.

January 23. The rest at Mr. Gregory's is much appreciated and represents considerable comfort in the jungle. He controls thousands of acres of tea, but his hobby is entertaining guests (for a small fee). He has been away from England for the last thirty years, with only a few return visits. He asks us to sign the guest book, and I see signatures of statesmen and newspapermen; Chiang Kai-shek stopped here, too. Mr. Gregory's real hobby is guarding the health of the thousands of natives who are under him. He is doing a splendid job. He plays tennis each afternoon, then has rum and ginger bitters. He tells interesting tales about the Japanese encroachments. He speaks the Naga language and was invaluable in negotiating with tribesmen in the rescue of

American fliers. We are all thinking and talking of tomorrow, when we go over the Hump.

January 24. Colonel Baker, our pilot to China, says this will be his 111th crossing of the Hump. We are first USO troupe to go to China since ban on civilians.

Weather unusually clear. Short briefing on use of parachutes and oxygen masks. This is first flight so far where parachutes are necessary. Someone remembers joke about them: at end of parachute briefing the inevitable question—"What happens if the chute doesn't open when I pull the cord?" Answer—"Well, just bring it back and we'll issue you a new one!"

Take off and begin gradual climb. Valley after valley with drifting cottony clouds above them. Seemingly endless snowy ridges to be crossed. Shining narrow ribbons far below—the Salween and Irrawaddy rivers. Ever higher—time for oxygen masks' grotesque disguise. In cockpit I see we are 13,600 feet and still climbing. Pilot points to a house on mountaintop, at 12,500 feet. How was it ever built way up here? Tibet, the roof of the world, to our far left.

Now, terraced grounds in regular designs below. Baker signals this is China. Descent bumpy.

We have landed in Kunming, capital of Yunnan province. First impressions: many women all dressed in blue coats and carrying little baskets filled with small stones—they maintain the airport runways. Reddish earth. Chinese soldiers, Special Services officers, all smiles. *Ding-ho!* Thumbs up!

Driving through Kunming to General Cheves's home. This is a different world. Stores and markets full of food, especially vegetables, but we are told prices are very high. Inflation terrific: 500 Chinese dollars to 1 U.S.

Talk to General Cheves about my desire to bring string players to China. He tells me the situation is difficult—transportation scarce and billeting quarters in the camps we are going to so meager. It will be impossible. With great regret we let the players know the bad news.

January 25. Our arrival coincides with the reopening of the Ledo and Burma roads, which merge at Bhamo and continue as one to Kunming. After two and one-half years the supplies to China can again move over land. During those two and a half years every ton had to come by air. I meet the driver of the first truck—cheerful young lieutenant from Oklahoma. "It was a long ride," says he. He is on his way to a short, well-earned rest at Hot Springs, near Kunming.

Thrill in the air because of the opening of the road. A map of China on the wall at headquarters with scribble "Jan. 22nd" Cheves put there two months ago, prophesying the day.

Cheves is a jolly-spirited man, very fond of showing off his cocker spaniel "Punjab" or "Pal" (like General Clark's dog in Italy). The dog performs amazing tricks. When the general yells "Japs!" Pal rushes, barking, to the door. At "Rotation!" (most popular word in China) the dog turns round and round on the floor. The general insisted he "will not put myself out to be hospitable," but he is a perfect host.

We are invited to dinner by the Special Services officer, Lieutenant Colonel Birch Bayh. He arrived in China just a short while before we did, so it is just as new to him as it is to us. The restaurant was dimly lit, and our private dining room was on the second floor. Cantonese food—fried rice, chicken and walnuts, sweet pork, tea, and Yunnan ham, which tastes somewhat like our Smithfield ham.

The stores are open late at night, and there is considerable hubbub in the streets.

No band or orchestra here. I face the task of starting from the very beginning. The call is out for any and all musicians. We succeed in getting "Pinkie's Pipers," named after General Dorn. Because he blushed easily the nickname "Pinkie" was given him at West Point and has remained with him. I will use the pipers as a nucleus and add other players. We start rehearsing.

January 26. First concert in China, at a hospital near Kunming.

Lieutenant Colonel Leonidoff, chief doctor of the hospital, tells me of his experiences as medical adviser to the Chinese. There is much disease here. Incidentally, the cost of constructing a hospital is enormous. Land is $10,000 an acre; one windowpane, $8; a simple chair, $15.

The band played very well, and when we signed autographs after the concert we were showered with fine comments.

Driving in moonlight back to Kunming was beautiful. Tall trees throwing black shadows on the countryside. But the bright light of a full moon is not welcome in this part of the world. It is perfect for bombing.

January 27. We are driven to our second concert over a road the first half of which was built by U.S. engineers and the second half by Chinese. It took one and a half hours to make 17 miles. See our first Walled City and Marco Polo's road, which is still used by bullock carts with wooden wheels.

Show is scheduled to be played outdoors in the afternoon, but due to sudden high winds and dust, it is transferred indoors. There are so many soldiers gathered that we give two shows in a row. During the performance men are called over the loud-speaker—"Lieutenant M——, report immediately to the operations office." Harsh impersonality of the loudspeaker intrudes on the music.

Hospital after the concert, dinner with the officers and men. Ranks mix more freely here in China than in other places.

Kunming Red Cross in the evening. Short speech.

Many new marble-front banks in Kunming. Fifteen to twenty percent interest on loans. No usury laws. All military personnel permitted by the finance office to change money where they wish, so you are usually surrounded by money changers as soon as you stop on the street.

January 28. Visit beautiful Buddhist temples in the mountains, at about 10,000 feet. Strange figures on walls. There are students and monks here. Profound peacefulness in their place of worship and in gardens. Enormous smiling gold Buddhas. Chinese soldiers help us translate our questions to the monks.

I am invited to visit the War Room. General Cheves drops in and explains intricacies of fighting in the Orient. "Everything I say here can be quoted, since it will be known in Tokyo tomorrow," he tells me.

A proposed broadcast to U.S. canceled due to security. Great disappointment. Returning from concert, we missed by only a few

One segment of the India series of concerts included a train tour through jungle areas on the Bengal-Assam Railroad. A baggage car had been converted to a most comfortable home for Lily and me. Frank Versaci, to Lily's left, continued as flutist. Our pianist this time was Ted Paxson, next to Frank.

Assam, the end of the line. I was unable to resist
filling in as temporary "switchman."

A hardworking member of the Air
Transport Command at the supply
depot, Bengal airport. From here,
fuel and equipment were flown
"over the Hump" to China.

(*Above*) In January 1945, we too were flown over the Hump to Kunming for a concert tour of the China theater. Thumbs-up represents the Chinese greeting, "Ding Ho!" (*Below*) Lieutenant Al Hoffman was our guide in Kunming. Behind us is the city's West Gate.

Shopping in Kunming. Poor flying weather often prevented us from keeping our concert dates on the scheduled day.

A concert somewhere over the Hump.

(Above) Our final concert in the China-Burma-India theater was during an all too brief stay in Burma, February 1945. (Below) Maj.-General Howard Davidson, at head of table, honored us with a farewell dinner in Burma. At Lily's left is Admiral Lord Louis Moutbatten, Supreme Allied Commander, Southeast Asia.

(*Above*) From Burma we flew to New Delhi, then to the German front. The burned-out tank is German. The whitish areas on the magnificent Cologne cathedral are accumulated battle dust. There was still quite a good deal of enemy action in this sector, March 1945. (*Left*) Before leaving for home in that final spring of the war, Lily and I took a little time to see her native Southern France and to visit with Henri Matisse at his home in Vence.

(Above) Ten Gracie Square, living room and terrace. View is north and east. *(Right)* Entrance hall. Spiral staircase leads to second floor.

(Above) Rehearsal. The baton is traditionally held in the right hand and is the tempo and rhythm guide. Expressing the emotion of the music is the province of the left hand and arm. I am unaware of any conceptual explanation for this, but perhaps it is because the left arm is closer to the heart. *(Opposite)* The control room, where music is transformed from what is played in the studio to what people hear on a record or on the air.

(Right) In Israel with Moshe Dayan. I had cut my finger, nothing serious, but a great fuss had been made, bandages applied. When Moshe saw it, he said, "You must have been conducting Wagner!"

(Left) In Puerto Rico with Pablo Casals and his wife, Marta. In 1957, the year after he moved there, Casals inaugurated annual music festivals in San Juan. *(Below)* With Irving Berlin, whose "shadow reached the Vatican!"

(Above) Rehearsing with Beverly Sills for one of the first concerts we did together, in Houston. In the ensuing years her lyric and coloratura soprano gifts took her from stardom to superstardom. (Right) Beyond the fact that Maria Callas could sing coloratura, as in *Lucia,* and dramatic soprano, as in *Norma*—and do both to perfection—was her genius at interpretation. She brought so much feeling to the words—like Chaliapin. (Below) Leopold Stokowski, innovator, iconoclast, lover of jokes, friend.

(*Above*) Rehearsing *Lincoln Portrait* in 1960 with the indomitable Carl Sandburg as narrator. There is a little story about those shoes he is wearing, which are so full of character! Once, in a dressing room at Carnegie Hall just before a concert, Carl was preparing for his appearance and in walked Phil-harmonic-Symphony manager, Bruno Zirato. Bruno noticed that the shoes were in high contrast to Carl's otherwise formal attire, but all he said was that they looked like good old friends. "These shoes," Carl replied, "are thirty years old. I would never give them up." (*Below left*) With Sir Thomas Beecham, conductor of London's Royal Philharmonic, 1961. Once, on a flight to London together, Sir Thomas told me he could not drink alcohol any more. So, while he entertained me with a fascinating history of his life, we shared the experience of consuming at least a case of Coca-Cola! (*Below right*) After a Hollywood Bowl concert in 1961, Carl Sandburg has the full attention of Ferdi Grofé and me. Grofé was one of the great orchestrators, a fine painter of music who used the orchestra as his palette.

(Above) With Sara Gene in Tahiti. We were married in 1960. (Left) Rehearsing with Peter Ustinov for the *Nutcracker*.

(Right) Ogden Nash's smile here belied his usual poker face. His delightful verses made many happy alliances with music: *Carnival of the Animals, Between Birthdays, The Nutcracker* and *Carnival of Marriage*.

(Above left) Noel Coward was delightful as narrator for *Carnival of the Animals*. *(Above right)* With Archibald MacLeish, whose *Magic Prison* was one of the new works presented during the Lincoln Center Promenades years. *(Below)* E. G. Marshall narrated *Lincoln Portrait* at an outdoor concert with the Philadelphia Orchestra and also performed *Magic Prison* at Lincoln Center.

(*Above left*) While Mayor of New York, John Lindsay took a turn as narrator for *Lincoln Portrait*. He then lived across Gracie Square, in the mayoral mansion, so we used a light-signal to let each other know when we were free to rehearse. (*Above right*) I engaged Shinici Yuize, pupil of Michio Miyagi, to play the solo part for koto of his master's *Sea of Spring*. The 13 strings of this Japanese instrument are made of silk. The placement of the left hand on a particular string determines its pitch. (*Inset*) With the Portuguese *fado* singer Amalia Rodriquez, who twice honored Promenades audiences with her superb voice and style. (*Below*) The White House, May 1978, a "command performance." During rehearsal in the afternoon I turned to see President Carter, who asked if he could stay and listen. He took off his shoes, lay down on the grass, and remained for the next hour and a half.

Reaching Out. Central Park, August 8, 1979.

minutes a Liberator that exploded full of fuel. Miraculous that only three were burned, and they will recover.

We see many hundreds of grass-covered mounds, which is the Chinese way of burying their dead. Kunming's east and west gates are most picturesque.

January 29. Begin our tour today. I now have twenty-one players, the smallest group of musicians so far, and no strings. The scores for brass band I packed are now being put to use. The limitation is coloring our selections, of course—we do a lot of marches—but we get around it. Particularly nice is a version of "Begin the Beguine." And we always have our "regulars"—Lily's accompanists Theodore Paxson, piano, and Frank Versaci, flute.

On the flights there are twenty-eight people: three crew, Lily and me, two Special Services officers, and the twenty-one musicians. The C-47 seems overloaded, the tail is jammed with instruments and baggage. Pilot has never landed at airfield we are headed for, which is in the Hump, 8,000 feet up and complicated to reach.

Landing strip surrounded by mountains. We hit tail-first, then nose goes up and down again, all in a matter of seconds. In a plane not equipped with safety belts you have to hang on to whatever you can—but, as the saying goes, "Any landing from which you walk away is a good landing." Special Services' greetings as we emerge from plane: "We thought you would all be killed." The plane was obviously overloaded.

Concert starts at 4:15. The sun goes down early. During the last part of the show it is extremely cold, wind blowing. Indoor "rec" (recreation) halls too small to accommodate audiences wishing to hear us. Everyone frozen. Lily looks blue. The C.O. offers us an extra plane to help us out, and his chief pilot, Major Watson. As we drive to the airport I notice a forest fire on one of the ridges—I'm told that Japanese sympathizers started it to pinpoint the airport. There doesn't seem to be any possibility of controlling it due to the enormous spaces involved. Takeoff in the dark, Major Watson at the controls. (He is a pleasant fellow with a Southern accent. He bets me a hundred dollars I will not recognize him when he comes to see me in New York.) I go into the cockpit and from time to time see more of those fires burning. The major's pet dog is with us in the plane, a brown mongrel. He yawns on takeoff to clear his ears. Fine landing; everybody applauds the major. In the other plane went the piano and baggage.

Lily stays with two Red Cross girls in a nicely appointed place. Orchestra and I go to unfinished quarters—plenty "rough." We are now a third of the way up the Hump. Extremely cold night—five blankets.

January 30. Movie at the Red Cross in the evening with Lieutenant Colonel McClure, the C.O. An inferior musical short. The men laugh derisively over some cheap sentimentality. Suddenly we are informed there is a fire in the wall of the Red Cross snack bar. "Lights on," says the C.O. Everybody files out quietly, no panic.

February 1. We meet the head of U.S. air task force in China, General Claire Chennault, who organized air defenses for Chiang Kai-shek and also the famous American volunteer group, the Flying Tigers. His face is rugged and very kind. Loves China—"this great mass of inertia that loves peace and has no aggression ideas." The General had shot some doves that morning, and his Chinese cooks prepared a dove-and-oyster pie according to a recipe that he brought from his home in Louisiana. Like all the generals, he has dogs, two dachshunds—father and son. On wall hangs an enormous Samurai sword and a Japanese general's campaign helmet. We have seldom met a man more gracious. To him and his men applies the phrase used by Churchill—"Never have so many owed so much to so few."

After dinner the general entertains his guests with a film—*The Conspirators.* It is a thriller. Life here in China, at the foot of the Hump, is a close competitor.

Black market in China: gallon of gas, $20; a carton of cigarettes, $15; ounce of gold, $90; bottle of Scotch, $100; one brick, $1—all U.S. dollars.

February 2. Seventy-mile headwind going through Hump today. Extreme turbulence. Circle field where we are supposed to land three times, but no use with a forty-mile cross wind. Radio message from the ground: "We regret the field is closed." Great disappointment to us. Meteorologist in Kunming told me those winds arose in about 15 minutes, and there was no way of predicting them. Many of my musicians and some of the crew are airsick.

February 3. Today, fine flight. On landing, my first trumpeter has temperature of 100 degrees. Taken to hospital. Quick rehearsal so second trumpet, despite a sore lip, can take his place. Musicians and I arrange a system of cue signals; during performance the melody is passed around like a ball.

Back in Kunming. City all agog—banners, arches being decorated—for the first convoy to come through tomorrow, all the way from Assam, over the Hump, twenty-four days on the road.

February 4. Great day! Over a hundred vehicles coming through. General Lewis A. Pick, builder of the Ledo Road since October '43, in the first Jeep. Big, jovial, looks and speaks like Walter Huston. Face extremely sun- and windburned.

At the gates where the road ends are enormous pictures of President Roosevelt, General Stilwell, and Generalissimo Chiang Kai-shek. The spittoons in the Custom House are glistening, and bunches of grass have been spread around to keep the chill away. Dignitaries of both nations on dais. The Governor of Yunnan appears with a cigar in his hand and three enormous stars, decorations, on his chest. Ceremony to begin with our playing of "The Star-Spangled Banner." General Davidson, commander of the Tenth Air Force, has told me that the Chinese felt that since we are the guests we should play first. So the moment Lily cuts the ribbon I start to conduct the first notes—and at the same moment the Chinese band begins their anthem! Everyone doubles over. According to tradition, once a national anthem is begun it must be finished. No stopping. Well, the second we finish the Chinese stop, too. Very strange—because you can start any music together, but to finish together is almost impossible. (Later I asked General Davidson if simultaneous playing of two anthems made terrible confusion. "Not really," he said. A very important Chinese general had turned up at the last moment, inquired about the procedure, and was told we were to play first. That was not right, he said, because if Americans play first they will feel awful that they make us lose face—so play at the same time. And, out of courtesy, the Chinese stopped when we did, although they hadn't finished their anthem!)

First truck rolls through. The Chinese play "Polly Wolly Doodle All the Day." The Generalissimo announces that the Ledo Road will henceforth be known as the Stilwell Highway. Then many speeches—and translations—last of which I make, finishing with two Chinese words I know very well because they are the names of our Tibetan dogs at home: *Shan Lo! Wah Ping!* Peace and victory. After that Lily and I invited to a hut by two colonels and a major—they are OSS—and eat (devour!) whole box of Blum's chocolates, which the major magically produces. Lily confesses she thought for a split second that I was calling our dogs in Connecticut when I yelled their names. The longing for home is always just under the surface, struggling with the desire to be *here* and make some contribution, some sacrifice, for the cause. How must these boys feel who have been so long away and face death every single day. . . .

Celebration continues in evening with concert and a Chinese opera. Asked earlier how long my concert was going to be, I said ninety minutes. The Chinese opera this evening is exactly ninety minutes long!

Concert audience eats nuts, peanuts, and tangerines throughout performance. Everybody smokes. We sit in the audience for the Chinese opera. Music mostly percussion, flute, and Chinese violin. Exceptional costumes and make-up, naïve plot. Generous portions of Chinese drink, Jingbow juice (bomb-explosion juice), available for those who wanted it (who dared!).

The Governor presents flowers to Lily, and we cable General and Mrs. Joseph Stilwell at Carmel, California: "We were honored to play at the opening of Stilwell Highway. Best greetings." Drivers and members of the convoy tell us they are leaving immediately after the show to go back over the Hump to India and start all over again.

February 5. General Cheves asks us to come downstairs (we have the entire second floor of his residence) and meet the deputy commander of India-Burma theater, Frank W. Merrill. General

Merrill—bespectacled, with a kind smile—thanks us for the twenty-seven concerts we gave in India in twenty-nine days. "It is too many," he says, but "good music is appreciated by the soldiers." When he and his Marauders were surrounded by the enemy in Burma, they wore out the record of *Peter and the Wolf*.

Later in the evening General Pick drops in upstairs for a chat. Regrets that we haven't come to Burma, but we tell him we will try our best. Last night's concert was the first live music he had heard since 1943. He says that he would drive 1,040 miles again in a Jeep to hear Lily sing. He is a great admirer of General Stilwell. Thinks highly of the Chinese and is very proud of his own men.

February 6. Scheduled for concert three hours away by air but the airfield there has been closed for the past twelve days. Weather incredibly bad. Combination of extremely high mountains, icing conditions, and unpredictable hundred-mile-or-more winds makes flying most difficult. Old-time pilots consider flying in China the most complicated on the globe.

Quick decision made to give a concert in the hangar here. This enormous building is full of soldiers. We noticed General Merrill in audience.

Orchestra is playing better each day.

February 7. Base we were supposed to play for yesterday still closed—"Even the birds are walking," says General Glenn, Chennault's chief of staff.

Lily and I visit with Dr. and Mrs. Brown, missionaries. They have three Tibetan dogs of the type we have back home. One is named Miss Lhassa. Lily delighted as she has been asking about the breed here but had no luck in finding any. The Browns had to leave their 150-bed hospital near Nanking when the Japanese came. Mrs. Brown is now managing the Hotel du Commerce for a small colony of French, mostly from Saigon, who came here via the little railroad built by the French many years ago.

We give a concert in a giant hangar on very short notice. Curtains had been hung on the doors to muffle the aircraft noise. Played for two hours. Cheers and whistles after everything. Lily sang the "Mad Scene," the "Bell Song," "Estrellita," "Silent Night" . . . a real potpourri. Once when a night patrol plane, the

Black Widow, roared down the runway there was a terrific vibration of the hangar door. At the end Lily sang "Ave Maria" very softly, and a hush fell over the huge audience. It was not broken by cheering or applause. Everyone filed out quietly.

February 8. Snow, first time in seven years. Reaction of the populace most quaint, with everyone watching snowflakes and laughing. Very cold. It is difficult to keep warm, particularly at night. Iron stove in our room which helps a lot because there are four yards of hot pipe stretching from stove to the window.

Surprise party given by Colonel McNeill after the concert today. He comes on stage at the end of the show and thanks us—"They came and took the same chances we did." The whole audience rises and cheers. Toasts are drunk with mulberry wine.

The Hump is acting up—planes lost, people missing. Even if you manage to land by parachute, it is difficult to walk out of these mountains. The men who fly the Hump have an extremely difficult job, and there is more traffic there than at LaGuardia Airport in New York. Colonel Rust, aide to General Tunner, in charge of Hump operations, says, "A ton a minute is being flown in." No wonder we are short of gas in the U.S., and when you consider this is only a single facet of the world-war operations, it is surprising we can get as much at home as we do.

February 9. Weather still preventing our appearances at outlying bases. Extremely disappointed, but there is absolutely no flying in that direction.

Colonel Maurice Sheahan arranges a real Chinese dinner in a private home. It is in Peking style with Yunnan specialties. Here is the feast, as noted by Lily:

1. Fish and apples, fried as cakes (very crisp and buttery).
2. Yunnan ham and Chinese bread. (Whole-wheat type, thinly sliced. You make your own sandwich.)
3. Bamboo shoots with a light, creamy sauce.
4. Grilled duck with special bread à la fancy brioche.
5. Chinese celery—cabbage with a white sauce, delicate flavor.
6. Grilled goat cheese, small slices—like pancakes.
7. Sweet fermented rice soup with sliced oranges cooked in wine. (Rice is brown. This is the dessert.) Boiled chicken with sauce—

hot cheese, chili—and the rice bowl, which indicates that the dinner has come to an end.

Throughout dinner rice wine, warmed in teakettles, is served in small goblets. After the meal coffee and Yunnan tea, which is very light in flavor and color, are served in another room. There is a large fruit bowl with tangerines and oranges, and a fruit called "Buddha's fingers." The last mentioned is not edible but merely put there because it has a strong perfume. It looks like a lemon with many shoots—somewhat like fingers. Finally a hot, wet towel is given to each person. At the table a knife and fork are available if one prefers, but everyone uses chopsticks. We did—but as neophytes we had great difficulty capturing every last morsel of this delicious food.

Regarding toasts, the Chinese have a quaint but most sensible custom which doesn't make you any less a gentlemen or lady if you drink only a very small amount of rice wine at each toast. The host says, *"Kanpay,"* literally, "bottoms up." If you want to drink a very small quantity, you reply, *"Swebien,"* which means "at our pleasure." It is then perfectly proper for you to take only a little sip.

One of the dinner guests was General Wang, wearing the rosette of the Legion of Honor and the *Croix de Guerre*. He was the only Chinese general commanding Chinese troops in France during the last war. Dr. Miao, quite a power in Yunnan, was dressed in a Chinese robe, the only guest who was. Not long ago he was in the States for an operation, and he saw *Oklahoma!* four times.

Lily and I talked for a long time with Dr. McClure, who is associated with the American Red Cross. He has spent all his life, except for eight years, here in China. Some of what he told us about the Chinese in the North: Honesty is the primary virtue— for example, municipal governments post their monthly balance sheets for everyone to read. Education and medicine stressed. Not much attention to religion and morality, as we understand them in the West. Fact that their women were molested by the Japanese probably accounts in large part for their fighting pitch. They are effective guerrilla fighters and repeat the famous wooden rail trick with great effectiveness: a piece of wood, well camouflaged, is substituted for part of a steel track. After the train derails, the guerrillas make short shrift of the Japanese. It is an old trick, they say, "but we never get the same audience!" The guerrillas are fond of wearing two left shoes, symbol of two enemy soldiers eliminated. The tall corn grown to protect soya bean crops makes a valuable hiding place for them. They are experimenting with trying to reform captured Japanese and turn them into farmers.

Saving a man from death, via suicide, for example, or from disabling disease results in his benefactor's having to support him for life. Dr. McClure's father, also a doctor in China, once saw a beggar outside his compound. He was almost blind from cataracts. The doctor operated on him and restored his sight. A short time later the ex-beggar appeared at the compound with his family, requesting life support because he had lost his earning power as a beggar. The doctor hired him as a guard at the compound for life.

Chinese will often jump in front of planes and cars to get rid of evil spirits that they believe are following them, and of course many of them die that way. There are still many women with bound feet, although custom has been abolished. Children are carried papoose-style.

February 10. No concert. Much conversation with other people who have lived in China for many years.

Everyone's opinion is that when war ends China will want, first, nylon stockings; second, radios; third, automobiles. Rents in Kunming sky high: two good houses on outskirts rent for $70,000 a year, U.S.

February 11. Weather still unflyable. Some of the concerts way up north have been dropped from our schedule.

Chinese soldier comes to the house bringing a personal invitation to a reception and concert given by General Ho Ying Chin, Chief of the General Staff and Supreme Commander of the Chinese Army. A Chinese soprano sang the aria from *Madame Butterfly.* During the reception and concert most of the women sat apart. The Governor of Yunnan and his wife were at our table. The Governor smoked cigars incessantly. A pianist and a violinist played some popular compositions. The hit of the evening was a juggler, really excellent.

An officer told us some footnotes to the 1943 Cairo Conference of leaders of Great Britain, U.S., and China: the British wanted to fire on each plane coming within six miles of the pyramids, beginning the day before President Roosevelt's arrival. The officer persuaded them not to do it until the President actually landed in Egypt. There was considerable discussion, but finally the British agreed. Next day the President's plane was three hours late—and flew directly over the pyramids. Churchill and Roosevelt had a party one evening, and a band was brought in. Churchill conducted—with a drumstick—their favorite number, the "Marine Hymn."

Cold rain, low, squally clouds. Everywhere preparation for the Chinese New Year. The streets are crowded with people. We receive a letter of introduction to Madame Sun Yat-sen for when—and if—we reach Chungking. Weather still keeping everyone earthbound.

February 12. Visit the new rec hall, Club 11. It has a small bar serving good and not overly potent drinks. A sergeant comes in and announces, "One-ball alert!" No one pays much attention since this means the Japanese are one hour away. But quite soon a two-ball alert is sounded and the sirens wail. It is the Chinese New Year, and the Japanese usually select holidays to come over. Use of firecrackers suspended in blackout. (Our number-two boy, Woo, calls them "crackerfires.") Planes must have been driven off because soon the sirens sound the all clear.

Meet Major Nichol Smith, the author of *Burma Road*, and Lieutenant Colonel T. de Sibour, the first to fly the Hump in a small plane—a British "Moth"—in the Twenties.

The streets are deserted now. New Year's is a holiday that the Chinese spend with their families.

We have eleven household servants! They are:

> Jim, number-one boy
> Woo, number-two boy
> Wong, coolie

Chung, coolie
Hou, stove boy
Leechoy, room boy
Cheuw, room boy
Lee, number-one cook
Lee, number-two cook
Mah, dishwasher
Amah, laundrywoman

Number-one boy is paid $16 a month, U.S. money. Number-two boy is paid $14 a month, U.S. money; and all the others less. All of them buy their own rice, which costs about $2 U.S. a month. Rice, before the war, used to cost ten cents (Chinese) for one and a quarter pounds. Now it costs $100 Chinese for same. They are all members of WASC—War Area Service Corps. It is a Madame Chiang organization for refugees from the coastal cities of China, and they are employed as servants to U.S. troops.

February 13. Spend most of time talking and resting. Met Lieutenant Colonel Ilya Tolstoy, grandson of Leo Tolstoy, who seems to know this part of the world well. Major Smith—who is known here as "Fantastic"—tells us of a dinner given by a local chieftain which consisted of elephants' trunks, bears' paws, and sinews of the muscles of deer!

February 14. Downpour. None of the U.S. personnel in China remembers such a spell of bad weather in February. We give another "extra" concert; grand success. Fellows come with valentines for Lily.

The little horse-driven carriages here use old auto tires as wheels.

New word to us: "Stateside," meaning the United States.

February 15. Early-morning phone call from Lieutenant Colonel Bayh telling me that the weather situation looks hopeless, flying north might be out of the question for many more days. A wire from Major General Davidson, commander of the Tenth Air Force in Burma, asking us to go there to give some concerts. We will leave tomorrow for Myitkyina in northern Burma.

Visit General Chennault to say good-by. He says, "Next time we hear you I hope it will be in the Opera in Tokyo, if there is still an opera house left there." Wire from General Wedemeyer in

Chungking, thanking us for the job done and regretting that weather conditions make it impossible for us to get to other bases. We are told that we played to about 80 percent of the personnel in China.

At farewell dinner Governor of Yunnan presents lovely gifts, including a Chengfu silver box and bracelet for Lily.

February 16. Breakfast with General Cheves at 7:00. We will leave China with regret. . . .

The Tenth Air Force sends in a C-47 which takes my China Band over the Hump. We go in another plane. All our friends are at the airport. Weather is clear. A good flight—on oxygen.

Land in Myitkyina (it's pronounced Mishino) on the Irrawaddy River. This is the town where the old Ledo Road joined with the Burma Road. Completely different weather, really hot. China Band has not arrived, so in the afternoon I start rehearsing the band here, teaching them the same numbers that the China Band played so I can join the two if the China players arrive at the eleventh hour. Everyone now very much concerned about their plane. There are no reports.

We give the concert with the Burma Band for enormous crowd outdoors. After concert news comes that China Band landed in Bhamo, 120 miles south.

February 17. Fly south over jungle at an altitude of only few hundred feet. Lily points out elephants in a clearing. Follow the Irrawaddy, winding through the thick growth, land on improvised airfield—recently vacated by Japanese.

Concert set for afternoon, and we are asked to give first broadcast over station WOTO (Wings Over the Orient) that night. (WOTO theme song is "Road to Mandalay.")

China and Burma bands play together for concert. Very effective performance for huge gathering of soldiers. Afterward, visit to recent battlegrounds. Jungle growth churned up by explosives. Some temples greatly damaged because the Japanese had established a radio station close by. Small temples everywhere, most in disrepair—it is apparently an act of devotion to erect one but not to see that it is kept up.

Major General Davidson is our host at dinner, and we meet

Admiral Louis Mountbatten, head of Southeast Asia Command and commander of Allied operations against Japanese in Burma. Talk centers around Indian and Chinese music. Consensus is Orientals understand Western music better than we do theirs.

Lieutenant Bert Parks, former CBS announcer, is emcee for broadcast, which is given in a small portable station. Everyone squeezes in. I close with a short farewell speech, for we are on our way tomorrow for the European theater. General Sultan asks for "Ave Maria." I give baton to Sergeant Jack Kollon, my assistant throughout China tour.

Walls of house we are billeted in are made of jute and strung on bamboo. For privacy all lights must be put out—the jute is almost transparent. Cries of peacocks sound through the night, which is very cold.

February 18. Leave Burma early morning for long day's flight. Everest visible—enormous masses of snow about 60 miles away. At sunset we see the incredible Taj Mahal below. Land in New Delhi.

First tub bath in two months.

February 19. Return to Taj Mahal, splendid in the midday sun. Everyone says that, like most of the great monuments of the world, it looks best in moonlight. To enter we take off our shoes and put on special sandals. Great echo in the tomb. When Lily sings a few notes, they are heard for quite a few seconds, a shimmer of overlapping bell-like tones. Outside, behind the tomb, is the Jamin River. Vultures are circling. The chant of the muezzin mixes with begging cries of the sick and lame. The beauty of this ancient edifice is a creation of man. What a pity that same being has so often turned his energy to the voiding of life and beauty. . . .

Talk with General Merrill in New Delhi. He loves music—plays the accordion well and is now studying the bagpipes.

February 22. Leave India, flying up the coast of Beluchistan. In the pilot's compartment I hear Lily's recording of *Lucia.* Land in Cairo late this night.

February 24. To El Adem, near Tobruk, then across the Mediterranean to Athens. Weather very bad. We fly fifteen miles from enemy-held Crete. The Turks declared war on Germany today.

We wonder whether the Germans in Crete will react, but all seems quiet.

Naples by evening.

February 25. Leave Naples early. Over Corsica and the coast of France—Riviera, Lily's birthplace, is clouded over. It is the first time in seven years she has seen her native land and she is much moved. At Dijon a crew of shot-down American flyers who walked out of Germany join us for flight to Paris.

In Paris streets deserted. Whatever shops are still in business are closed as it is Sunday. City impressive and dignified, but like someone dazed and not yet recovered.

Full moon in evening as we walk through the quiet streets. We had been told there were no air alerts here, but all at once all lights go out and sirens wail. The first alarm in months, but the all clear sounds soon.

February 26. We are going to play at the front in Germany! Briefing at USO headquarters at Chatou. Nonfraternization highly emphasized—reports of young boys and girls shooting and knifing Americans. We are issued gas masks and steel helmets. There is quite a problem about the organization of the orchestra, and I am busy getting it together.

A tale of Paris. When the Nazis were ready to leave Paris they camouflaged their vehicles with greenery. The next day everyone from small boys on bicycles up to men in trucks did the same thing.

One of General de Gaulle's aides tells us the General likes to listen to Lily's Mozart records. Meet Mrs. Anthony Eden in a smart British uniform—gray and red, with service ribbons. She asks for our autographs for her son.

Lily and I lunch with Marlene Dietrich, who says the table will now be known as the "Lily-Marlene" table!

March 2. Six months overseas; we are due for our first stripe—"hash mark."

By car through France to the forward areas in Belgium. Lunch at Rheims, near the sandbagged cathedral. Intermittent sun, rain, snow. It is strange to go through Château-Thierry, Belleau Wood

—cemeteries of the great sacrifices of the last war. It is an all-day drive, and we see the first German prisoners working on the roads, and our soldiers guarding them with rifles. Driver watches constantly for enemy strafing.

Arrive at our destination in Belgium and find the town—a rest center for combat troops—completely blacked out. Spring shows in the green grass. Only military cars on roads; civilians ride bicycles. The children we pass on the road give us the V sign, reminding us of China's *ding ho*—thumbs up!

March 3. More German prisoners, and they do not look like the Master Race. Their faces are blue from the cold, and they have scarves tied around their heads to cover their ears. Everyone wears steel helmets and pants stuck inside mud boots. Results of the buzz bombs everywhere. Block after block of buildings with blown-out windows.

I have a good orchestra—the First Army Band, with strings added. We give an exciting concert, first in Europe. From Burma to Belgium.

March 6. During concert, just as I finished the *Showboat* number, the emcee, Sergeant Friedlander, came to the apron of the stage and shouted, "Cologne is ours!" Yells and cheers from these men of the First Army, who did the fighting to capture the city. Concert continues in a glowing atmosphere.

The theaters we play in were built some time ago. Despite some bomb damage they have fine acoustics, which obviates the necessity of a mike. "Cologne looks more devastated than Stalingrad," said Bill Downs of CBS. Germans creep out of cellars, we are told, with, "Heil Eisenhoffer," and remarks like, "We haff been vaiting for you."

March 8. Leave Belgium for Germany and lunch with Major General Huebner, victor at Aachen. ENTERING GERMANY—says huge sign. Lily leans out of the Jeep and spits. Cold fog, rain, snow. Devastation—a few civilians dragging themselves along. General Huebner thanks us for coming to entertain his forward troops—"Some of them have been on the line fifty-three days, and this is their first rest."

Drive through Aachen shows us close up what modern warfare can do to a large town—there is not a house standing.

Rest center on the border of Germany, splendidly organized. The soldiers come in dirty and battle weary. They are given hot showers, clean clothes, clean quarters, good food. There are no set hours. Soldiers' night club called Chez Dog-Face. USO and Belgian shows are playing there, and every 48 hours—the length of the soldiers' stay at this camp—brings a complete change of entertainment. We are eager to play Cologne but are told it is still very "hot." Everyone anxious to know about CBI.

Siegfried Line—white and green "dragon's teeth" camouflaged with twigs. Each tooth like a Chinese tomb or a little pyramid. Tremendous pillboxes in grotesque ruins. After a while it is difficult to describe ruins; somehow they all look alike, Bengasi, Bhamo, Cassino, Aachen. . . .

March 10. Air-raid sirens blow almost daily in this border town in Belgium, but the German planes must be intercepted or shot down because we don't see them. Great disappointment, Cologne concert called off.

March 11. First concert in Germany, in Stolberg. Ride through Germany at night. Completely deserted except for American MPs. Gratifying to play American music on German soil.

March 12. Farewell to the First Army. Colonel May, Special Services officer, lends the First Army Orchestra to the Ninth Army (where we are going), and I intend to add some strings from the Ninth Army to this group. Closing concert in Liege is immense success, enormous audience.

March 13. Three-hour drive to Krefeld, Germany, captured March 5. It is a few miles from the Rhine, opposite Duisburg. Drive through Aachen, Julich, and many other cities and villages now famous as battlegrounds. Everything destroyed—houses leveled, dead cattle and horses. There are many minefields—some of them marked by Germans, some by us. Enormous quantity of burned and overturned tanks. A few German civilians.

Arrive at house in Krefeld where we are billeted. Nearby, a road sign: Dusseldorf—20 kilometers. Essen—18 kilometers. In front of house is burned German truck, and on the spring grass lie

German bazookas and mortars. Deep roar of steady, heavy artillery, with occasional particularly loud blast. We are about three miles from the Rhine and front lines.

Owners of the house at the door, greet us with exaggerated obsequiousness.

On drive to the Mess for dinner we see that Krefeld did not escape—most of its buildings are laid waste but still bear, in enormous white letters, statements of allegiance to Hitler: We Will Not Capitulate. Victory or Siberia. What Did You Do Today for Germany? Innumerable Heil Hitlers and, of course, countless swastikas. Many white flags, obviously hastily made, hanging out of windows or affixed to what remains of the houses. We are less than 4,000 yards from the Rhine. At the Mess hall there is suddenly a tremendous concussion and explosion. The soldiers hasten to explain that it is our 155 howitzer battery, located close to the Mess hall, going into action.

Krefeld was taken only about a week ago, so it is suggested we get home before dark—there are still snipers around. German civilians are off the streets at five o'clock, and it gets dark about seven, but conversation with the men who do the fighting makes us late for curfew, and we drive at night. No lights on the streets or car, so it takes us some time to locate our house. Steady cannonade. An eerie feeling to drive in this dead town. We creep along, careful not to get off the road and into possible minefields.

Candles inside of the house. Windows rattle at every blast.

March 14. In bomb shelter adjacent to house are several people in German uniforms, obviously discards by Nazi soldiers. MPs are posted at the house to keep out all unwanted visitors.

The German couple in our house excessively and artificially solicitous. They just can't do enough for us. This morning Lily opened the door to a room near our bedroom and discovered about ten Nazi uniforms lying about, as if hastily discarded. Sometime during the night, despite the U.S. soldier guarding the house, some Nazis must have slipped in, changed to civilian clothes, and slipped out again. A little disconcerting. We realized then that you could never tell just by looking at someone whose side he was on. . . .

Visit a dugout next to a battery of 155 howitzers where the officers are surrounded by radios and phones. A target is selected, and Lily writes with chalk on a big shell, "Catch this one, Hitler!" It is loaded. Terrific roar. When noise subsides, a sergeant says blandly, "Hitler, count your soldiers."

Security does not permit any announcement of concert, but I see little posters in a few places with an arrow pointing to Caserna, which is where we are going to play. It is a huge building, probably once a warehouse, with many holes in the ceiling and walls.

Concert is in afternoon because of evening curfew. Enormous gathering of combat G.I.'s overflows through the many doors. We are greeted with tremendous enthusiasm. Throughout the concert, cannonade persistent. Airplanes overhead continually. The audience sits with rifles and battle helmets within easy reach. Rapt attention—I do not think they are nearly as conscious of the bombardment as we are.

After concert many soldiers come to talk to us and, noticing the CBI patch on our sleeves, express amazement at our having been there. Great curiosity about that part of the world. Many think they might be there eventually themselves. One soldier tells us about the deep caves in Holland—not far away—where the paintings of Rembrandt, Van Gogh, etc., are hidden.

In the evening there is a knock at our door, and a sergeant comes in to tell me that he heard my records being broadcast by the Nazis with an announcement that I am touring the Western front!

March 15. Second concert at the same place, at 2:30 P.M. A truck with recording equipment stands at the door, and I meet Vick Knight, whom we know from New York. He is here on orders from SHAEF to record the show. Audience seems to be even larger and refuses to let us go. Same type of accompaniment, occasional extra-heavy blast. My very good drummer tells me: "I have too much competition."

Warm spring day. Blue skies, forsythia and pussy willows beginning to bloom, but no one picks them, since there are still many mines around.

Windows rattling particularly loudly this evening, and from

time to time the house shakes. High steady roar signifies our bombers going over.

We are called outside. Two big planes coming down, afire. One dives to earth quite quickly; the other continues semilevel flight for a while and finally settles behind the hills, far away. No sound —as if he had landed on a downy pillow. They must have dropped their bombs, as they were on the way back, but very white flashes continue for a time. It is the ammunition going off. They were RAF planes. No word yet whether the men have escaped death. . . .

A passing soldier offers us a bottle of cognac, which he has "liberated." Battle noises are getting heavier. He tells us that today the Germans strafed the street that leads to our "concert hall." We hear the irregular wavy hum of the German planes. "That's Bed-Check Charlie making his regular nightly visit," he says. It is an observation bomber, and he does some desultory bombing. Our ack-ack opens up.

March 16. Colonel Barret tells us there will be an artillery barrage on Duisburg and wants to know if we would like to see some of the battle action. We drive for half a mile along the Rhine and climb to an observation tower 400 yards from the river. From the platform we see the German lines on the opposite bank. Factory section of Duisburg very well outlined, despite rain and some fog. One of the guns will be a German 88 manned by a crew of our soldiers who were wounded by this type of gun. Colonel Barret orders antitanks to attack first. A few seconds later we see bright flashes and the antitanks reveal their location in a clump of trees. A smokestack is hit. Then a set of cannon open up on pillboxes on the far shore. Flashes from all sides, explosions. Once 12 batteries— 120 guns—fired 2 shells each simultaneously—240 explosions in less than a minute. They burst over the entire riverfront. . . .

Back in Krefeld I spend an hour on field telephone, trying to revive the issue of giving a concert in Cologne. There is hope.

March 17. Lunch with "Railsplitters," the 84th Division, which with the 102nd, the "Ozark," took Krefeld only weeks ago. "We have a 56-piece military band in our outfit," says Warrant Officer Scott, so I ask him to get all the musicians together and suggest that they appear with us on the show. It is 1:00 P.M., the concert is at 2:30. We rush to get everybody together and rehearse on the street. From every nook and cranny Germans keep coming out to watch. I climb on the hood of a Jeep to conduct. Music by Victor Herbert is punctuated by bombardment in the German street. In the concert hall the two orchestras fill the stage—over a hundred musicians.

Dinner at Munchen-Gladbach, Goebbels's hometown, which is in poor shape.

"Bed-Check Charlie" is over again and is responsible for some damage. His flight is timed to coordinate with those of our big bombers going over, which makes it difficult for antiaircraft to shoot at him without jeopardizing our planes. German soldiers are being found every day in town—some in civilian clothes—a Gestapo agent was caught today.

The planes sound like low cellos moving in chromatic thirds, somewhat irregular major and minor sequence.

During the evening Warrant Officer Scott tells us he has received orders authorizing him to augment his 56-piece band to 90 pieces. Lieutenant Rooney, our Special Services officer, tells me: "You turned the trick. The C.O. was so pleased with the concert that he ordered this expansion."

March 18. Visit the displaced persons' camp. Every nationality seems to be represented.

Wonderful to have 100-piece orchestra. After concert a soldier says, "War is misery, but you brought us joy." Lily and I feel humbled. . . .

Ominous silence tonight, broken now and then by small-arms fire quite close to the house. A sergeant rushes in and calls Lieutenant Rooney and myself to the phone, which is across the street. Message: the concert in Cologne is set—2:30 P.M., March 20! Overjoyed, we step back outside into the pitch-darkness. After a few paces I ask Rooney if he knows the password for the evening. He says no and stops in his tracks. We start to retrace our steps. Suddenly a guard appears from nowhere and follows us. For some reason he doesn't ask any questions, and we are relieved to reach the telephone post, where we are given the night's password. Luckily. As we went back home we were stopped abruptly and challenged. Last night a general was out walking and was challenged. He didn't know the password, so he began explaining who he was. One MP interrupted with, "Who is Frank Sinatra?" "A damn poor singer," said the general. The MPs laughed and let him pass.

March 19. Lunch with General William Simpson, commander of the Ninth Army, who promises, "If my army gets to Berlin first, I will send for you right away!" This command performance is accepted with pleasure.

Farewell finale at concert. We arrange a party for the orchestra on a field next to our house as thanks for their fine playing and wonderful cooperation.

March 20. Morning drive to Cologne. Delayed en route by enormous military traffic going forward. Finally reach outskirts of the battered city. Cathedral spires visible on horizon. No time for lunch. Go immediately to concert location, New University. Much battered—the rear stage wall is gone; a cloth hangs in its place. But there are 2,500 G.I.'s gathered, each one holding a gun. The German line is only three-quarters of a mile away, across the Rhine. As I greet the audience and announce the "American Patrol," there is a great blast that jolts the stage. I'm sure the beginning of that piece—bass drum and snares—has never sounded so feeble! Smell of cordite fumes on the stage and, as I go off after the first number, someone shouts, "It's an outgoing!"—a 155 howitzer battery behind the thin stage wall attending to the serious business of war. Throughout the performance there are firings at the most unexpected moments, which release dust from the ceiling each time. Atmosphere triumphant. American music for American soldiers on the banks of the Rhine. . . . The men cheered us on, and we added encore after encore.

Our request to visit the cathedral causes a conference of MPs. Finally we are driven off in a Jeep through the shambles of the city. Opera house in ruins. A narrow winding street, made even narrower by rubble, brings us to the great cathedral. Everything around it is down. Cathedral looks particularly light in color because of the battle dust that has settled on it. There is some damage, but the fact that it stands at all is testimony to the skill of the Allied fighting men and fliers.

Lily and I cross narrow street and move nearer the cathedral, in front of which a giant burned-out German tank is standing. "Make it fast," the MPs tell us. A few shells fell during the day, and the big square is out of bounds.

Long drive back to Belgium and a most welcome dinner. Sirens start just as we sit down, but it is a short alert and everyone relaxes.

March 21. Receive message that the great United States Army Band and Major Glenn Miller's orchestra will be combined for our two concerts in Paris. I look forward to conducting them. In the now relatively peaceful town of Namur, on the Meuse, we give our closing concert in Belgium, in old opera house. Soldiers are everywhere—in the orchestra pit and on stage. A cold evening, and there is a draft on the stage. When I ask the stage manager whether he can remedy the situation, he points to the roof and says only "V-one." There is much destruction in this part of the world from a weapon that made its first appearance at the tail end of Hitler's career.

March 22. General Simpson's Ninth Army not to be first in Berlin, after all, so concert tonight is our last USO appearance overseas—the 112th. Phone rings about six o'clock, a friend telling us to turn on the radio—a broadcast of the recording made of our concert on the Rhine.

Opera house is jammed to the rafters. The musicians absolutely fill the stage. No heat, so Lily wears her coat throughout evening. The moment I begin to conduct the electric power fails. Emergency lighting equipment for about half an hour, then lights come back on.

Cheers and whistles of G.I.'s in appreciation of music unrivaled in our professional life. Encore after encore. "The national anthems!" announces Lieutenant Rooney. We start with the "Marseillaise," then "God Save the King." Turning to audience, I conduct "The Star-Spangled Banner." Everyone sings. . . .

PART FOUR

Blessings

Home

I CAN STILL HEAR THE excited voice of Lily's secretary, Tiri, as one day thirty-five years ago she told Lily and me the alarming news: "This apartment is becoming a co-operative!"

It is difficult to imagine, in the present-day wave of apartment buying, that there was ever another meaning attached to *co-operative*. But to us Tiri's words conjured an immediate vision of a radical change in life style: sharing living quarters with other families—rooms divided up, duty rosters, cooking schedules—something we thought went on in the Soviet Union! We knew that war work had concentrated people in some areas and there was a serious housing shortage, but the situation must have deteriorated critically in the months we were away on the USO tours. No time to lose. Tiri was asked to please drop everything and look for an apartment.

I've no idea how she did it, but that same day she called to say she'd found a lovely place, superb view, a little large, maybe—could we come right over and see it?

One look was all we needed. Within twenty-four hours we had signed the papers and were the proud owners of a beautiful penthouse apartment. Ten Gracie Square was, as it turned out, a co-operative, American-style.

Our apartment on Fifty-seventh Street had been a gracious place to live. Ten Gracie Square was—is—to me a fantasy come true, a dream I never knew I had until I walked in here. To this day it works its charm on me—the space and light, the river views on three sides, the terraces from which I can gaze at the universe, listen to the world. On days of perfect cloudless sky and sweet air the balcony view is sharp and scintillating, as if seen through polished crystal. The buildings on the eastern horizon are deeply etched in a random series of projections into the blue; the sounds of river traffic and children playing in the park far below come up clear, unambiguous. The balcony on such days is for breathing deep, for rejoicing in the pleasure of sights and sounds, for giving thanks. There are other days and other views—when fog rolls up the river, tucking under itself as it moves all traces of earthly reality; when a storm approaches and the chromatic vitality of a sunny day is shaded down to several tones of gray. And there are the nights—some with the low-hanging starry sky of a desert; some filled with total darkness and the noise of howling winds, and I feel I am riding the deck of a great ship that is holding its own against the elements. The displays of sky and river and earth are ever-changing, seemingly infinite combinations of color and light and sound that correspond to every mood of the spirit, inspire the mind to consider so many things.

To have had the serene pleasure of such a home for so much of my life increases my strong belief in luck, for it is hard to imagine what I've done to be so rewarded. I have always indulged my taste for travel; perhaps one reason I do so is for the sweet anticipation of coming home again. I've lived the happiest times of my life here. Lily. My second wife, Sara Gene. Plans made and triumphs celebrated. Hours spent with dear friends.

For over a decade Leopold Stokowski was a neighbor. In 1945 he and his new wife, Gloria Vanderbilt, moved to Gracie Square—which he always called Crazy Square. Their apartment adjoined this one; we shared the north balcony. In those years we developed a deep and lasting friendship.

He was one of those vital people who seem to live several lives in the time it takes the rest of us to live one. Iconoclast, innovator, genius; passionate, fearless, self-possessed—all accurate enough descriptions. Yet he also possessed the homelier virtues, which are, happily, sometimes found in the breasts of giants.

He was a loving father to his two sons; in fact, he loved all young people, perhaps because an essential element of him remained youthful. Part of his charm was his outspokenness, his love of fun and of anything new. Once, in San Francisco, we had arranged to lunch at the Palace Hotel. I arrived early and decided to play a little joke on Leopold. There was nothing on the list of drinks that was "special," so I asked the bartender to please bring two Old Fashioneds with plenty of fruit in them, no matter what I actually ordered. Stokowski arrived and, true to form, immediately asked what was new in the drinks department. Something called a Seventh Veil, I told him. Wonderful! So I asked for two. Leopold sipped his disguised Old Fashioned, then asked with obvious enjoyment and air of intense interest, "What is this? How is it made?" Had he seen through the prank, turned the tables on me? Given his love of a joke, I can never be sure.

He did love to laugh and could come up with some pretty brisk retorts. One day I asked him what he thought about sex before a concert. (I had just been reading that a well-known boxer doesn't make any secret of the fact that he and his wife abstain for two weeks before a bout.) "Well," said Stokowski, without missing a beat, "it depends on the girl!"

In the Thirties he gave a series of young people's concerts, the first prominent musical figure to do so. For his presentation of Saint-Saëns' *Carnival of the Animals*, he arranged for live animals to be on the stage (including baby elephants)—Stokowski was not one to skimp when it came to providing the fullest possible sensory experience!

Leopold formed the All-American Youth Orchestra in 1940 in order to give talented young musicians a place to gain experience. And this was after a formidable career as conductor of the Philadelphia. Among orchestras there had always been the big three—Boston, New York, and Chicago. By the time Stokowski left the Philadelphia, in 1938, it had become the fourth.

He was the first to play Gustav Mahler in the U.S., to give the American composer Charles Ives a hearing, and to introduce *Le Sacre du Printemps* here. He loved the Stravinsky work; in fact, he loved all that composer's music, a feeling, however, that did not carry over to Stravinsky the man. And it was mutual. Stravinsky felt that his music was too freely invaded by Stokowskian interpretation.

It is true certainly that Leopold was not shy about his readings of scores. What conductor is? The tools of a conductor's trade have to do with subtleties such as phrasing, tempo, bowings, and what to do in the absence of composer notations. And sometimes he will even become convinced that certain minor changes will improve the piece. Now, Toscanini had the reputation, in the main, of playing only what the composer had written, but I know, for instance, that he reworked the ending of Respighi's *Pines of Rome* somewhat—I have copies of those changes—and edited other works, among them Debussy's *La Mer* and Schumann's Symphony No. 3. Toscanini also once added a notation to a score that had been conducted and annotated by Mahler (scores are passed around to various conductors, so will often show the variations in interpretation): "These changes are unworthy of such a musician!"

Leopold luxuriated in music; when he wasn't conducting or rehearsing, he could be found studying scores from his huge collection. Rare was the conversation that he would not, sooner or later, direct toward music. Music swept him up, thrilled him, and he responded to the pleasure with the simplicity of a child. The morning of his ninetieth birthday, which was to be celebrated by an evening party at the Plaza Hotel, he was rehearsing Beethoven's Ninth at Carnegie Hall. I went down to wish him birthday congratulations. He acknowledged my greetings with a smile and nod, but what he said was, "This music is so beautiful!" He cared little, if at all, about being ninety, or the party, or anything but that which was the center of his life.

Without a doubt, Stokowski was among the more vigorous of interpreters, always looking for what he considered the most beautiful possibilities of the music. He worked under the assumption that "if the composer could have heard it this way, he would have preferred it!" And he welcomed inspiration for his labors in any area that might present itself.

There is a small museum on Manhattan's Upper West Side that contains the paintings of Nicholas Roerich, an artist, archaeologist, and philosopher who was born in St. Petersburg in the latter part of the nineteenth century. To me his work is an exultation in the magnificence of nature and its mysterious power to uplift the human spirit and simultaneously remind us that we are part of the beauty of the universe. "In beauty we are united," Roerich had written, "through beauty we pray, with beauty we conquer."

The mountain paintings are especially appealing. To contemplate Roerich's visions of the Himalayas—those "abodes of snow" where he lived for so many years—is to feel their energy and the deepest secrets of life, which they seem to hold serenely within their snowy swells. Immutable, indestructible, holy. Approachable but never entirely known. Sometimes, looking at them, I've had the impression that I was experiencing music visually.

Interestingly, Roerich in one period of his life had designed for the stage—operas and ballets, including decors and costumes for the 1912 Paris presentation of *Le Sacre du Printemps* ballet. I thought of Stokowski when I discovered this, and I took him to the Roerich museum. Stokowski was very much impressed with the paintings. I was not surprised. Some time later he told me that Roerich's visions had inspired him to fresh interpretation in his conducting of the Stravinsky ballet music.

Stokowski loved to experiment with sound transmission, whether by way of rearranging the orchestra seating—which he did, putting all the violins on the left, violas in the middle, and cellos on the right, horrifying perhaps at the time but the typical arrangement today—or through the complexities offered by electronics. For Disney's film *Fantasia*, in the 1940s, he used eighteen separate sound channels, which gave the audience the illusion of sitting right in the middle of the orchestra. He used the music of Beethoven, Bach, Schubert, Moussorgsky, Tchaikovsky, and his old favorite, Stravinsky. (He had to do a bit of talking to convince Walt Disney that *Le Sacre du Printemps* would work well; its atonalities had so far prevented it from becoming the popular selection it is today.) And of course when the film was released Stokowski was attacked once more for tampering with great music. It didn't bother him. He was sure of his dedication to music and of his skill in bringing it alive in the most effective possible way.

In what I think is one of the marks of a truly creative person, Stokowski didn't cling stubbornly to an interpretation once he'd found it; he was always alert for new ways of expression. "There is no such thing as a correct interpretation," he used to say, adding that it grew more difficult every time he approached a piece, no matter how many readings he'd given it.

What happens inside a conductor as he is bringing forth music? No conductor I've met—including myself—could describe those inner workings in any detailed way, but that there definitely are such drives is obvious, and in various combinations they are what make each conductor unique. I doubt any two could lead an orchestra in the same piece of music, follow its notations, determine not to "tamper," and still produce the same effect. Individual style pushes through, efforts and intentions to the contrary.

Some years ago, Bob Sherman, who had organized a lecture series at New York University, asked me to give a talk on the ego of the conductor. Having a healthy conductor's ego of my own, I naturally accepted. I prepared a tape with the first three chords of Beethoven's *Eroica* as conducted by Arturo Toscanini, Bruno Walter, Eugene Ormandy, Sir Thomas Beecham, and Dimitri Mitropoulos. Amazing how differently three chords can be played —and the differences are easily recognizable even by the uninitiated: Toscanini, very dry, brittle; Walter, just the opposite, with longish chords.

There can be variations in tempo and loudness, and these may arise from the composer's instruction—if any exists—which might read, "a little faster" or, "a little louder." Well . . . but what *is* "a little"? A conductor's gestures are musical Esperanto, universally understood, so once the downbeat—the tempo—is established, that's it. It can be fast, slow, in between. But not only the tempo, or speed, of a piece is open to interpretation; the emphasis within each measure can also be a matter of conductor's choice. If there are three beats to every measure, for instance, then the 1-2-3 can be 1—2-3, a slight lingering on the first beat, called rubato.

The New York Philharmonic keeps chronological track of conductors' total time for performance of various works. It is a useful reference when planning the details of a concert program. And it incidentally demonstrates that tempo varies not only with each conductor but with different performances of the same music by the same conductor. For Beethoven's Fifth, for example, in minutes: Toscanini—31:15 and 30:10 (his tempi got faster as he got older, as if he might have been compensating for age by adding the vivacity of speed!); Bernstein—32:40 and 34:45; Mitropoulos—29:20 and 31:10; Szell—31:45 and 32:37; Rodzinski—27:00 and 27:35.

And then there is the matter of the composer's instruction—or lack of. The greats of the past, of course, cannot be consulted where there is some doubt as to how a piece should be played or, less frequently, whether a certain note is really the one wanted. With contemporary composers—well, you can always ask. Once, with Villa-Lobos, it was a question of whether a certain part was playable at all. I still have the score of his *Songs of Childhood*, which he brought to me to introduce. I began to read it, and on the third page a passage for cellos riveted my attention. It called for fourteen cellos to play *together* what was really a piano arpeggio—not even one cello could have played all the notes he had packed into the scale, let alone fourteen in unison. So I said, "Tell me, how is this played?" And he said those words that bring sweet relief to a conductor: "I trust you." So I changed it, reducing forty notes to about fifteen. (I think what must have happened was that he'd told the copyist to put in an "effective passage.")

I remember having to prepare Stravinsky's *Firebird* some years ago for a concert, and there was one place where the note could easily be either C or C-flat. So I asked the composer which he wanted. And Stravinsky said he didn't know. (I wonder what he would have said if Stokowski had asked!)

Conductors are very much aware of their individuality and, whether or not they admit it, make strenuous efforts to preserve it. That is what distinguishes them from one another. I am fond of a joke about the subject of music makers' egos—and I have heard many of my colleagues laugh at it, a hopeful sign that we do not always take ourselves *too* seriously!

Three of the greats, Böhm, Bernstein, and Von Karajan, are engaged in conversation.

"I've conducted Mozart for eighty years," says Böhm, "and am no doubt the best for Mozart."

"You know," Bernstein pipes in, "as I was conducting Mozart last night, God came to me and looked right into my eyes. 'Leonard,' he said, 'you are the best interpreter of Mozart.' "

Von Karajan studies Bernstein for a moment. "Isn't that strange," he remarks. "I don't remember speaking to you!"

Leopold came here to lunch one Sunday with his two little boys. We had our usual good time. Watching him with his sons, I thought he loved to play as much as they did—more, maybe. He didn't tell me the saddening news until after we'd eaten and the boys were out of earshot—that Gloria had asked him to move out, she wanted a divorce. He held back expressing just how deeply this hurt him, but I knew he was suffering terribly at the thought of not being able to live with his children any more. "Life is an art," he said. "I have not quite mastered it."

Of course, we would remain friends, but the closeness of our homes had allowed us to share our lives with each other on an almost daily basis. I would miss him.

He lived for twenty-two more years, to ninety-five, but he did not marry again: "I've been married three times, and now is the best . . . I do what I like."

Leopold had an endearing habit of always remaining in view after I would drop him off at his apartment on Fifth Avenue. I can still see him standing on the sidewalk, somewhat stooped with age yet elegant, and waving with one white-gloved hand until my car pulled out of sight.

It is strange the little things one remembers. Thinking of Leopold, gone now, has reminded me of Lily, of the years we had together in this island in the sky. We had festive parties, and visits with some glamorous and famous and successful acquaintances, quite a whirl of excitement—sometimes I felt we had prominent roles in a play by Noel Coward. But those are not the images that linger in my mind. I like best to look across the room now and see Lily sitting on the divan, her back to the nighttime heavens visible just beyond the terrace door. So often after a performance at the Met she'd say let's just go home and have *"un peu de potage."* And there we'd sit, relishing the little soup and the quiet. . . . Of course, there were weekends at the house in Silvermine and sunny days in Palm Beach, but home was New York, here.

Even in these later years, when the cold winter makes me threaten (but only to myself) to schedule no concert above the Mason-Dixon line, I cannot be truly serious about changing my home base. But it was not, in the end, so compelling for Lily.

She decided, in 1958, to retire from the Met. I have read that she left that organization in "undisguised disenchantment" with Rudolf Bing, then the Met's general manager. I don't remember her putting it quite like that to me; in any case it was only part of the story. Lily was ready for drastic changes in her life, ready to leave her professional career, to leave New York for Southern California, and, since I did not feel at all comfortable with that idea, to leave without me.

I cannot say it came as a shock, really. Our careers had sometimes overlapped—we did guest appearances together, for example—but as my broadcasting career gradually gave way to more and more live concerts, I began to travel farther and wider every year. In sharp contrast, Lily's commitment continued to center around the opera in New York. By the time she made her decision to retire she had discovered Southern California. The climate and the beauty of the land appealed to her. She wanted to close the door on her professional life, ease the pace of days so that there would be time for the enjoyment of nature, which she dearly loved. I simply was not ready for that kind of radical change. I did not ever entertain the idea of retirement, anyway. But I did understand. And so did Lily. We were friends and we remained so.

Lily went to Juarez until the divorce was arranged. To escape the press, I went to Puerto Rico. We telephoned each other every day. One evening on the way to a restaurant with some friends I saw the headlines in the papers some little boys were selling: LILY

PONS Y ANDRE KOSTELANETZ DIVORCA. Inside the restaurant I opened the huge menu, and my eye was caught immediately by one of the entrées: "Filet of Sole Lily Pons."

There was no bitterness about the end of our marriage. We had come to it gradually; we were not aware as we went along that we were growing apart. Our lives were essentially directed by our careers, which after all was true even before we met.

Reaching Out

Soon after Lily and I returned to our brand-new home from the USO tours, we answered a "command performance" call from San Francisco. The occasion was the founding conference of the United Nations—a term first used by Franklin Roosevelt early in the war to refer to the nations of the world united against the Axis powers. The conference convened April 25, 1945, ten days after Roosevelt's death, and went to June 26, by which time the world delegates had drafted the UN charter. The war in Europe had ended, the war with Japan would go on for two more months; still, the mood was victory and, as the UN meeting reflected, it was underwritten by the urgent hope for lasting peace. The "world of tomorrow" was going to have a second chance. . . .

It was after that concert, which celebrated the new international consciousness, that I began to realize what effect the tours, the war itself, had had on me.

In the first days of making music for soldiers who had fought and would have to return to battle, my only thought was to provide immediate relief for them in the hope that music would give solace and pleasure. But as the weeks and months went by, that prevailing purpose began to lengthen to a feeling of responsibility, an urge to reach out more than I ever had with what I treasured and believed in most—music. To give concerts as often as I could and in as many places as possible was not just a wartime goal. It became a lifetime intention.

I was especially proud to be asked to conduct the Liverpool Symphony in a concert in London in 1946, because it was to be a benefit for a celebrated group of World War II fighters, the commandos.

In India during the second USO tour, I had met and talked with some of these men. But it was not until after the war that I found out more about commando activities. These irregular units of highly qualified volunteers were ruggedly trained for particularly dangerous work. Drawn from every level of Britain's population, civilian as well as military, they were formally called Combined Operations Force and were small bands capable of surprise attack by land, sea, and air. One of their famous missions was a series of raids on Field Marshal Rommel's tank corps headquarters in North Africa in 1941. On another, in 1944, a commando group captured the Dutch island of Walcheren, in the North Sea. Soon after, British troops landed there and drove on into Antwerp.

Clearly the concert was meant to express deep appreciation. To permit the attendance of as many people as possible, it was to be played in Albert Hall. An impressive place—not ideal for music but, because of its capacity, ideal for bringing together a huge number of people. Among them would be the royal family. With this knowledge beforehand—and with my personal delight at being able to participate in the tribute—you can be sure I was determined all would go well.

Prior to the concert a droll, gentlemanly official and I had a brief meeting. His voice still echoes in my mind, polite, definite, British. "I must tell you," he said, "that the royal family like the anthem played very slowly—and I must say, it is wonderful that way. Here is what I suggest: you go on onstage in about five minutes. The public will greet you, and then you remain standing facing them and the royal box. Presently, you will see a small red light go on right next to the box, and that means the royal family are arriving. And at that moment you begin the anthem . . ."

Grateful for such clear instructions, confident, I went onstage, acknowledged a warm greeting, and then remained in position facing the audience. I could barely see them in the almost total darkness. Now, the red light would come on "right next to the box." I glanced in what I was sure the proper direction . . . Where was the box? Was it that faint bulging outline at least two miles away? "A small red light. . . ." The question of when it would go on was now academic because how would I see it?

So I stood there, half smiling out into the darkness, and waited. And then there was suddenly an unmistakable sound, thousands of people rising to their feet. That was enough for me. I began the anthem. "Very slowly."

I experienced a thrill of a different sort after the performance when I was presented to George VI, the queen consort, Elizabeth, and their two daughters, Elizabeth and Margaret. The Queen told me she very much enjoyed the concert version of *Porgy and Bess*— once again confirming the British fondness for Gershwin. Princess Margaret said she had all my records—and a standing order with Columbia for all my new releases!

I am smiling to myself because that remark reminds me of the time a few years ago when I was asked by the producers of *Goodbye, Columbus* if I would mind the use of a similar remark in the film. The script called for a rather one-dimensional, sports-minded teen-ager to ask his sister's sophisticated New York beau if he would like to see his Kostelanetz record collection. I said I didn't mind at all, and the remark went into the film.

To dismiss a nagging notion that the incident was an affront to my work, I concentrated on a healthier interpretation: that my efforts to reach out with music, good music, were successful. Indeed, many of those who shun classical music do so because it seems too intricate, too unintelligible, too formidable. Perhaps the label "serious" music is forbidding, suggesting anything but the enormous pleasure that is the intention of composers, the goal of interpreters. And so the mixing of the "light" with the "serious" is my way of making a stranger to music an acquaintance and, perhaps, a loving friend.

And sensitivity to music is, I think, to a large extent inculcated and thereby a matter of chance. People can discover it at any time. It might be a revelation leading to lifelong delight or only a brief encounter of no consequence. Say a nonlistener is invited to a concert by a music-loving friend; the music is extraordinary and the friend's enthusiasm contagious. A revelation. On the other hand, a child might be forced to sit through a long foreign-language opera or to take the unwanted discipline of piano lessons; he has not been thoughtfully introduced to music but has had it pushed upon him. It might be a very long time, maybe never, before music will weave a spell for him.

I once received a brief note from a young lady in junior high school. This is how she expressed her revelation: "I attended your concert on March 28. I enjoyed the piece called *La Valse*. It woke me up"!

Lily and I spent some happy weeks traveling in France after the war. In Paris we met Lew Kowarski, whom I had not seen since his family sheltered me in Vilna on my way to Warsaw. At that time he was a young boy. I doubt I would have recognized him so many years later, but when we were introduced the name was an immediate echo of those long-ago days. Lew had studied science in Lyons and Paris. After France fell in 1940, he went to England to continue his work in nuclear physics, bringing with him the French supply of heavy water, an oddly prescient action since he had no knowledge at the time of the part heavy water would play in the creation of the atom bomb.

Sadly, that visit in Paris was the last I would have with him. I read occasionally of his work, but our paths did not cross again. Just recently I saw the notice of his death in the paper. Strange how people, sometimes perfect strangers, can touch your life at a certain moment with just the help needed—for a second in time instruments of your fate—and then are gone.

Lew was not the only echo of earlier days I encountered. I recall a particular lunch with Rachmaninoff—in fact, the last time I would see him, too—and there at the table was Alexander Aslanof! Dear Aslanof, who had hired me at the opera in Kislovodsk. That was quite a long lunch, there was so much to tell. But what I remember most is how he laughed when Rachmaninoff took out his beautiful, jewel-encrusted cigarette case and offered us a smoke. There, neatly side by side under the gold spring bar, were the smallest cigarettes we'd ever seen. The composer explained that his doctor had ordered him to "cut down" and he had, quite literally!

In the late Forties I did return to broadcasting for a while, conducting the Chrysler program, but concert appearances and recording began to take up the larger part of my time. The listening ground was widening, and one of the most rewarding and inspiring developments was the outdoor concert.

Minnie Guggenheimer, an art patron and successful business-woman, started the project—destined to endure as a great tradition —in New York City in 1918. The idea was to provide good music to many people at low prices. So Lewisohn Stadium, way uptown at 138th Street and Convent Avenue, was for many years New York's only open-air concert hall. Prices could be kept to a mini-mum because soloists and conductors accepted nominal amounts instead of their customary fees. (Orchestra members received their regular rates.)

When I conducted there for the first time it was with an orchestra I would become very happily attached to in the ensuing years, the New York Philharmonic-Symphony (the "Symphony" was later dropped). Our association with one another can be counted in decades; I have come to think of these ladies and gentlemen as my family.

My first contract with the Philharmonic was signed in 1953, and my first assignment was to conduct three special Saturday night concerts at Carnegie Hall, the orchestra's home before Lincoln Center was completed some years later. The "special" part of these concerts was the fact that they would be entirely nonsubscription, which meant that each performance would not have the security blanket of a virtually presold house. For as much faith as I had in music and in myself, I must say that the challenge caused me to swallow hard a few times. The idea was Arthur Judson's. He had been managing the orchestra for many years—thirty, I think, by that time—and had seen the same faces in the audience season after season. It was time to do something about that.

Well, the day came and with it a genuine full-fledged snow-storm. This would be a real test. I deliberately avoided checking on how many seats were filled when I arrived at the hall and went directly to my dressing room for some last-minute words with my librarian and old friend from CBS, Lou Robbins. Just before I was to go out to the stage, Judson's chief associate, Bruno Zirato, stuck his head in the door and said the magic words: "Sold out!" Suddenly I felt elated, floating among the peaks. "Lou," I said, "where do we go from here?"

At the program's conclusion I expected the audience to waste no time getting away, especially in view of the weather. But they just went on applauding. The Philharmonic did not play encores at subscription concerts. The orchestra was officially opposed to the idea and did not like even a soloist to do it. (In fact, Yehudi Menuhin once caused a minor shock wave by playing an encore.) I never thought to prepare any, even though this concert was a departure from the norm. So I found myself in an embarrassing situation—everybody sitting out there clapping and we did not play. After that, though, we always played at least three encores at the nonsubscription concerts, at times as many as five or six. Once, we did seven. Five encores is one thing, seven is going out on a limb! By the time we reached number five, Zirato confessed later, everybody backstage was getting a bit nervous, but we got through the seven, our listeners' enthusiasm undiminished. And then somebody came up with the idea that encores, which are relatively short and musically appealing to everybody, would make perfect recording material. Soon after, I did make a record, called *Encores*, and that idea turned out to be true.

The underlying idea of the Carnegie Hall special concert series was to expand the audience for good music, and it was a success, continuing as part of the musical season in subsequent years. The programs ranged widely; on a given evening the audience—invariably a full house plus standees—might hear Rimsky-Korsakov, Khachaturian, Beethoven, Toch, and Grofé. This was another demonstration of the "democracy of music" I believe in, and New

York, the proverbial "melting pot" that has always welcomed a variety of cultures, was an ideal setting.

One duty of a conductor is to be resourceful in enriching the music repertoire. This can be done in several ways: by revivifying music too long ignored (yes, there are fashions even in music); by discovering works and giving them their first performance; and by acting as a kind of catalyst through the commissioning of new music. Koussevitzky was a great one to commission, but not many conductors do. I don't know why. To me being on hand for the birth of music from composers like Aaron Copland, Paul Creston, William Schuman, Virgil Thomson, Ferde Grofé, and Alan Hovhaness—the catalyst role—has been my favorite. Each experience was special in its own way, and, of course, there was always the suspense of the premiere—how would the music be received?

In the case of one of Hovhaness's works, suspense was an element right from the beginning. I received a phone call from Carlos Moseley, president of the Philharmonic at the time. Three young men had appeared in his office with a tape of whales singing. Would I like to hear it? Why not?

Within half an hour I was listening to the sound patterns of the humpback whale . . . a bewildering variety of pitches, startling wails, low, almost oboelike moans, altogether fascinating and at times very moving.

I subsequently learned that one scientist in particular, Dr. Roger Payne, had for some years been studying the humpback—sadly, a nearly extinct species because of illegal killing of these magnificent animals for their oil. The modern method of killing is particularly horrible; a small cannon, mounted on the forecastle of a fast vessel, fires a harpoon containing an explosive charge into one of these gentle giants. From the safety of their invulnerable craft, the hunters can watch the last agony of a dying creature, a dying species. Greed seems to bring out the very worst in the human being. Dr. Payne had made tapings off the coast of Bermuda to gain better understanding of how sea animals communicate. Some of the details are fascinating: the songs are transmitted over distances that can reach an astonishing number of miles through a sound channel, a path of water that has special acoustical qualities; each whale probably sings a distinctly individual song; nobody knows how whales sing, since they have no vocal cords.

My first thought was how to bring man-made music into the picture. My second thought was to call Hovhaness, whom I knew as a gifted composer, always interested in new ventures. He was intrigued and immediately inspired to compose. I suggested selecting segments of the songs and surrounding them with music. We sat down with the tapes—there were several, not just one—and listened for hours. It wasn't easy but finally we agreed on four sections.

Hovhaness had to go to London, but he said he would write whenever he could and send the results to me, which he did. Within two weeks his contribution was complete. Finding a title took almost as much time. Finally we went to the Bible for inspiration, and there it was, Genesis 1:21—"And God created great whales . . ."

The composition was amazingly beautiful, I thought, a new language of sound. The premiere was in 1970. The critics were, on the whole, receptive.

There were disappointments, too, of course. In the case of a Virgil Thomson commission there was plenty of excitement beforehand, just as with the Hovhaness, but as it turned out, the show was virtually over before it started. It was during the war. On the advice of a friend who said that Thomson had written many musical portraits, I approached him to ask if he would compose one of a great American, as Jerome Kern did of Mark Twain, and Copland of Lincoln. And Thomson said he would— how about Roosevelt? A wonderful choice, but since for every portrait Thomson wrote the subject had to "sit" for him, I said it would be impractical . . . the President during a world war? And the same was true for his next suggestion, Mrs. Roosevelt. So he said why not Fiorello La Guardia, Mayor of New York? That was fine. I said I would call him myself and ask.

La Guardia was most congenial. By all means, he said, let Virgil

Thomson come to City Hall, and while I transact the city's business he can write the portrait. Of course, we all landed in *Time* Magazine.

Virgil called his composition *Mayor La Guardia Waltzes*. I have no idea what there was about the mayor that suggested a waltz. But, worse, the music just didn't seem substantial to me; it was in fact rather silly. Nevertheless, I conducted the premiere in Lewisohn Stadium, and naturally invited the mayor to come.

Mayor La Guardia was late for the concert; we'd finished playing the *Waltzes* by the time I heard the sirens approaching. I'll never know if La Guardia had somehow sensed it would be better to arrive late or whether he was simply very busy. In any case, since he hadn't heard the music he wouldn't have to comment on it one way or the other. Alas, others did.

———

For one of the Carnegie Hall special concerts I added a piece to the program at the last minute, something I had recently "discovered." Without knowing it, I had begun my "Cambodian adventure."

There was a State Department packet among my mail one day in 1954. I opened it and discovered that it had been delivered to the United States by D. R. Heath, American Ambassador to Cambodia, and that it contained, of all things, a music score by Norodom Sihanouk, then king of that country! My immediate reaction was, to say the most, casual. There was no note, so I confess I did not even glance at the score itself that day, but simply laid these "Cambodian Sketches" on a shelf and in a very few moments had forgotten all about them. The day would come when I would appreciate the ignorant bliss of such casual negligence.

The "Sketches" had been sleeping peacefully for weeks by the time I noticed them again. I don't know what prompted me to read the score then. Curiosity? And a mild attack of conscience, too, perhaps. Well, the music was not what I had thought it would be—not a far-fetched notion of an otherworldly king and, most surprising, not bad. Not at all bad. In fact, the more I looked at the score the more I realized it was delightful, full of *nostalgie* and grace. Certainly the French influence was not so unusual when I came to think of it. After all, Cambodia had been connected to France, politically and otherwise, for more than a hundred years. I determined to bring the music to life.

After making a few minor adjustments in the orchestration, I rehearsed it with the Philharmonic and, as I said, added it to one of the programs of the Saturday night concerts as the *Cambodian Suite* in three parts, "Berceuse," "Nostalgia," and "Dance."

The cablegram arrived not too long afterward. One doesn't normally think of a cablegram as a particularly elegant form of communication, but this one was an exception. It was two pages long, all in French, and signed "Le Roi de Cambodge, Norodom Sihanouk." I started to read. "Mon cher maître . . ." The king first explained that a radio listener in Canada had happened to tape the performance of the Suite and was thoughtful enough to send the composer a copy. And then, with all the style and grace of the French language when it is so well mastered, he expressed his delight, his gratitude, his happiness . . . and would I honor the warm feeling of friendship he had for me by accepting his invitation to come to Cambodia as his guest?

It was my turn to feel honored. And, as it happened, I had already made plans to take advantage of a twenty-nine-day break between concerts with the Philharmonic by making my first round-the-world trip. Why not add Phnom Penh to my tour? It was, or so I thought then, readily accessible from Bangkok, which was already on my schedule. I wrote to the king that I accepted his invitation with the greatest pleasure.

My fascination with the Orient was born during the World War II tours. I had returned several times and now once again I was surrendering to the lure of the Eastern cultures.

By the time I reached Bangkok I was filled with anticipation about the trip to Cambodia. It was a country I had never seen. I would have to make arrangements fast to get to Phnom Penh by the next evening because the king had planned a banquet in my honor. Discovering that there were no commercial flights to

Phnom Penh was a minor problem—I would just go to the U.S. ambassador's office and see about engaging a private plane. I was secretly delighted because I thought I might persuade my pilot to take a detour over Angkor Wat on the way.

At Ambassador Putifoy's office I found two old friends from the wartime days, Lowell Thomas and Jim Thompson. The famous author and traveler, Jim, and I had all been members of the F.H.B.'s—Fair Haired Bastards—a service club established by Dr. Margaret Chung in San Francisco for pilots who had served humanity in some special way. We all had numbers and now I heard my own: "Hello, four-three-four! And just what brings you here?"

It was Jim. In very short order he arranged for a plane. The pilot would pick me up at my hotel the next morning.

And there he was, at 6:30 A.M., a serious-looking young fellow beckoning me to his car. I settled in the backseat to enjoy my parting views of the exquisite city as we rode to the airfield.

My pilot was not the talkative sort, and so offered no explanation as to why the car slowed suddenly and came to a stop in front of a pagoda. Well, the reason was soon evident in any case: he did not get out of the car but simply joined his hands and bowed his head in silent prayer. It was only for a few moments and then we resumed the ride. I was admiring a second temple that was coming into view—and then I realized we were slowing down again. The pilot repeated his ritual. There were six more pagodas on the way, and six more such acknowledgments. I could not help respecting such devotion—and I am not prone to undue anxiousness—but as we drew away from the final scene of prayer I wondered just what the pilot had been praying *for*. . . .

The plane was a twin-engine Cessna. We climbed in. The pilot began checking various switches and then the radio. "Cessna three five double oh calling tower. . . ." Several times. No response. . . . I said nothing. Somehow I felt it would be impolite and might cause intense embarrassment for the pilot. But I was very glad we had all those prayers on our side.

As we became airborne the pilot assured me that he knew the route very well and everything would be all right. I told him I used to fly myself and that I would appreciate a short turn at the controls. He agreed. The day was perfect for flying. In the pleasure of it I forgot everything else. When the pilot took the wheel again I asked if we could see the ancient temple ruins of Angkor. Of course, he said. There would be no problem.

It was warm in the cockpit, the sun was strong. I felt myself dozing off. It was so easy. . . . Some time must have passed before I woke up. The pilot said Angkor Wat was just below. I was completely thrilled with the sight: the magnificent temple, the vast moat, the causeway across it in the form of giant Nagas (divine serpents), the towers and colonnades . . . all of it spread just 300 feet below us.

I noticed that the needle on the right gas gauge was all the way over to the left. Empty. Remain calm. Check the left gauge. The needle was all the way left. Well, surely the pilot was aware of the situation.

I said, "How far is it to Phnom Penh?"

"Twenty minutes," he said.

"And how much gas do we have?"

"Six minutes."

He explained that some gasoline must have leaked. I think we both knew, though, that this was not true, that he had, in fact, failed to check before leaving, but we chose to ignore further discussion on that matter. We had to find a place to come down. At once. Preferably safely. The terrain was mostly thick jungle. Not hopeful. But then we saw water below, a river, and—the important thing—a narrow strip of flat land alongside it wide enough to land on. But was it clear of stones and rocks? Crash-landing a small plane on a rocky surface can be disastrous. One fair-size stone can turn the plane over. But no, my optimistic pilot was certain the strip was smooth enough.

He asked me to turn all switches to OFF and, as soon as we landed, throw open the door.

The ground was coming up fast now, and we could see, yes, stones. They were everywhere. But it was time to throw the switches. I swept my hand across the panel as if it were a xylophone. We hit the next second. Great noise, thunderous, as the stones bumped and pounded against the fuselage. The plane skidded and rocked crazily and then stopped. Neither of us was hurt. It was all right. We remained in our seats.

"Good landing," I said.

I resisted the urge to remind him of what every pilot knows: *any landing you walk away from is a good landing!*

It wasn't long before we realized we had been observed. Faces were visible through the trees, and soon a crowd of wild-looking men (I later learned they were Anamites) came close to the plane. They were dressed in tatters, and their eyes seemed to threaten although their movements did not. They did not speak. We got out of the plane, and the pilot tried Khmer, the Cambodian language, and we both tried French, but without response.

Finally one man stepped out from the group, and as he began to speak to us in French, I noticed that he had only one tooth. He agreed to take me to a nearby village—when I asked the name, he would not say. Or perhaps he did but I could not make it out. The pilot would stay with the plane until I could get gasoline sent back to him.

I followed my one-tooth rescuer through the jungle. We waded streams and cut through brush and tramped dusty trails. It was a strenuous walk but luckily not too long. The first thing I did in the village was telephone the Phnom Penh airport. The secretary to King Sihanouk was at the phone. I explained what had happened and asked help for the pilot. The secretary said he had a good idea where we might be and would be leaving immediately to find me. Since there was only one road out of the village, we would be sure to meet eventually. Then I looked around for possible transportation.

I noticed a bus apparently ready to leave. Its motor was idling, and I saw passengers inside. The driver agreed to let me aboard and said he was heading for Phnom Penh. I thanked my rescuer and stepped into the bus. When my eyes got used to the dimness I saw clearly who the other passengers were. It was an arresting sight: twelve monks seated two by two, all in saffron robes, all silent with eyes straight ahead. They were grand in their immobility. I think it was their profound quietness that struck me the most. They were like some voiceless background chorus to the whirlwind of thoughts and feelings I was experiencing. I backed slowly into a seat at the front of the bus, and we began to move.

Progress was bumpy and very slow. From time to time puffs of red dust came up through the floorboards of the bus.

I attempted some conversation with the driver, but it was mostly a silent ride. Occasionally I looked at the monks. Never once did they acknowledge my glances or give the smallest sign that they were aware of any of their surroundings. An hour or so must have gone by before the secretary's car met us on the road. During that time I was in a state of consciousness I cannot fully describe. Certainly exhilaration at having come so close to death and surviving—all my senses were sharp and tingling, released from the tension of fear. But there was another, subtler element, a peacefulness that seemed to drift through me like a mist. I will always wonder if the presence of those monks had anything to do with it.

Night comes early in countries near the equator. By the time the king's secretary and I reached the cottage on the palace grounds that had been prepared for me it was dark, although only about six o'clock. Just before the secretary left, he asked that I be ready for the king's banquet at eight, a half hour before the rest of the guests arrived. The king wished to greet me privately.

I went inside to make myself presentable for the events of the evening. My first inspection of myself in the mirror was quite a shock. The face looking back at me was completely covered in red dust. What fine manners the secretary had not to have shown any reaction whatsoever to my alarming appearance.

Just before eight a chauffeur called for me. The ride through the grounds gave every indication that we were approaching the palace of a king. The long road was lined on both sides with palm trees, and posted at each was a soldier holding a lighted torch. Mysterious shapes and shadows in the distance hinted at magnificent landscaping beyond the light of the torches. Treetops were silhouetted against a red sky, the afterglow of a splendid sunset. It was eerily lovely, a perfect dramatic prelude to my first sight of the king.

He stood alone, a silhouette against the glowing marble steps of the palace, waiting for me. I had heard him described as full of *joie de vivre* and with a grand sense of humor. But there was no laughter in his face now. His eyes were grave as he came to embrace me.

"You have risked your life for me," he said. "And you have played my music."

I've made many trips to the Orient, each time with increased anticipation of its utter foreignness. The eyes see new colors, the ears hear new sounds. Experiencing the East is a matter of absorption, of applying to your senses and instincts for directions. Beauty is ever-changing forms, delicate extensions into mystery. What Archibald MacLeish calls the "inner landscape" is soothed, enticed, expanded.

No matter how much time is spent in a watchful drift through the streets of those hot, dazzling cities—Bangkok, say, or Singapore, Hong Kong, Kuala Lumpur—through the noise, odors, dust and heat, contrasts of old and new, the attraction does not fade. I suppose the core of that attraction is the mysteriousness, the exotica of the Orient. And when you finally leave, it is with the feeling, as Somerset Maugham has said, that "you have missed something," that some secret has been kept from you.

The temptation to take photographs is especially strong in such places of closely guarded mystery. Perhaps something significant but unseen at the time will reveal itself in a picture. I had done dutiful picture-taking on other trips, and would again, but for this first round-the-world adventure I'd decided to take a tape recorder instead of a camera. Of Ceylon (now called Sri Lanka), for example, I have echoes instead of snapshots. To record the pera hera, or full-moon celebration, I simply hung the tape machine in a tree and left it on while a magnificent procession passed: shouts of young boys dancing; bells tinkling as decorated elephants swayed by; songs, fifes, tambours . . .

That tape proved to me that sounds can be a forceful sensory reminder of an experience, as stirring to perception and memory as any photograph. And they not only bestir a visual image but re-create its aural dimension, the beauty of which is often otherwise forgotten.

Subsequently I took a tape recorder on many other trips. In London I got permission to tape the Tower closing ceremony, which had gone on for eight hundred years, even during the Blitz in World War II. Piercing, almost menacing shouts of "Close the gates! Close the gates!" And then they come together in thunder-ous finality. Listening, you shudder to think of the grimness of the Tower's prison history. In Paris, I taped the ancient chimes of Sacré-Coeur and the bells of Nôtre Dame; in Kyoto, a deep, earth-trembling gong; in a Granada garden, the song of a nightingale, which was quite a challenge as I didn't want other sounds to in-trude. Once, in a café in Israel, I heard a wonderful song played by a gypsy fiddler. I taped it and when I came home transcribed it for piano and then asked Julius Burger, assistant conductor at the Met, to arrange it for orchestra. It appeared in the *Rumanian Fantasy* album. Oscar Levant later told me that once as a guest in Toscanini's home he'd heard it over and over on the record player —and very loud. The maestro was apparently much taken with that gypsy melody.

On my way to Hong Kong and then home after the Cambodian episode, I returned to Bangkok for the first of several visits over the years with Jim Thompson. I'd met Jim originally the day the Burma Road was reopened, in February of 1945—he was one of the OSS officers with whom Lily and I ate those Blum chocolates by way of celebration. Toward the end of the war, orders took him to Thailand. He liked it so much he decided to make it home after his Army discharge.

By the time of this visit with him, some ten years later, he had nourished the almost extinct Thai silk industry to the level of a thriving business. Thai handwoven silks have become internation-ally prized, with colors that shimmer like forest pools. They have been gifts for queens, and they have been used for costumes in Broadway shows, *The King and I* for one, which is set in Siam (the old name for Thailand).

Jim was a man of great charm. He had lived in Asia so long and was so open to its ways that he had become almost Oriental himself. The inner calm, the delight in simplicity, the special Far Eastern rhythm and deliberateness of his movements.

Jim had studied architecture at school and retained a love for it. Thai architecture was particularly appealing to him, understandably. Whether for domestic buildings or wats, the temples, it is a combination of the imaginative and the practical, simple, light, and upward-reaching in feeling. The houses, unlike the temples, are not colorful and have a minimum of decoration. No nails are used in the construction, which is basically premade sections hung on a superstructure. Jim's home was made by joining several old Thai houses and nestling the whole on the bank of one of the klongs (canals) that flow through Bangkok. Because of its snake-like twists, it is called Maha Nag, which means "Big Naga" after the half-human, half-serpent water spirit of Hindu myth.

The house contained Jim's collection of Oriental art, the most arresting I had ever seen—tapestries, Buddhas and demons of various periods in Thai cultural history, and pottery, including the stunning five-color Bencharong porcelains made in China after Thai designs. I felt I was living in an exquisite personal world that was made so as much by the charm and modesty of its owner as by the intrinsic beauty of the art itself. It was my first real encounter with Asian art, and I was completely taken by it. There is about it an inner life of serenity that seems to reach into the soul. The house was a perfect setting for the appreciation of its treasures. The light that entered through the long, wide windows was filtered by the closeness of the tropical plants just outside. There was a certain amount of traffic on the klong and tree-life sounds from luxuriant gardens—to which Jim's pet cockatoo, "Cocky," might murmur a response—but nothing disturbed. The tranquil beauty of the place had aural as well as visual dimension.

I thought I would like to begin a collection of my own, so Jim took me to a dealer one morning—and there it was, a lovely Buddha, not large, with the most arresting expression. . . . Jim said I must own it and not worry about getting it to New York—he would take care of the shipping. The price was not high, only a few hundred dollars; yet I hesitated. Why I will never know. That was not the last I saw of the piece, though. Some time later I was visiting Asia House here in New York, and there in one corner was "my" Buddha. As I gazed at it I indulged myself in a fleeting but comforting fantasy: the dealer had known I would regret my hesitation and so had arranged a situation where there would at least be a chance for me to see the statue as often as I wished!

After an early lunch one afternoon, I went with Jim on a small boat through the klongs to visit one of the families who made up the Thai Silk Company. There were only five looms in use when he had first arrived in Bangkok. Now the system of silk-weaving families totaled almost 4,000 workers. There was no factory; instead, the weavers worked in their homes. Jim dropped in on one or another of them periodically, as he was doing this day, to make suggestions about colors and design and to keep track of production. I still have some of the utterly beautiful silks, with which Jim was always so generous.

He was interested in music though not very deeply. Still, he helped me to hear some of the Thai players. There are no concerts, or at least I never heard one. Music is a more personal matter, enjoyed on a much smaller scale. If you visit a friend for dinner, for example, you might well expect to hear an intimate concert from a single musician, who might have brought a clarinet-like instrument or a gamelan, which is a Javanese xylophone. The music is completely different from anything we produce in the West and so, while it is interesting and pretty, it takes some time to get to the realm of familiarity where a true appreciation can begin.

It has been about thirteen years since I've seen Jim Thompson. One day he simply disappeared. The circumstances were utterly casual and yielded nothing in the way of clues. He was visiting friends in the Cameron Highlands, a popular Malaysian resort area some 5,000 feet above sea level. After lunch he decided to take a walk by himself. The last sound of him was his footsteps on the gravel path as he walked away from the house. He undoubtedly hadn't planned to be gone long, because he left without his cigarettes and bottle of pills he always had to have with him.

Search parties never found a trace of him. At one point there was high expectation that word would come about a ransom demand, since bands of kidnappers were known to operate in the area, preying chiefly on wealthy Chinese businessmen. But weeks went by without any information whatsoever turning up. The mystery took on a new dimension a month after Jim's disappearance when his sister, who lived in Chicago, was murdered at her home. There was no evidence that her dogs had been aroused by an unwelcome stranger.

After so many years it is not reasonable to expect to see Jim again, and yet the very unreasonableness of the situation keeps hope alive. I can't help thinking there was some significance in the fact that he was in the OSS during the war and that he had dealt with all the prominent Communists in Malaysia. Perhaps he was caught in some awful embroilment in international politics. . . . When someone close to you dies it is awful enough, but the finality of death can be, must be, accepted eventually. By contrast, a disappearance leaves nothing final to come to terms with.

Those who knew Jim will treasure their memories of his generosity of spirit. Unwittingly, he left a legacy of beauty to the world at large, too; his house and its collection of Asian art is now a national museum.

I think of Jim walking into the jungle that last time. Has he entered some other scheme of things? Somerset Maugham was right—the Orient does keep its secrets well, and Jim Thompson has become one of them.

————

The first time I met Maugham was in the Columbia studios in New York about thirty years ago. He was preparing material for televised versions of some of his short stories. I noticed that for the recording sessions he was completely untroubled by his well-known stutter.

In Istanbul a few years later I saw a notice of his arrival in the paper, and so I called him. He said we should have dinner that evening—could I meet him in the hotel lobby at six-thirty, just after his press conference?

When I came down, however, Maugham was still surrounded.

At his suggestion I went up to his suite to have a drink with his secretary, Alan Searle. And there we were, Alan and I, gazing out at the view—the Bosporus and the Sea of Marmara beyond—and having a quiet chat when the door flew wide open to reveal Maugham in the grip of absolute rage. His face was a deep violet. For a moment I thought he was close to a stroke.

"These awful Turks," he yelled. "They've been reading my books for years, and I've never received a cent in royalties!" That didn't seem to justify the alarming state he'd got himself into. And it was not quite over. A few minutes later an unsuspecting news-man came to the door and asked for an interview. Of course, Maugham was just then in no mood to give anything away, so he was quite strong in his refusal. But hardly had the door closed when he was assailed by self-doubt. He turned to Alan. "Do you think I was too short with him?" Suddenly the incident had be-come a comic vignette, and we all laughed.

Travel was the centerpiece of our conversation. Maugham, then in his eighties, continued his lifelong habit of spending time in foreign places. He was partial to Spain and the Far East and had returned many times to both places. When I asked him if revisit-ing a city where his first experience had been entrancing had ever been a disappointment, he turned the tables on me. Did con-ductors get tired of doing the same music over and over? And I fell for it, reminding him that Jeanne Eagels had played Sadie Thompson for several years on Broadway in *Rain*—a play adapted from one of his own stories, "Miss Thompson." "Apparently there is always something new to be found," I wound up.

"Exactly," said Maugham. He liked to return to places where he'd had a wonderful time to see if he could find greater wonder. He willingly took the risk of disappointment.

Of course, he'd maneuvered our conversation so I'd answer my own question. I realized I had just had a lesson in the Socratic method.

One of the grandest things about the profession of conducting is the opportunity to travel and work at the same time. On my occasional vacations I do travel to places that have no orchestra, like Tahiti, for instance, but inevitably I miss giving a concert. Then there are countries that make up for that. Like New Zealand or Australia, where you could give a concert a day for a week, each in a different city. Sydney, Melbourne, Adelaide, and Perth all have orchestras, and a visiting conductor will be asked to perform in all of them.

Something I realized early in trying to expand the listening ground with live concerts was that the more I gave in music the more I received in the way of discovering the wonders of this world, human or otherwise.

On the ride in from the Denver airport one summer morning I noticed NO WATERING caveats everywhere. Nature was showing shades of only one color, brown. I could not help thinking that this was one outdoor concert that wasn't in danger of being rained out.

Denver's Red Rocks Hotel is in arresting surroundings, where the dramatic beauty of nature is left unmarred. I had the impression of entering a Wagnerian stage setting. There was plenty of time after rehearsal for a rest, so I went to my room, drew the curtains, and lay down.

It was late afternoon when I woke up. The room was almost completely dark—my first thought was that I had slept through the concert. I hurried to the window and opened the curtains. It was dark outside, all right, but not because of the hour. The view was hidden by thick gray sheets of rain! I laughed out loud. One of the pieces we had rehearsed that morning was "Cloudburst," from Ferde Grofé's *Grand Canyon Suite*. Need I say that there was no outdoor concert that night?

The human spirit, too, can loose its wonder on the world. I knew Irene Gubrud for some time before she sang with me in Minnesota in 1975, a beautiful woman endowed with an extraordinary lyric soprano voice. When she was thirteen she was thrown from a county fair roller coaster and suffered severe damage to her spine, which kept her in a wheelchair and on crutches. Six years later she broke her left leg in thirty places. Neither accident prevented her from developing her voice or her spirit, but her professional career was necessarily limited to concert recitals. Her goal was opera, but that meant she had to walk.

Irene spent three years in Chicago with John Scudder, a therapist whose technique combines physical exercises with meditation. Some people have called him a faith healer as well. Finally Irene was able to take her first steps without crutches in eighteen years. It was just then that we were to appear together. At rehearsal she was using crutches, and I expected she would at the concert, but she asked me if I would mind if she walked without them for the performance.

I alerted the string players, just in case, as she would be passing them as she came onstage, but I knew instinctively she would be all right. Her determination was totally convincing; she left no room to doubt her strength. Her singing was brilliant, and the audience gave both of her performances a standing ovation.

John Scudder has been a friend of mine for years. I was once able to do a small favor for John's daughter. He was very grateful and asked what he might do in return. Since I had an upcoming outdoor concert I asked him to ensure good weather. Well, the evening was perfect. Ever since then I have not hesitated to call him before a park concert to ask if he can "arrange" a rainless evening. It is half in jest on my part, but so far he has a perfect record!

In any case, I have even more direct experience with unexplained though demonstrable power. During my time of refuge in the Caucasus so many years ago, I joined a group of young people who had made friends with a man who was a poet, writer, and master of Zen. We would meet him in the morning and then proceed up narrow mountain paths to the higher plateaus. There he would teach us breathing, meditation, and concentration on a single small thought, and we would practice for an hour or two.

One morning when we got to his house we found him lying in bed in an awkward position, with one arm at a stiff angle. I asked what was wrong. He told me he had terrible pain and would be unable to go with us that day. When I asked exactly where it hurt, he took my hand and placed it on his arm. Almost immediately he declared that the pain had vanished and—to my amazement—

that I had the power of healing in my hands. Natural skepticism caused me to dismiss the matter—until an opportunity arose. The next person I was able to help was my mother, by curing her of a headache. It took only three or four minutes of simply holding my hands over the area of pain, very close to it but not actually touching. I've had occasional success with helping others, too, although I have no effect on my own pains.

I've always had some resistance to taking this phenomenon with seriousness. But the idea of doing good, even without understanding the causality, is compelling and one that I gladly embrace.

I have not always been able to philosophically overlook a review —as Lily once pointed out, enthusiastic applause at the end of a performance is wonderful, but the *New York Times* is read by 2,000,000 people! But I try not to take reviews too seriously because ultimately reviewers are not the ones I want to reach.

There have been many times when I have found a reviewer's comments useful and been grateful for them; and there have also been many encouraging responses in the press to what I've tried to do. But the ones I remember best are those that have given me great amusement.

In Buenos Aires some years ago, the concert manager met me at the plane with some "very sad news"—the concert I was to conduct had been canceled because of a musicians' strike. A month or so later, Peter de Rougemont, then the director of Columbia Records in Argentina, sent me a clipping from a posh monthly magazine there. His note said I might be interested. Indeed, I was; the clipping was a review of the Buenos Aires concert I never gave! I read that the oboe in the symphony's second movement had been too loud, that the last movement was too fast. . . .

(The composer Deems Taylor did pretty much the same thing when he was the New York *World's* music critic. It so happened that laryngitis had afflicted key members of the cast of *Faust*, so the Met substituted *Aida* at the last minute. Taylor did not know of the change, nor did he attend the performance. The next day his review of *Faust* appeared in the *World*. He was fired, but there were no hard feelings, at least not on the part of the Metropolitan. They subsequently commissioned Taylor to write two operas, which he did. *The King's Henchman*, with libretto by Edna St.-Vincent Millay, was performed in 1927, and *Peter Ibbetson* in 1931.)

To be sure, reviewers do have an educative function. Their readers can rightfully expect music to be identified correctly and discussed with intelligence. However, as a general rule it is not wise to deferentially take the reviewer at his word. There must have been quite a few mystified readers of a newspaper review the morning after I had conducted in New Orleans. I had opened with the Mozart Symphony in G (K.318), unique among his symphonies in that the work is only one movement, this in contrast to the usual structure of several movements with pauses between them. To follow the classical selection, I had chosen something from the typically esoteric impressionism of Ravel's ballet music, *Mother Goose Suite*. The two traditions are as different as a century and a half of musical developments could make them. But those differences were no problem for my imaginative reviewer. The Mozart symphony, he wrote in his column, had a beautiful if unusual second movement!

That same city was the scene of a much more unsettling occurrence. A good number of years ago I arrived at my hotel there and, as was my habit, immediately asked the manager if he could send someone to help me get organized for the concert and go with me to the hall to be there for my change at intermission. The manager said fine, someone would be up at six.

Right on time a young man appeared, and we began the preparations. Just as it was time to leave he said he would put me in a cab and meet me at the hall. Very curious. Well, he explained, the fact that he was black meant he could not ride in the same taxi with a white man. I had traveled in this country enough and read enough to know there were deplorable injustices against blacks, but I had never encountered it firsthand. I felt a warm flush begin at the back of my neck. What struck me most was that the man was apparently so accustomed to this kind of abuse that he showed no reaction. This was simply the way things were.

I told him that if I couldn't find a way for us to go together, then I would not conduct that night. An old friend was the only person in the city I could think of who might help; how, I could not imagine. I immediately called him and told him the story. He said only, "Don't do anything until I get there."

Before I knew it, there was a call from the desk. We went downstairs, and there was my friend saying he had arranged everything. The three of us went outside, and there at the curb was the biggest hearse I had ever seen!

"Please, get in," said my friendly undertaker. And off we went to the concert hall. I thanked him for his spirit and for his imagination—it wasn't every day that one experienced being driven in a hearse while still alive!

Of necessity there is a certain scheme to every conductor's engagements, whether he is playing at home or out of town—a routine that acts as a safety net for the random shocks of the unexpected. The idea is to make the pattern sufficiently firm for support but elastic enough to allow for the little surprises.

Arrival in the city where I am to guest-conduct. It could be Houston or Vienna, Tokyo or Cincinnati. Greeted at airport and ushered to hotel. I have brought the music the orchestra will use; it will be distributed in time for rehearsal. (For every concert I play, Lou Robbins makes sure that all the musicians' parts are well and clearly marked with whatever editing adjustments we've worked out. It is not as easy as it may seem. Orchestras can buy music, but not always. Some has to be rented. Usually there are about twenty-five sets of a given piece available but, even so, all may have been used so many times by other orchestras that the parts are too marked up to read. It is against the law to copy them fresh for your own use, so Lou must somehow clean them up.)

Rehearsal. The score is in place in front of me. I pick up the baton. The players are fully concentrated on my raised arm, ready for the downbeat. In the course of this rehearsal for a concert of about two hours I will make at least five thousand movements with the baton, which becomes an extension of my conducting arm. Every conductor's baton is made especially for him. For years mine have been made after the design of I. A. Cary, who had the idea of fitting the held end of the featherweight rigid birch stick with a slightly bulbous piece of cork.

The orchestra begins well, but the first piece is a commission, brand-new to the musicians, so I must stop them frequently for a discussion on how I think a particular section will sound better. I must accomplish this without sounding as if I am imposing my will. (Which, of course, I am!) After two or three of these breaks I feel my concentration begin to falter. What is going on between the first and second bassoon players? Every time I stop they begin to talk. I am now concentrating on controlling myself, but fuming inside nevertheless. Don't they want this concert to be a success? After all, it is a benefit for their own orchestra's retirees. . . .

At intermission I find the orchestra manager and politely ask if he can shed some light on the behavior of his bassoonists. Oh, he neglected to warn me that the second bassoonist has a mild hearing problem, just troublesome enough that the first bassoonist has to tell him everything the conductor says! I thank the manager.

Rehearsal finishes around noon. Usually there is only one, although in some cities the orchestra is well enough endowed to allow for two or even a luxurious three. Light lunch, then a massage and rest.

Conductors' activities vary before and after a performance, but all have some sort of routine that will least interfere with their concentration and allow the maximum rest. I know of very few who eat large meals, for instance, either before or after. On the way to the concert, Koussevitzky would sample some chocolate bars, which his driver would have placed in the car. I remember sitting with Pierre Monteux in his hotel in Chicago about an hour before he was to conduct the Chicago Symphony. It was a hot July evening, no air conditioning, so he sat near a fan while eating half a ham sandwich and drinking some black coffee. After the performance he would have only a bowl of cereal. We talked little. Reserved quiet was part of his preparation.

Fritz Reiner's pattern allowed for a postconcert treat. He would put on a velvet smoking jacket and relax over a meal of two little salami sandwiches and two martinis, which his wife had prepared for him.

After the afternoon rest, I have some fruit or a salad. If there has been no opportunity for rest, I am not concerned. I know the fatigue will conveniently vanish in the urgency of the performance.

The concert. From the moment I raise the baton there is nothing in my mind but the music. It weaves a connection between me and the orchestra, an invisible web of fabulous intricacy. Only the final applause dissolves that connection and restores us to our physical surroundings. We acknowledge the applause of the audience. I've been virtually unaware of their presence up to now, but their response is as necessary to me—and as gratifying—as the music because it assures me that I have accomplished what I came to do.

I avoid whatever parties there might be; I must travel tomorrow and begin preparation for the next concert engagement. A quiet chat and a drink with a friend in my hotel room is my preference, but tonight the opportunity does not present itself. I will be alone.

A situation has changed with breath-taking speed: minutes ago I was being applauded by thousands, accepted, thanked. Now a silent hotel room. For the moment the exhilaration has no place to go, but I know from experience that it will dissipate, slowly. Plenty of time to let a little air out of the ego! And I will make a long-distance call to a friend. It is not easy to accept being alone at such a time of excitement, but not having someone to share it with is, however unnatural, a fact of life for a conductor. It is, like stage fright as described by Artur Rubinstein, the "price I have to pay for my wonderful life."

A small price, however, when measured against the anxieties that plague the orchestra musicians. Being subject to the "ordinary" nervousness of performing is familiar to virtually all of them. Add to that the relatively recent phenomenon of players' reactions to the noise level and discord of certain forms of modern music. I must say I was astonished when I read a newspaper article a few years ago that said German psychiatrists studied two orchestras, one that played chiefly modern music and one that concentrated on the older, more conventional repertoire. Ninety-five percent of the modern orchestra suffered a variety of far-reaching physical and psychological complaints, including headache, irritability, sleeplessness, earache, and depression. However exaggerated and unscientific these findings may be, they do suggest the vulnerability of performers.

But many musicians suffer before and during the performance of any concert, whether or not modern music is on the program. The orchestra's stress is well camouflaged from the audience, but I can sometimes see the telltale signs of paleness, trembling, perspiration. When a player's solo is coming up, his normal look of concentration can harden into stone. Two hours is a long time to be completely attentive, and yet each player must be—to the conductor's signals and to his own timing, probably the most important thing because the orchestra succeeds at its job only if it plays as a team. That means, too, that the musician must derive his satisfaction from that success of the whole because rarely will he be singled out for separate praise. For a mistake, on the other hand, he is sure to be criticized.

Sometimes the tensions of preparing for a concert can deteriorate the resources of the players so that progress is temporarily blocked. I can remember one situation when a rehearsal got bogged down because the orchestra was having trouble with an especially difficult passage. After trying to take them through it several times without success, I realized that repetition wasn't the answer, so I simply stopped the rehearsal altogether. There was to be a dress rehearsal on the morning of the concert, and I decided to rely on that. It worked. The orchestra played smoothly all the way through.

But I did not come by such insight by myself. I had the help of the painter Henri Matisse. He taught me a lesson in nonconfrontation.

Many years ago I was on the Riviera for concert engagements, and I had been invited to visit with the master one afternoon. That morning I had discovered that my music bag with all the marked scores I needed for the next concert had been lost, a special nightmare for the conductor on tour. The rest of the morning was spent in trying to deal with that problem, in addition to finding time for a rehearsal with a piano soloist, an interview, and the inevitable telephone calls. By the time I arrived at Matisse's house I was in such a state of anxiety that I found myself launching into a nonstop monologue about my morning difficulties. Matisse had some pretty odd words to say when I finally finished: "My friend, you must find the artichokes in your life!" What?

He then took my arm and guided me outside for a walk in the garden. We stopped in front of a patch of artichokes. He then explained that every morning after working for a while he came out to contemplate the play of light and shadow on the leaves of these plants. It seemed to loosen his mind, relax him, and he always found "new combinations of colors and fantastic patterns." No one was allowed to disturb him during what he called his "ritual of discovery," which was, I realized, his way not only of finding new perspectives for his work but also of restoring psychic and physical energies he had expended that morning.

The first time I experimented with discovering my own "artichokes" was when I had reached an impasse in learning Spanish. The fact that I just couldn't grasp the intricacies of the overall structure surprised me, since I had mastered other languages, so I just stopped paying any attention to it for two weeks. At the end of that time I went back to where I had left off. Amazingly, everything seemed to make sense. Since then I have used Matisse's technique successfully countless times. The key, I think, is to realize that a seemingly unsolvable problem is quite often simply the result of a clouding of the perceptions brought on by mental fatigue. Putting the whole thing out of mind might seem a bold step, but it does work.

The problem of musicians' stress begins in the conservatory or school where music study is undertaken in driving earnestness. Emphasis, deliberate or not, seems to be on striving to be best. Students are exposed early to the competitiveness that is necessary for future survival in the profession. The knowledge that they are being constantly judged, that they are only as good as their last performance, must surely plague them for the rest of their lives.

And the worst of it is that their performances suffer from this constant fear of failure. What is needed, I think, is some recognition of and attack on the problem right where it begins; perhaps some sort of program designed to give psychological insights to the problem, and to develop resources to deal with it, should be part of the regular curriculum of every music conservatory.

I have often seen stage fright at its most aggravated—in solo performers, especially pianists, The last-minute cancellation of a concert appearance is not always for the reason given by the performer; the "stomach virus" or "flu" is actually a tacit admission that panic has triumphed over well-founded trust in his talent and ability.

Sometimes a performer will not cancel but will let it be known that he is "ill"—it is really what the French call *malade imaginaire*. Thus if he makes mistakes he will be forgiven because he was playing with a handicap. And, of course, all symptoms disappear right after the performance.

I do not envy the life of the concert pianist. In addition to the fact that he is heir to the stresses of virtually all musicians, he must also worry about the instrument he will be playing. A Horowitz or Rubinstein or Michelangeli will travel with his own piano—and piano tuner. (Sometimes just five minutes before the concert begins the instrument is still being tuned to absolute perfection.) But that is not a luxury available to most performers.

Every piano is different, has its own personality, just as violins and organs do. And not all are great. Whenever a pianist has an engagement in New York, the first thing he does is go to his favorite piano company and choose from among the ten or twelve concert grands there the one he thinks will be best for him. And it makes a difference. When John Browning rehearsed with me two years ago, he used the grand at Avery Fisher Hall, but for the concert he played the Steinway he had selected. It gave a much stronger sound.

In the larger cities there is a choice of concert pianos, but in most other places the pianist just has to make do with whatever is provided.

Years of Grace

THERE ARE TWO CATEGORIES OF risk, I think. One, probably the most frequent, is taken deliberately. Dangers have been weighed against advantages and found wanting. The gambler's step is taken, knowingly. The other is much more the child of impulse. A nod to instinct. A surrender to chance. The fact that it is a risk at all is not relevant, or even apparent. Only much later, upon reflection, is it clear there was ever a risk at all.

My first impression of Sara Gene is still intact, after twenty years: utterly lovely, somewhat shy, full of graceful simplicity—all adornments that youth wears especially well. We talked for some time, and the discoveries I made about her lingered after we parted: the shyness that hid warmth and a charming ingenuousness, the simplicity and grace that seemed to be true reflections of her inner being. . . .

As it turned out the attraction was mutual. We became wonderfully close friends. We traveled together: to Japan, where we marveled at the splendor of temples in Kyoto and dined on the finest steaks in the world in Kobi; to Hong Kong, where we blazed a trail through the tightly packed bazaars; to visit Jim Thompson, in Bangkok, who was enchanted by Gene and gave her some beautiful silks for dresses; to Tahiti, where we reveled in the absence of "civilization" and found native paintings to bring home. Everything was fresh and wondrous for Gene, and I discovered the sweetness of sharing familiar treasures with someone for whom they were new.

We were married August 1, 1960, in Honolulu. And from that day we were rarely separated. Ten Gracie Square was set aglow with candlelight and the excitement of gala dinner parties. In far-off places we unearthed more new treasures, in people, in art, in nature.

Sara Gene had not traveled extensively before. She loved music, but she had not attended rehearsals or listened to a soloist rehearse in her living room. She loved art but had not collected it. It was a brand-new life for her and, seeing and experiencing these things through her eyes, it was brand-new for me, too. Everyone loved her and said we were "radiant" together. And I was radiant inside.

We were married for ten years. Then, suddenly and completely, everything was over. One day Sara Gene left—I thought only for a restful visit with her mother. But she did not return to me, not ever. I didn't understand why at the time, hadn't seen the calamity coming . . . happiness can be distracting. From the beginning I was ignorant of the risk we were taking. I can see it now, though, very clearly in the light of reflection. The considerable difference in our ages, while a mere fact by itself, did affect the final outcome. Sara Gene was caught up in the energy of youth; virtually everything in her life changed when we married, and she embraced the differences wholeheartedly. She involved herself in the details of my needs. Nothing was too much for her—she was there at concert intermissions, backstage, to make sure I had a massage and a change of shirt, eschewing the valet. She watched over me, and so lovingly and beautifully that I accepted it as her way of expressing her love. I didn't see that her own needs as a separate human being went unrecognized—by both of us. And the price of that gross oversight was paid by both of us, too.

When Sara Gene and I were approaching our tenth anniversary, I suggested we celebrate by inviting to dinner the couple we knew who seemed most in love. Well, it was a happy evening. And within a year we were all divorced. People change, and truth is too often discovered too late.

Still, I choose to remember those ten years as a blessing. There were risks taken, affection shared, genuine purpose in everything.

If we are lucky, in time we remember happiness. All else fades. Time is the magician and he worked his magic for me.

The idea had been germinating at the Philharmonic for some time: New York's winter season of fine music should be extended through the spring. Not a new idea, at least in other parts of the country and in Europe, and not always a successful one. But tempting. Everybody was pretty sure what to avoid—a repetition of the type of repertoire familiar to the winter subscription audiences, the heavier classics that seemed appropriate in the sober months of the year. But more than that, there would have to be a new dimension, something fresh, different.

One evening Sara Gene's candlelight dinner was just over here at Gracie Square. I suddenly realized that the composer William Schuman, who was then also president of Lincoln Center, was telling our guests that Andre was the person who could do it, make the adventure happen. And that is how I became artistic and musical director of the spring concerts at Lincoln Center, the Promenades. I was thrilled, flattered, excited, eager—and at the moment fresh out of ideas.

I waited for Necessity to do what it is famous for. And I waited, but Invention apparently does not always respond immediately to an urgent request.

Many weeks later, on an island in the British West Indies where we had gone, I to contemplate my "artichokes," the thought came: spring was a time that appealed to the senses, particularly to the eye. Why not apply that to the spring music season? Flowers, buntings, art, lighting effects; mimes, actors, dancers. . . . The idea blossomed into full-blown plans. I sat down and began writing. By the time I got back to New York I had a fair-sized sheaf of notes.

The concerts for the month, approximately nineteen, could be broken up into five or six units, each with a different theme— Viennese, Russian, French, Spanish, American—that would be reflected in the decorations of Philharmonic Hall. The musical programs would be designed to avoid symphonies and the established concertos, concentrate on new or relatively new works and on those that hadn't been heard for so long that they would seem to be new. And if I ever ran into trouble finding little-known works I could always get help from my friend James Michener. Jim likes music. He is especially fond of finding obscure pieces, and takes delight in asking me about them. "Oh, yes, Charpentier," he might say. "His *Impressions d'Italie* has such a beautiful section called "Mules"—do you know it?" I always give him his satisfaction by answering, "Never heard it." (Which is quite often true, too!)

The month of May, 1963, was merry indeed. Talent came together from all directions. Roger Englander produced the entire series. There were designers, like Thomas DeGaetani and Peter Wexler; soloists, like Beverly Sills (whose lovely soprano voice the world hadn't heard nearly enough at that time) and Andre Previn; dancers and choreographers, like Patricia Wilde; poets, like Ogden Nash and Carl Sandburg. There was a night in Vienna, a salute to France and to Spain, evenings with Tchaikovsky and with Gershwin. Andre Previn conducted three concerts of his own design in which he was also piano soloist, and the two final concerts included dancers Danny Daniels and Royes Fernandez.

The opening-night concert was "An American Gala," music by Gershwin—some of whose paintings we borrowed from private collections and exhibited at Lincoln Center—Gottschalk, Kern, Schuman, Copland. It was a tremendous success. The spirit of the audience told us that, even before we read it in the reviews. Huge talent, enthusiasm, and hard work had blossomed into a lovely spring flower, a perennial, as it turned out, at least for fifteen seasons.

Copland's *Lincoln Portrait* seemed especially appropriate for the first Promenade concert, and I wanted very much to have Carl Sandburg narrate, as he had done on the memorable Washington occasion some twenty years before. His Lincoln Center performance turned out to be his last public appearance—he was well into his eighties by then—and it almost didn't happen at all.

The first step was to call Carl's wife, Paula, to see if she thought he would be up to the demands of travel and performing. Paula said he was in good health, but she was not sure he would accept— why didn't I come to Flat Rock and talk to him?

On the flight down to North Carolina I thought it would be best to approach Carl positively, to assuage whatever the doubts might be. The material would certainly be familiar to him, and I was sure that after a little rehearsal at the piano Carl would agree to do it. But as soon as I arrived I noticed that Carl seemed anxious to avoid any discussion about the project. Every time I suggested we go to the piano, he would find a way of turning the conversation in another direction. Once he said he must read me some poems he had just written. Paula later whispered to me that he had composed these newest poems over twenty years ago.

After supper we all took a little walk. It was pitch-dark, and we had to cling to one another so as not to fall. I suggested we should go back to the house—and perhaps try to go over the *Portrait* before bedtime. But again Carl said no, we would do it "later." I had thought perhaps our closeness there in the black night would prompt him to confide the reason for his hesitancy, but it didn't. And since he was so reluctant, I was a little apprehensive about taking the responsibility of trying to persuade him further. There wasn't going to be any rehearsal just yet, but I did want to talk to Paula to try to discover the reason behind Carl's attitude. It was not like him to miss an opportunity to perform.

My plane was to depart at noon the next day, and I had to be on it, so I thought I would have a chance to talk to Paula alone at breakfast; Carl's habit was to read very late and then sleep late the next day. I probably wouldn't even see him before I left.

In the morning over coffee I put the question to Paula—should I persist? Was Carl's health really good enough? Paula became a little flustered then. There was really no problem at all, she announced rather briskly, except that Carl was just too vain—he didn't want to appear in public wearing glasses!

Shades of Toscanini, who conducted without a score, I'm sure, for that very same reason.

Well, if Carl needed glasses for reading it meant he was far-sighted, and in that case there was every possibility that a certain new invention, the TelePrompTer, was the answer. I said good-by to Paula, telling her I was going to try something new.

The minute I got back to New York I telephoned Edgar Vincent, my public relations manager—and one of my closest friends. Edgar always knows exactly what the next right step should be. He immediately arranged a meeting for us and the Philharmonic at the hall to try out the new invention. Eventually we got it working. Carl would be able to see what he had to read, at the exact moment he had to read it, in clear, large type, without his glasses—and without the audience's knowing a thing about it. (Indeed, the *New York Times*'s review marveled that this gentleman of such great age had such a grand memory!)

As I've hinted, Carl was quite theatrically inclined, and so he was delighted with the news. In the course of discussing the other details of his performance I mentioned that the light on him would be extremely strong, so intense as to be blinding if he wasn't careful. Oh, he said, that would be quite all right; he'd avoid looking anywhere near the powerful flood lamps. But he knew also that the effect would be marvelously dramatic, with his dark suit and great quantity of contrasting white hair.

And it was, of course. The whole thing went very beautifully. One newspaper reported that Carl had dozed during the musical introduction. But that was no nap—he had just closed his eyes to avoid the glare!

Carl was one of the most spirited and outspoken yet gentle men I have known. He was not one to hesitate at expressing, in that wonderful basso voice so deliberately measured, whatever it was that puzzled or offended his great integrity of spirit. We happened to be in California the same week in the late Fifties, so I asked him if he might like to come with me to the Hollywood Bowl, which he had never seen and where I was to conduct *Porgy and Bess*. Our drive there was interrupted by an immense traffic jam, the kind where you know immediately you will be late, no matter how much extra time you have allowed.

The policeman I consulted was not impressed, either with who we were or with the immediacy of our problem—it was no reason to "change the traffic pattern." The one piece of advice he gave us turned out to be a dead end, literally. In spite of that we were only ten minutes late. Carl was hurried onstage and introduced as the proverbial "legend in his own time." He stood there, smiling and bowing at the applause, which went on for some minutes, and then rushed backstage. "Can you imagine? I am a legend in my own time," he said to me. *"What* is that fellow talking about?"

I think he was genuinely mystified by the fact that the man had resorted to cliché rather than risk sounding clumsy or inadequate by saying something sincerely his own.

How important Carl felt it was to speak what is really on your mind was demonstrated the very next evening at a reception to which we had both been invited. At one point I introduced him to Norman and Buffy Chandler. Buffy, I told Carl, was devoted to the improvement of cultural life in Los Angeles, particularly that of the fine Philharmonic orchestra there, and her husband, Norman, was publisher of the Los Angeles *Times.* That was it. Time to speak out. "What kind of paper are you publishing?" Carl boomed. "So much nonsense!" Silence. What *could* anyone say, after all, to a "legend in his own time" who was blowing his top?

Cost was the ultimate downfall of the Promenades. Attendance was always high, but, so I am told, even with a sold-out performance of any concert there was a $2,000 deficit the minute the doors opened! Even so, those fifteen seasons were enriching in other ways.

The music repertoire grew. There was the excitement of unearthing neglected music; of "importing" foreign works and then waiting for clearance on the performing rights; of searching for playable orchestral parts for seldom-heard operas, like Rimsky-Korsakov's *The Tsar's Bride*, for example, and then editing them —always with the inspired assistance of my old friend from CBS radio days, Charles Lichter. And there was the pleasure of rediscovery that came with finally hearing the results—Poulenc's *Babar, the Little Elephant*, perhaps, or Reizenstein's *Concerto Populare*. Puccini's *La Rondine*, which we presented in an orchestral version, had had its last Met performance in 1936; Tchaikovsky's *Pique Dame* was last produced there in 1910. There were new works—in 1967, *Magic Prison*, a dialogue for music I commissioned; Ezra Laderman and Archibald MacLeish collaborated on it after letters written by Emily Dickinson to Thomas Higginson, Anne Draper and E. G. Marshall spoke the dialogue—ballets, puppet shows, folk singers from foreign countries. One season we acquired film from NASA and projected it as a backdrop for the artistry of mimes and the music of Holst.

In 1965 the season was extended to five weeks, a total of twenty-five concerts. Guest conductors like Sir Malcolm Sargeant, direct from the English Promenades, and Andre Previn. That year audiences who attended the Spanish theme program heard what a zarzuela (or Spanish musical comedy) was like with Chapi's *La Revoltosa*; and the next season we imported Amalia Rodriguez from Portugal to sing the haunting fados peculiar to that country. "Blues go away"—"*Sandade vai-tea embora*"—floated out over the hall to the traditional accompaniment of guitars. It was yet another beautiful discovery.

Ogden Nash contributed his talents to the success of the Promenades as inventor of countless ingenious lyrics. I never met anyone more facile with the English language. He was so full of humorous turns of phrase that sometimes I suspected it must be downright difficult for him to speak plainly. Ogden had a seemingly endless supply of charming verses. Those that went so beautifully with Ravel's *Mother Goose Suite* and with music from Tchaikovsky's *Children's Album*, which became *Between Birthdays*, might have been written by a child prodigy, which in a way Ogden was all his life. He just couldn't resist the impish point of view, and it was equally compatible with adult themes, as in *Carnival of Marriage*.

My first association with Ogden came quite a few years before the Promenades were even dreamed of. I was in St. Louis conducting a program that included *Carnival of the Animals* for two pianos and orchestra. While the pianists were playing I turned my head slightly toward them and also caught a few members of the audience in the line of vision. There was complete absence of expression. Saint-Saëns had meant this music to be a collection of portraits of his confreres, each "seen" as a particular animal—sort of an inside joke. My observation of the audience told me that the joke was still safely inside; they had no idea which music went with which animal. I decided to do something about it.

Back in New York I called Ogden, told him my thoughts, and wound up by asking him if he could write a little verse for each animal that could then be narrated at the appropriate time during the piece. Oddly enough, considering the musicality of his poetry, Ogden was not particularly interested in music. Not surprisingly, he said he had not heard *Carnival*, but he would do the verses. I told him I'd give him a recording and a list of the animals to work from.

The project was delayed somewhat because Ogden had other commitments, so I didn't see the verses until some months later. And they were perfection. Each animal had been captured with wit and precision. I was delighted. Ogden was delighted. And then he made a little confession. "You know, Andre," he said, "it's a lucky thing you gave me that list of animals with the record, because I never did get to hear the music—my machine broke down!" (So much for music as inspiration!) It made a wonderful album, with Noel Coward doing the narration. His voice—devilishly smooth, full of implication and wit—was exactly suited to the text.

We collaborated again a few years later with Tchaikovsky's *Nutcracker*, with Peter Ustinov's perfect storyteller's voice for the narration. By then I was a confirmed fan of Ogden Nash verse, and when I came across some of his poems about marriage, I couldn't help thinking what wonderful vocal interludes they would be if I could find the right music . . . Saint-Saëns' "Wedding Cake" came immediately to mind and music by Strauss (Jr.) and Liszt. Ogden was agreeable. Could I fly up to his house in New Hampshire to discuss it?

I hired a private plane to get there as it was a bit out of the way. My pilot was a young girl; she looked no more than sixteen and, I would say, wasn't yet twenty. She was wonderfully skillful at handling the controls, but after we were up for a while I could see by the shoreline below that we were headed in the wrong direction. It was nothing serious—she had simply misunderstood when I had told her my destination. But, of course, we arrived a bit late. There was Ogden's upturned, absolutely serious visage as we climbed out of the plane—you would never believe he had a drop of humor in him if all you had to go by was his poker face. "The soufflé is flat" was his greeting. Then, with a glance at my young pilot: "Please, Andre, introduce me to your granddaughter."

Carnival of Marriage premiered June 2, 1971, just two weeks after Ogden's death.

One January day in 1976 the phone rang. I picked it up and heard a familiar voice speaking French to me. And in between the phrases she drew trembling breaths, as if struggling against tears. It was Lily, calling from a hospital in Dallas. She didn't know what she had, and she was terribly frightened. I tried to calm her and said all the things that seem to come to mind in such a situation, and that are so inadequate: I knew she would get better, overcome whatever it was, be home soon. . . . And they were inadequate, because she was dying. But neither of us, whatever our suspicion, would admit that. Within a month she was gone. She never was told what she had, but it was what she had always feared the most, cancer.

I was in Dunedin, New Zealand, when the news came. Very far away and with many things to do, yet all I could think of was how beautiful she looked and how magically she had sung just four years before . . . Lily's return concert at Lincoln Center.

She had sent me a tape someone had made of her singing at a party. There was no accompanying letter saying what reason she had for sending it to me, but when I played it I understood: it was very good, wonderful—and I think she must have known that, too, and wanted to share it with me, a kind of salute to the past. But I had another idea.

A week or so later I played the tape at the monthly Philharmonic conference, without saying whose voice it was. Carlos Moseley, then president, was impressed. I said the voice belonged to Lily. No one could believe it. Carlos immediately asked if I thought she would sing with us. I said I didn't know and let it go at that. Privately I thought there was a good chance, if the approach was just right and if she didn't know so far in advance that her old "nervosity" would gain control and take all the pleasure out of it for her. It was then late fall. If there was to be a performance, it wouldn't be until late the following May.

In the meantime one of my conducting engagements took me to Los Angeles, and so I went to see Lily at her house in Palm Springs, the first and only time I saw it. It was charming and so was Lily, as always. We had a grand visit. At one point I casually wondered if she had ever considered singing in public again. She laughed. "I don't sing any more," she said. "All my music is in the basement." I let it go at that for the time being, but I left with a teasing suspicion that she just might be influenced to change her mind.

I did nothing about it until the beginning of May. By then Lily was in Dallas, where she also kept a house, and I called her there. This time I asked her point-blank, "Will you come to New York and sing a concert with the Philharmonic?" "*Non.*" But a week later she called me and said yes she would sing—the "Bell Song" from *Lakmé*, the "Mad Scene" from *Lucia* . . . Two of the most difficult songs in the repertoire! At one time there was hardly anyone who could do them well except Lily, but now? No. I knew it would be impossible for her to sustain her old quality. Clearly, Lily had been stricken with what the French call *la folie de grandeur*, where you think you can do anything. Naturally, I kept quiet about all these things; I didn't want to discourage her. But I got myself down to Dallas fast. There was very little time.

All through Lily's delightful lunch I was trying to think how to get her to sing something that would show off her voice, not destroy it, and at the same time avoid making her lose confidence. Then I remembered that Joan Sutherland had sung Donizetti's *Daughter of the Regiment* within the past year. It happened to be another one of Lily's specialties and, more important, it was something her voice was still equipped to handle.

So I began to give Lily some news of what had been going on the past season. Did she know, by the way, that Sutherland had enjoyed enormous success with the Donizetti opera? Lily's reaction was instantaneous disbelief: Why, Sutherland couldn't know how to sing that! She was not fit for it . . . et cetera. Music to my ears! So, I said, why don't you sing it at the concert? After that there was no more talk of *Lakmé* or the "Mad Scene."

We planned the program right away. It would include Delibes' "Les Filles de Cadix," Rachmaninoff's "Here Beauty Dwells," Bachelet's "Chère Nuit. . . ." Then I called Moseley and said we had Lily Pons.

When I got home, Carlos said there were only forty-seven tickets left for that May 31 concert—what were we going to do for tickets once the announcement about Lily was made? The only thing I could think of was for us to ask everyone we knew who had a ticket already to relinquish it. And that is what we did. It turned out to be a great way to make tickets available. And also a great way to test friendships!

Lily arrived in New York two days ahead of time. She was excited but seemed confident. *I* was the nervous one—the only time I ever was with her. What if this idea of mine backfired? A New York audience with its array of professional critics . . . her nervousness . . . what if this one time nervousness conquered her? But the rehearsal went very well. I began to relax.

When she came onstage everybody stood and applauded. It was a very emotional few minutes. As I stood there looking at her, so straight and smiling, so calm, I thought of other times—so many and so long ago. The Fifties, outdoor concerts in Grant Park, Chicago; Lewisohn Stadium, New York, the thousands of clapping hands and cheers rising into the starlit evening; the San Carlo Opera in Naples, 1944, G.I.'s whistling and shouting; a hospital near Kunming in the last year of the war, soldiers in wheelchairs or on crutches but grinning with delight at Lily's magical voice and her petite dark beauty. . . . Silence. The audience has resumed their seats. We begin the concert.

From Lily's first notes I knew she would weave her spell again. And she did. Her voice had, indeed, as the *Times* noted the next day, kept its "golden sheen."

To Lily it would have been unthinkable to give anything less than her best, no matter where she performed or for whom, be-cause for her music was the closest human creativity had come to spiritual perfection. She regarded it with reverence; her talent was a blessing to share, a gift for the soul.

I have an office here at Gracie Square, or at least there is a room with a desk in it facing the windows and equipped with the appropriate paraphernalia for doing the kinds of things one does at a desk. But I confess I am much more in favor of doing those things while lying down in bed, so the desk is neglected but not the room. It has become a sort of gallery of mementos, photographic portraits I have collected over the years. I was never shy about asking someone I admired if they would give me a picture, whether or not I had ever met them until that moment. So now the alcove in one wall of the "office" is filled with faces, and it gives me great pleasure to wander in and look at them.

My collecting has been rather casual and sporadic, something I was simply moved to do at various times in my life. But, reflecting on it now, I suppose it is my way of paying tribute to the people who enriched my experience of the world. Stokowski is there, and Sandburg, Grofé, Koussevitzky, Ormandy, MacLeish. . . . There is Jerome Kern's photograph. It is over thirty-five years old—I had yet to meet Kern when I wrote and asked for it. And there was no response for quite a while. But then one evening when I happened to be here alone, there was a knock at the door, and when I opened it there was Kern himself. I recognized him, of course, and invited him in. He told me he and his wife were moving to California within a few days, and he wanted to bring me the photograph himself. I was very touched by this.

I have two photographs of Toscanini's handsome face. By the time I requested a picture I had met him on quite a few occasions. Very quickly I received a package, which he had marked in red: Air Mail Special Delivery. Inside was this wonderful note: "My dear Kostelanetz: It was embarrassing for me to choose between these two pictures. I like the old one taken in my studio in Milano by my son [Walter]. Maybe you like the one recently done in

New York. So I punish you, sending you both, the old and the new. Remember me please to Madame [Lily] very cordially. And believe me I am most sincerely . . ."

He was to my mind the most brilliant, energetic—and strictest—missionary for great music who has ever lived. It will never be known exactly how many people were touched by his artistic genius. He had traveled all over the world, lighting it up with his special fire. When he died millions mourned him. The day the news came of his death—January 16, 1957—I was rehearsing the Philharmonic. I told the orchestra to go home, the rehearsal was over. That night I announced the program would begin with Bach's Suite No. 3 in D major, in memory of Toscanini. The audience spontaneously stood, and there was complete silence at the end.

I don't remember the occasion of receiving Irving Berlin's portrait, only that it was very long ago indeed. He was one of the most universally known composers of popular music. It is safe to say that his songs have been and still are played in every country in the world—although, as I once discovered, while the music's attractiveness might be recognized, the little details of title and composer are sometimes not. I had just visited the Vatican in Rome, and I decided to stop in a souvenir shop and perhaps find some objects that had been blessed by the Pope to send home for my Catholic friends. The shopkeeper hurried over and asked if I was American. I said yes. And he promptly showed me a little crèche made of some sort of plastic. He said it opened to show the Madonna and Child, and it also played "Ave Maria." Oh? I said. And he opened it and it played "White Christmas!" So I immediately told him I would like to have one sent to the composer. "Oh, no, signore," he said, "the composer is dead. . . . Anybody who writes the 'Ave Maria' is gone!" No, he was not dead, I assured him. I wrote out a little card to go with the package: "Dear Irving: Your shadow has reached the Vatican." Weeks later in New York I ran into Irving and his wife having dinner in a restaurant, and, of course, he thanked me for sending him that wonderful crèche from Rome. And then he paused for a moment. "Andre, do you think I'll be getting royalties from this?"

I am on my balcony, at the edge of the city and at the edge of the universe, too, between the world and the sky. From here I can observe the seasons replace one another and marvel at the ever-changing displays of nature. The late-afternoon air is clear and dry today, and the light is casting longer shadows. Nature is making her first announcements of autumn. The soft summer loveliness will surrender soon to the bittersweetness of fall.

It is a long road from St. Petersburg to now. From the start it was Fortune's way to smile on me, to give me music, a gift I could share with the world. And the world has shared its gifts with me—friends, nature, places, beauty, love. Blessings. I look back on many seasons of happiness. I look forward with hope to more. But to stand still now, in the center of this moment, and say, "I am happy"—that is the greatest blessing of all.

Yes, it has been a long road. And here I am.

Closing Note

ANDRE COULD NOT KNOW THAT the autumn of 1979 was to be his last full "season of happiness," and I am not sure it would have changed his plans if he had. He was a man who walked forward meeting the future straight on. That was his chosen direction, forward. At that moment on the balcony his schedule for the coming months was already filled with music, concerts that would take him near and far. There would be time for a rest somewhere in between the old and the new year, but his choice of Haiti for that rest was not made until almost the last minute—I think part of the enjoyment of a vacation for Andre was combining the elements of chance and difference.

My last memory of him is a hug and smile. "Till soon," he said, and he was off to a San Francisco concert. We spoke on the telephone Christmas Day just before he left for Port-au-Prince. He died there January 13, 1980.

During the many months we worked together on this book there were frequent "till soons" as he left to conduct—in Salt Lake City, in Toronto, at the White House. . . . He scaled down his concert schedule somewhat "for the book," but even so there were the necessary times we had to say good-by–for–now. Such was Andre's sense of the ironic that once, with a twinkle in his blue eyes, he said, "Well, if something should happen and I don't come back, you'll at least have the ending for the book!" Inevitably, I remembered those words when the news came of his death, but the irony did nothing to console me. I had lost a dear friend.

He had left a large part of himself with me—hours of taped

CLOSING NOTE

thoughts and opinions, anecdotes, adventures; boxes of notes, clippings, letters, pictures; and, the most elusive yet significant legacy, countless impressions of the inner Andre. We had special "off-duty" times together—at Lincoln Center listening to Beverly Sills sing *La Loca*, in the audience of a Zubin Mehta concert in Central Park, over a fine dinner at one of his favorite restaurants and many lunches at Gracie Square. And these were the times when I saw newer dimensions in his gentleness of spirit, irrepressible humor, and most imaginative thoughtfulness.

We had many discussions of what to select from the material and how to bring it into focus, and it is from those talks—and with the spirit of Andre—that this book was made.

To Andre's family and friends who helped, first of all, by encouraging him to embark on this new adventure and, second, by being always ready to share their time and memories of him with me, I give my deepest thanks—and, without risk of presumption, Andre's: to his sisters, Mina Afan and Marion (Maria) Frank, and her son, Robert; to his brother, Boris, Boris's son, Richard, and daughter, Lucy; to Lily Afan, his niece; to Efrem Kurtz, Louis Robbins, Edgar Vincent, Carlos Moseley, Helen McGranahan, Maria Reichenbach, Paulette Thuillier, Harriet Pilpel, Joan Judge, Rose Ann Ferrick, George Jellinek, Horace Sutton, Sir William Stephenson, William Stevenson.

One August evening in 1979, in Central Park's Sheep Meadow, some 250,000 people gathered to hear Andre conduct a Philharmonic concert. A full moon appeared just as the maestro raised his baton to begin. At the end of the program the sky was filled with fantastic fireworks. And in between was the inspiration of the music and his joy at sharing it with us. Andre, thank you.

GLORIA HAMMOND

Index